FACETS OF WOMEN'S DEVELOPMENT

FACETS OF WOMEN'S DEVELOPMENT

Editors

Anuradha Mathu
Rameshwari Pandya

Publications

KALPAZ PUBLICATIONS

DELHI-110052

Facets of Women's Development

Rs. 750

ISBN: 81-7835-459-4

Published in 2006 in India by
Kalpaz Publications
C-30, Satyawati Nagar, Delhi-110052
E-mail : kalpaz@hotmail.com

Laser Typesetting at : Master Computers, Delhi
Printed at : Salasar Imaging System, Delhi

Contents

Preface

This book - "Facets of Women's Development", though a new concept in India but has its deep roots in history and development of women in India which has been its dawn in pre-historic India in the 'Vedas' and 'Puranishad' and is coming to the twentieth and Twenty first century women of India - Kiran Bedi, Indira Gandhi, Kalpana Chawla and the Countless beauties of the World.

The history and development of women in India has gone through paradigm shifts of 'Women and Welfare' approach to 'Women and Equality', to Women and Development to Empowerment'. The word 'Empowerment' though a key word to day for judging women's status in changing India, there is still lot of scope and work for improvement in this direction.

It is with the brief background and concern that the authors feel that there is great need for having a book of this kind. This book would help all students of Undergraduate and Post-Graduate studies as ready reference for several perspectives on women's issues—

- Status of Women
- Gender and Women
- Women and Health
- Women in Media
- Women and Law
- Women and Environment, and so on.

This book would also help the teachers of the two very important courses.

- Women in Changing India
- Gender and Development

Overall, this book would go a long way in helping policy makers in the UGC, the women activities and NGO's working for and with women as it focuses on specific aspects of gender and development. This also takes care of current needs and problems of women in India.

The book is very informative useful and stimulating. It provides comprehensive synthesis of major problems and issues related to women and development. Each chapter has a variety of references which can be used for further information on various topics related to women and more in-depth reading for variety of view points.

This book is ideal for those people who are genuinely interested in gender issues and women studies, such as students, teachers, social scientists and researchers scholars.

Gender and Development is a topic of perennial interest and importance. In a country of India's size and population, these topics acquire greater significance.

Editors

Acknowledgements

We express our special gratitude to Prof. Veena Gandotra - Dean, Faculty of Home Science, The M.S. University of Baroda, who has been a constant support.

We also feel highly indebted to Prof. Uma Joshi - Head, Department of Home Science Extension and Communication, who has inspired us for taking up this challenging task.

We owe our special debts to all authors whose books we have either cited in our book or have given in our bibliography.

This book has been an exhaustive work conducted by the authors from various libraries and sources. However, no writers, editors or authors write without support from various sections.

We are also thankful to the following Libraries and number of sources and we offer our thanks to them-

R & D Centre of the Department of Home Science Extension and Communication, Faculty to Home Science, The M.S. University of Baroda, Gujarat.

- Hansa Mehta Library, The M.S. University of Baroda, Gujarat.
- Women's Studies Documentation Centre, Delhi and Baroda.
- S.N.D.T. Library, Mumbai.
- I.C.S.S.R., Documentation Centre, New Delhi.
- Lady Irwin College, Library, New Delhi.

We would not be truthful if we did not express our gratitude towards our families who have shown their unstinted love, support and encouragement while writing this book.

Last but not the least, we are thankful to our Publishers who have been kind enough to take extra pains for publishing this book in time.

Rameshwari Pandya
and Anuradha Mathu

List of Contributors

Dr. Rameshwari Pandya

She has an impeccable academic record having Gold Medal and Ph.D. She is senior lecturer at the faculty of Home Science, M.S. University of Baroda, Gujarat.

She possesses vast and rich experience of both classroom teaching and fieldwork in the discipline of Women's Studies and Non-Formal Education. She has written extensively in the area of Women's Studies.

At present she is in-charge of the Urban Extension Wing of the Department.

Dr. Anuradha Mathu

She is lecturer in the Department of Home Science Extension and Communication, Faculty of Home Science.

She is Ph.D. and ICSSR fellow.

She has guided many research students in the area of Women's Studies and Extension.

She has been in professional organizations such as ICWS, BUTA, HSAI and HSECAA.

Ms. Risha Kapoor

She has been teaching Home Science at the college level. Her area of interest has been Non-Formal Education and Adult Education.

She has worked as an instructor, organizer and supervisor in the field of Adult Education. She is life member of HSECAA.

Ms. Preeti Shah

She has specialized in Women's Studies. She has research experience in the area of Women's Studies.

She has membership of several professional organizations. She possess a rich experience of fieldwork in the discipline of extension education.

1

Programmes and Policies for Women

Anuradha Mathu, Rameshwari Pandya

Abstract

We have witnessed a paradigm shift in the approaches for women in our country after independence. From welfare, to development to empowerment.

There are gender blind policies, gender sensitive policies, gender neutral to gender specific policies.

The birth of Community Development Programmes in the year, 1952 to National Policy for the Empowerment, 2001. We have very good educational policies on economic policies, like National Policy on Education 1986, and equally good economic policies like STEP–Support to Training ane Employment Programmes. Amongst the recent policies we have 'Kishori Shakti Yojana'. Yet, there are limitations of the programme and policies as women themselves are not at all involved for planning of such programmes and policies. Further, there are many constraints which impede the development process. Many a times women are not at all motivated to participate in such programmes. Women themselves may have lot of biases ane rigid attitudes towards accepting such changes.

It is here that the involvement of Academicians, Researchers, Womens Studies cells centres would go a long way in making the so called programmes and policies–'A Dream come true'?

Introduction

As we step into the next millennium, a much-needed exercise is an assessment of trends in public policies, past and present, continued or changed and their impact on women across the country.

During the last few decades, we have been preoccupied with development and economic policies in view of the deteriorating economic conditions for a major section of women. In the field of judiciary and legislation, personal laws and rape laws have dominated our attention. Public policies on health care and health services have been an area of critical concern. Programmes of poverty alleviation, developmental thrusts, tackling dowry, age at marriage, domestic violence or scores of other such issues demand exposition.

The primary objective of this chapter is a critical assessment of public policies, historical and contemporary, in shaping women's lives and setting an agenda for the next millennium.

In more recent times, policy initiatives have induced some concrete structural changes. To cite a few : reforms in law and legal processes, institutional reform in policies, constitution of women's commissions at the state and national levels and gender sensitizing programmes have induced changes in public policy.

Gender Sensitive Programmes and Policies

Gender sensitive policies are those which are in favour of activities and resources which are likely to be controlled by women or which are beneficial to them. Some policies and programmes though planned for women, were being planned and supervised by men folk only. Thus, the focus could never be on women specific issues and problem. Due to these reasons, the sincere and well planned programmes could not benefit the women target group policies. The need for gender sensitive approach was found out and thus the gender neutral policies were renamed as gender blind policies.

Historical Overview

In the first twenty years following independence, Indian policy makers were primarily concerned with overall economic growth of the country. The third decade of independence witnessed an increasing concern for equality and poverty alleviation. But, gender issues were still overlooked. As a result, policies and programmes specifically aiming at women were limited in scope and resources.

It is only in the last twenty years, that it became evident that though women constitute an overwhelming majority of poor and that programmes of economic and social development are structurally biased in favour of men. This bias is now being openly acknowledged and corrective policies and programmes are being formulated, which calls for a systematic gender and development approach.

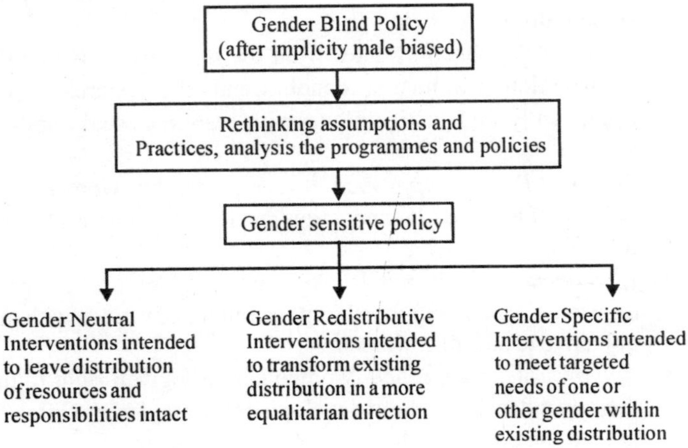

1952	Community Development Programme was launched to promote agricultural development and to provide village with welfare services.
1953	The Central Social Welfare Board was established to fund and support the activities of voluntary organization in field of social welfare.
1954	Decision was made to appoint two Gram Sevikas in each block and establishment of Mahila Mandals were encouraged.
1974	The Committee on the Status of Women in India submitted its report "Towards Equality".
1980	The Sixth Five Year Plan introduced with some major changes in Programmes for women.
1982	Development of Women and Children in Rural Area (DWCRA) was introduced which had women as its specific target.
1988	National Perspective Plan for Women.
1992	National Commission for Women.
2001	National Policy for the Empowerment of Women.

Change in the focus and target group compelled the variety of approaches used to take some different forms.

Shift of Approaches

- *Welfare Approach*–A top down approach which takes women as passive recipients rather than active participants and decision makers and considers that women are the deprived section of society urging for help.

- *Equality Approach*–It dates from the mid 1970s. It highlights contribution of women in economic and other spheres and equal opportunity and justice along with resources and support to women.
- *The Anti Poverty Approach*–It recognizes that women are the poorest of the poor. It encourages small scale income generation projects.
- *Effectiveness Approach*–It takes into consideration the gender division of labour and social responsibilities of women with major objective to mobilize women.
- *Empowerment Approach*–Women here are given right to make their own decisions about development strategies and integrated to lead the complete development of the society.

(I) Education Policies

1. University Education Commission

- Special colleges and schools and educational counselling with special course content for women was designed.
- Between age of 13 years and 18 years the schools were separate for girls and boys but education could be started with.

2. Secondary Education Commission

It was established in the year 1952-53. This commission in contrast felt no need to deal with women's education separately. Instead it suggested more interaction among boys and girls at school time. Co-educational schools were thus started at that time. Special courses and teachers could, however be planned keeping in mind the female students enrolment in the schools.

3. National Committee on Women Education

Started in the year 1958-59 to systematize the efforts towards women's education, which was given to the needy. Transportation facilities and scholarship were also provided.

4. Committee on Differentiation of Curricula for Boys and Girls

This committee was established in the year 1961. This emphasized that textbooks should be designed keeping in mind the girl students. Vocational courses were started and transportation was arranged for women teachers and students to motivate them.

5. Committee to look into the causes for luck of the public support particularly in rural areas for girls education and to enlist public co-operation

This committee in the year 1963 aimed at improving schools to overcome problems related to women's education. More and more incentives were given to women teachers. They were posted in nearby villages to help them solve problems of transportation.

6. Education Commission (1964-66)

This commission was established in the year 1964-66. The role of women in economic and social sector outside house was also identified. Vocational courses were started and incentives for girls like scholarship, free uniforms, etc. were given. Provision for hostels were also made. Research units were set up in university to deal with women's education. Employment of women teachers was encouraged.

7. National Policy on Education

It was established in the year 1986 to empower and improve their social status. Redesigning of curricula and textbooks was also done. Women's studies were promoted. Adult and non-formal programmes were geared up for women.

8. Condensed Courses of Education and Vocational Training for Adult Women (CCE and VT)

The programme of Condensed Courses of Education and Vocational Training for Adult Women provides new vistas of employment through continuing education and vocational training for women and girls who are school dropouts. In education, instead of strengthening the mainstream system and making it deliver to fulfill its mandate for ensuring full, free, primary education to all, alternate agencies have been mooted. While these are commendable, they also raise certain basic questions. Why do girls and women deserve only 'non-formal' education with a ragbag of micro programmes? The year 1986 New Education Policy raised a lot of hopes for the first time but as yet there is no evidence that this too will not remain on paper.

By public policy, we do not mean only policy documents actually released from time to time by the government in power but by all public agencies in all sectors of life–in institutions and their functioning, in the prioritisation for the allocation of resources, in the modus of implementation in addition to policy directives, explicit or implicit.

(II) Economic Policies

1. Socio-Economic Programme (SEP)

One of the major programmes of employment and training for Women is the Socio-Economic Programme (SEP) implemented by the Central Social Welfare Board, provides work and wage to needy women such as destitutes, widows, deserted, economically backward and handicapped. SEP takes care of trades of literate, semi-literate and illiterate women, promoted under this programme which includes both traditional and agro-based industries, besides non-traditional trades.

2. Employment-cum-Income Generation-cum-Production Units

This scheme was launched in the year 1982-83 with a specific objective of extending training and employment opportunities for women in non-traditional and upcoming trades. Training is imparted to women belonging to weaker sections of the society including school dropouts in non-traditional trades such as electronics, computer programming, printing and binding, weaving and spinning and garment making and so on.

3. National Commission on Self-Employed Women and Women in Informal Sector

This commission was established in the year 1987. It stated that working women should get certain incentives like free textbooks and mid-day-meal for sending their girl-child to school. It created a revolving fund from which money could be used for training women.

4. Support to Training and Employment Programmes (STEP)

This programme was launched in the year 1987. It aims to upgrade the skills of rural women to be utilised constructively. It makes attempts to provide employment to women in traditional sectors such as agriculture, dairy industry, fishing, sericulture, handlooms and handicrafts. It created support services like day-care centres for children of working women.

5. Shramshakti–the Report of the National Commission for Self-Employed Women and Women in the Informal Sector (1988)

The Shramshakti Report, for the first time underlined the critical contribution of the marginalized poor women in both rural and urban areas, to the growth of the formal economy. The situation of women in the informal sector, including self-employed and wage labour, paid and unpaid workers, as well as contractual employees was studied by the Commission. Based on detailed analysis many valuable recommendations were submitted in the Report which recognised women's work as homemakers, as social /

economic producers, enlarging the definition of women workers in all subsequent data collection efforts to embrace all paid and unpaid work and setting up of an exclusive credit-body for the poor and the self-employed and linking all training programmes to employment with the objective of increasing their remuneration and improving the living conditions of poor women.

6. Mahila Samriddhi Yojana (MSY)

This programme initiated in the year 1993 was a major step to empower women by raising their economic status. This scheme aims at women to create a financial source on their own to start a small scale enterprise. It enables them to exercise better control over household resources. It promotes the rural women to develop a habit to save. The Yojana offers facilities of small deposits with attractive rate of interest through the network of post office.

7. National Credit Fund for Women

This fund was created in the year 1993. It aimed at supporting developmental programmes for women. It made the fund accessible to assetless women so that they could start a small unit of production of their own. It provides credit services to women to boost self-employment, micro-enterprise and small business. The fund is also known as 'Rashtriya Mahila Kosh'.

8. Indira Mahila Yojana

With the aim at developing a new sense of awareness among women, particularly those in rural areas and empower them to become active participants in the process of social transformation and regeneration. This scheme visualizes an integrated delivery of services to women and children.

(III) Other Women's Empowerment Policies

1. Committee on Status of Women (1971)

It was appointed in India in the year 1971 to examine constitutional, legal and administrative provisions that have a bearing on social status of women. Co-education was encouraged. At university level, more relevant courses were introduced for students. Secondary education was made free and compulsory for all girls. Admissions were even made more flexible so that more and more girls enrolled in the education.

2. National Perspective Plan for Women (1988)

The National Perspective Plan for Women (NPP) was drawn up to facilitate main streaming women's issues in policies and programmes. It is linked to national targets determined for the end of the century in respect of certain standard development indicators and is the first comprehensive report since the year 1974 on women and development in India.

The NPP has recognized the need to highlight women's concerns and stated that a parallel substream of women's development, even if possible, would only perpetuate discrimination and sub-ordination. It has flagmarked the initiatives required and set out a series of action points relating to sectors of rural development, health, legislation, political participation, education, employment, support services, communication and voluntary action.

3. National Commission for Women (1992)

The NCW, a statutory body set up under the National Commission for Women Act, 1990 to safeguard the rights and interests of women. The NCW set up on 31st January, 1992 under the Chairpersonship of Ms. Jayanti Patnaik.

The major objectives of NCW are :

(i) Review of the implementation of both women specific and women-related legislations and suggest amendments whatever needed.

(ii) To function as an agency to keep surveillance and facilitate redressal of grievances of women. The commission also holds public hearings to listen to the grievances of the affected women.

4. The National Plan of Action for Girl-Child (1992)

This plan was implemented in the year 1991 as a part of programme to improve the status of girl-child. Sex determination tests were banned in order to prevent female foeticide. Survey was conducted regarding status and problems of girl-child and conclusions were drawn. Use of multi-media was promoted to develop a positive image of girl-child. State Governments were made responsible to fulfill the local requirements and ensure holistic developments of a girl-child.

5. Reservation for Women in Grassroot Level Democratic Institutions (1993)

The 73rd and 74th Constitutional Amendment Acts of the year 1993 mark historic events in the advancement of Indian women as they ensure one-third of total seats for women in all elected offices of local bodies, in rural areas and urban areas.

Kishori Shakti Yojana

Objective

- to improve the nutritional and health status.
- to provide the required literacy and numeracy skills through the non-formal stream of education, to stimulate a desire for more social exposure and knowledge and to help them improve their decision making capabilities.
- to train and equip the adolescent girls to improve/upgrade home-based and vocational skills.
- to promote awareness of health, hygiene, nutrition and family welfare, home management and child care and to take all measure as to facilitate their marrying only after attaining the age of 18 years and if possible even late.
- to gain a better understanding of their environment related social issues and the impact on their lives.
- to encourage adolescent girls to initiate various activities to be productive and useful members of the society.

State / UT / District may choose options as per their area specific needs and requirements :

- adolescent girl groups can be formed at AWCs and regular supply of IFTA and deforming tablets may be ensured along with provisions for nutritional and health education.
- to emphasize life education which may include knowledge of physical and psychological developmental processes including the psychosexual development.
- emphasis on education with particular attention on school dropouts and functional literacy among illiterate girls.
- educational activities should be conducted through non-formal education pattern.
- emphasis on life education aspects including physical, developmental and sex education.
- adolescent girls may be congregated at AWCs and the education should be provided through experts, consultants, NGOs and specialized government functionaries.
- vocational training activities may be undertaken for their economic empowerment.
- a group of 20-25 girls at AWCs may be identified by the Supervisor (Mukhya Sevika). Of these, nominations of 2 selected girls from each AWC may be sent to DPO.

- DPO in consultation with CDPO, officer's in-charge of these sectors and NGOs will organise vocational training courses, non-formal education course, life education courses, health and nutrition education, legal literacy etc.
- after completion of training, the group leaders (2 adolescent girls from each AWC) will provide training to remaining adolescent girls at AWC.
- additional requirement of funds may be proposed to be met under out of the funds available under ICDS (UDISHA) training programme.
- AG's who have been trained in various vocational streams may be given preference under these schemes.
- formulating a Plan of Action for improvement of social status of adolescent girls.
- focus on enhancement of self-esteem, addressing the problems of social abuses, strengthening of will power and self-confidence.
- ill-effects of early marriage and pregnancy with gender equity and equality could also be included in the curricula.
- legal literacy and knowledge of rights.
- a module for training in AWCs for empowerment of adolescent girls should be developed in consultation with local experts/ consultants.

National Policy for the Empowerment of Women

The government has approved the National Policy for the Empowerment of Women on 20th March, 2001. The Policy was drawn up by the Department of Women and Child Development in the Ministry of Human Resource Development through a process of consultation with non-government organisations, women activists, academicians, women Members of Parliament, Central Ministries and departments and the State Governments and UTs.

The origin of the policy lies in the recommendations made in the National Perspective Plan for Women (1988-2000 AD). A commitment to adopt a National Policy for Women was also made in the Fourth World Conference on Women held in Beijing in 1995.

Goal and Objectives of the Policy

The goal of this policy is to bring about the advancement, development and empowerment of women through a process of change in societal attitudes towards women, elimination of all forms of discrimination against women and active participation of women in all spheres of life and activities. It will empower women both socially and economically.

The policy will guide and inform action at all levels and integrate women's concerns and perspectives into all macro level initiatives.

New Initiatives

The policy prescribes affirmative action in areas such as Legal System, Decision Making Structure, Mainstreaming of Gender Perspective in Development Process, Economic Empowerment through increased access to resources like micro credit, better resource allocation through Women's Component Plan, gender Budget exercises and development of Gender Development Indices and Social Empowerment of Women through, inter-alia, universalisation of education, adoption of holistic approach to women's health etc.

The policy commits to making compulsory the registration of marriages and to eliminate child marriage by 2010. Under the Convention of the Rights of Child, all persons below the age of 18 years are considered 'child' and more than 40 per cent marriages in India take place below this age.

The policy takes into account the new developments initiated by the process of economic reforms and the impact of globalisation and liberalization on women, particularly in the informal sector.

Initiatives will be taken to review and amend the provisions of various legislation including personal laws, which are discriminatory against women with the support and initiatives of concerned communities. Review of women oriented legislations will be completed by 2003 and necessary changes be introduced before the Parliament.

The National Policy for the Empowerment of Women also provides that restriction on women to work in night shifts in factories should be removed to enhance employment opportunities for women.

Implementation of the Policy

The following implementation strategy has been prescribed in the National Policy for the Empowerment of Women:

(i) Action Plans

All Central and State Ministries/Departments would be required to draw up Action Plans with measurable goals to be achieved in a time frame of the next 10 years. Ministries/Departments would be free to launch new programmes/schemes to operationalise the policy in their respective sectors. During the current year, the Department of Women and Child

Development (DWCD) has already initiated action to formulate a new programme for women in difficult circumstances such as destitute women, widows, etc., DWCD is also launching an integrated self-help group based programme for empowerment of women (IWEP).

(ii) Financial Resources for Implementing the Policy

Implementation of the National Policy for the Empowerment of Women will be an intersectoral exercise that would aim at the convergence of resources of all the ministries/ departments. The Ninth Five Year Plan has already initiated the process of formulation of Women's Component Plan whereby 30 per cent of funds/benefits in all women related sectors shall flow to women.

(iii) Monitoring of Implementation of the Policy

The policy envisages setting up of a council at the national level to oversee the implementation of the policy. The national council will be headed by the Prime Minister. Similar councils will also be set up at the State levels to be headed by the concerned Chief Ministers.

The department has circulated the copies of the National Policy for the Empowerment of Women to Chief Secretaries of all State Governments drawing their attention to the new commitments and operational strategies contained in it. They were also requested to formulate time bound action plans to implement the policy and form State level councils headed by the Chief Minister to monitor its implementation, the copies of the policy document has also been circulated to various ministries/departments of the Government of India for implementing the policy.

Census of India 2001
Provisional Population Totals
Figures at a glance

1,027,015,247 Persons	
495,738,169 Females	531,277,247 Males

180,627,359 Persons	
88,683,339 Females	91,944,020 Males

Density of Population (per sq. km.) 324 per cent
Sex Ratio (Females per 1,000 males) 933 per cent

157,863,145 Persons	
75,952,104 Females	81,911,041 Males

566,714,995 Persons	
226,745,947 Females	339,969,048 Males

Inspite of so many programmes for women, there is not much progress and improvement in women's status due to the following limitations.

Limitations of the Programmes and Policies for Women

1. Women are not involved at all, at the planning stage of the programmes meant for the welfare, development and empowerment of women.
2. Most of the programmes that are planned for women have no relevance to the prevailing conditions, circumstances and existing time.
3. There is a general lack of basic resources and funds for buildings and infrastructure for any women's programme for implement.
4. The heterogeneity of women's mass according to age group, working group, caste etc. poses a great challenge.
5. The programmes for women generally lack supportive services as they are not planned for, in the beginning.
6. The incentives given are either very low quality or are less in quantity and numbers.
7. There is usually no or very poor effort to motivate women to participate in such programmes.
8. Again, there are very few women in these programmes in the implementation committees and working groups.
9. To make a bad situation worse, there is lack of co-ordination between all involved in such women specific programmes.
10. There is rigidity to change on the part of the beneficiaries of the programme.
11. There is inadequacy in terms of identifying and awaiting finance for women's programme.
12. Usually all government programmes have poor evaluation and supervision which also holds true about women's programmes.
13. Lastly there is no proper, planned or systematic follow up of these programmes.

Thus, keeping all these limitations in view, some suggestions for future action have been planned.

Suggestions for Future Action and Improvement

1. All women's programmes need to be decentralized and more women need to be involved in these programmes, right from the grass-root levels to the top.

2. In women's programmes and policies there is a great need to involve women in
   — Planning and conception
   — Implementation and administration
   — Evaluation and follow up.
3. The official authorities, in women specific programmes should be female members instead of male to make it convenient for the women beneficiaries, to interact forcefully.
4. The involvement of media should be more rigorous and a major method instead of a supplementary resource, in these programmes.
5. We should involve more methods of traditional and cultural values such as
   — Folk media
   — Puppetry
6. The focus of the women's programmes should change according to changing
   — Needs of beneficiaries
   — Interest of beneficiaries, i.e., women
   — Availability of resources
   — Availability of time.
7. The women participants in these programmes should be given more desirable incentives.
   — In jobs
   — In cash or kind or some benefits.
8. The women's programmes can be run well with the help of identification of women leaders.
9. The women beneficiaries should be made aware about the relevance of the programmes for their
   — Self development
   — Family welfare
   — Society at large
10. Follow-up and repetition of the programme needs to be taken up with all seriousness and adequacy.

Conclusion

From the above discussion we can conclude that, today women are in the need of various programmes to ease their development. These issues have to be tackled carefully. The policies today are increasing in number but their actual work has remained the same. Thus, the changes should be brought about so that the gap between the benefits and its beneficiaries is linked.

More and more women are able to develop through the programmes conducted by government, NGOs and by others. They are able to use their potentials and mould them in constructive way to obtain desirable results. It will help them to develop confidence and become independent and thus become self-sufficient.

Thus, programmes and policies are the fundamental or basic steps which lead women towards development and improved status. Therefore, they should be supported and strengthened. The government should link-up and network with NGOs for more successful implementation of women's programmes and policies.

The involvement of academicians, researchers and women studies cells and centres would go a long way in making the so called programmes and policies–'A Dream come true'.

Inspite of programmes and policies these are the areas which need immediate attention :

- Institutional mechanisms for advancement of women need to be improved and made more adequate in terms of :
  — Buildings
  — Infrastructure
  — Allocation of funds
- Persistent and institutionalized discrimination against girl child needs to be reduced.
- Gender-blindness in macro-economic policies need to be addressed to.
- Women's contribution to the economy and environmental sustenance needs to be made visible.

All the above points can be taken care of by having :

- Seminars, symposia, workshops, conferences at national level.
- Rallies and protestations at local level.
- Publicity and awareness regarding women's issues through healthy involvement of media.
- Use of folk and cultural media at local level to bring about awareness.
- Awareness to students at college and university level through exposure to courses like–

- 'Women in changing India'
- 'Women and Development'
- Media Appreciation of women's programmes.
- Gender sensitization of biased societal norms.
- Reducing of negative portrayals and perpetuation of gender stereotypes in mass media.

References

Aggarwal, N. Women, Education and Population in India. Chugh Publications, Allahabad, 1993.

Arputhamurthy Savitri, Women Work and Discrimination, Ashish Publishing House, New Delhi, 1990.

Azim Sherwani : The Girl Child in Crisis, Indian Social Institute, New Delhi, 1995.

Country Report - Fourth World Conference on Women, Beijing 1995. Department of Women and Child Development, Ministry of Human Resource Development, Government of India, 1995.

Critical Issues on the Status of Women, ICSSR, New Delhi, 1977.

Dasgupta Kalpana (1976). (Ed.). Women on the Indian Scarce, Abhinav Publications, New Delhi.

Desai Neera and Krishnaraj Maithreyi, Women and Society, New Delhi, Ajanta Press, 1987.

Desai, N. Patel, V., Indian Women - Change and Challenges, Popular Prakashan, Bombay, 1990.

Govt. of India (1988). National Perspective Plan for Women : 1988 - 2000 A.D. Ministry of Human Resource Development, Department of Women and Child Development, New Delhi.

Kumar, A., (1988). Indian Women Towards 21st Century, Criterion Publication, New Delhi.

Mitra S.M., The Position of Women in Indian Life, Neeraj Publication, 1981.

National Perspective Plan for Women - 1988-2000 A.D. Department of Women and Child Development, Ministry of Human Resource Development Government of India, 1988.

Reinconrt de Amaury, (1989) Women and Power in History, Sterling Publishers Private Limited, Bangalore.

Report of the Committee on the Status of Women in India (1974) "Towards Equality". Government of India, Department of Social Welfare, Ministry of Education and Social Welfare,

Shams Shamsuddin, Women, Law and Social Change, Ashish Publishing House, New Delhi, 1991.

Sharma U. and Sharma B.M. Committees and Commission on Women Education, Commonwealth Publishers, 1977.

Shramshakti. The Report of National Commission on Self Employed Women and Women in Informal Sector, Government of India, New Delhi, 1988.

The Constitution - Eighty First Amendment Bill 1996. Discussion Organised by the National Commission for Women, Compiled by Women's Studies Research Centre, M.S. University, Baroda.

UNICEF (1980) Assistance for Rural Women and Children Programme, An Approach Paper Association of Voluntary Agencies for Rural Development, New Delhi.

Varma S.C., Women's Vital Role in Rural Development Integrating Women's Programmes in the Rural Development - Strategy and Women's Programmes as Part of Rural Development Efforts.

2

Women and Health

Anuradha Mathu, Rameshwari Pandya

Abstract

WHO defines health as

"State of complete physical, mental and social well-being and not merely the absence of diseases or infirmity."

Health status of women is influenced by many factors:

- Economic status of the family
- Dietary intake of women
- Discriminatory behaviour towards a girl child
- Preference of son
- Early marriage and so on.

Gender discrimination which is further made worse because of amniocentesis, sex discrimination, female infanticide, female foeticide and so on.

There are many organizations working for improving health status of women in India but there is still underutilization of health services by women which is mainly due to:

- Lack of awareness
- Ignorance of women
- Poverty stricken families
- Lack of importance for their own health
- Superstitions amongst low socio-economic families.
- High illiteracy amongst women.

The condition of women and their health in particular can be improved by :

- Timely health care.
- Awareness regarding health care and family planning.
- Stringent laws and policies to stop misuse of sex-determination tests.

To sum up, women should be made aware of four A's of health.

- Awareness,
- Availability,
- Accessibility and
- Affordability.

Thus, to conclude it is women's health which is almost like lost wealth, so let us all make concerted efforts to improve their health status.

Introduction

WHO defines health as "State of complete physical, mental and social well being and not merely the absence of diseases and infirmity". The fundamental determination of health apart from the genetic constitution is nutrition, environment and lifestyle. The health of any rural Indian society is directly linked to its value system, cultural traditions, socio-economic setup and political organization. Each of these has a profound influence on the health of an individual or community.

Any health education programme cannot be limited to health care delivery but should also be directed to bring about the cultural, economic, social and political transformation of a society as a whole through the process of education.

What is Health?

To be healthy is a basic human right of all people, physical, emotional and mental well-being, lead to sufficient energy, physical strength and harmony and allowing people to be productive and deal creatively with the development of society, family and themselves. Having control over one's health means possessing the knowledge of what needs to be done in order to be healthy, the money with which to purchase health care, and the capacity to make the necessary decisions. Good health is a primary resource for development. Without it, life is more painful, slower and happiness more elusive.

Health is a basic human right. Health for all by 2000 A.D. is not just a slogan but a commitment made to the people of the world by the world health organization and UNICEF. This declaration was made by Alma–in

1978. India is also one of the nation to have signed to Alma–declaration. Thus, the Indian government has publicly undertaken the responsibility of providing health to each of its citizens. Health is therefore, a fundamental right for all of us.

What is health? Is it just the absence of illness or diseases? No, because what is considered as a serious ailment by one person might be a minor problem for the other person. The concept of illness is not being well differs according to age, sex, social status, class, occupation. Therefore, the concept of being well differs from person to person. Thus, health is not just the absence of illness or ailments.

The international concern with the position of women and the reflection of this concern in treaties, policies and world conferences like these–is not at all a new phenomenon.

The Women's Empowerment Year 2001 began with lot of fanfare. The issues of pre-natal diagnostic tests, girl child's rights, maternal mortality and various associated health related investment are being addressed in big world conferences, national fora and even at local levels through small group workshops, seminars, debates and discussions. In a 1980 UN Report, it was reported that "women constitute half the world's population, perform nearly two-thirds of its work, receive one-tenth of the world's income and own less than one hundredth of the world's property". The declining sex ratio has to be examined in the social context of discriminating practices and attitudes that are in store for and usually the lost of the girl child. The female foeticide is still a practice in many parts of our country not only amongst the low SES strata but middle and high income level families as well. The majority of foeticide cases take place in relatively larger towns where sex determination clinics are mushrooming up and proliferating.

Thus, investment in women's health promotes equity, it ensures wide spread benefits for this generation and the coming generations. Many of the health problems that affect women of reproductive age, begin in childhood and adolescence. Further, improving equity and quality of life could save millions of women and let them lead fully productive lives.

Facts at a Glance

In September 1994, the world focussed on population : delegates to the International Conference on Population and Development (ICPD) in Cairo, debated the relative importance of various population and reproductive health issues and made influential policy recommendations.

Issues concerning youth were given considerable attention. The reproductive health status of young people, in terms of sexual activity, contraceptive use, child-bearing and sexually transmitted diseases, lays the foundation for the world's demographic future.

To highlight youth concerns, six major international youth organisations had joined together to organize a youth consultation just before the ICPD. Over 100 young people from around the world participated. The consultation resulted in a statement reflecting the views of young people on ICPD's main issues and providing decision makers with a guide to the needs, aspirations, and hopes of youth. PRB and CPO had compiled the information on this data sheet to help draw attention to the crucial issues affecting youth around the globe. In general, the data illuminates several important points:

- More than half the world's population is under age 25, and most of the world's youth—more than 80 per cent—live in developing countries.
- Around the world, a significant number of adolescents are sexually active at early ages, with an increasing proportion of this activity occurring outside of marriage.
- Many sexually active teenagers are not using any method of family planning. Even among married youth, contraceptive use is low: in the less developed world, only about 17 per cent of married women aged 15 to 19 years use contraceptives.
- Fifteen million teenage women give birth each year, accounting for up to one-fifth of all births worldwide. The vast majority of these births are in developing countries.
- At least 1 million and as many as 4.4 million adolescent women have abortions in developing countries each year. Most of these procedures are performed illegally and under unsafe conditions.
- Each year, 1 out of every 20 teenagers contracts a sexually transmitted disease (STD). Some STDs can cause lifelong disabilities, such as infertility, or even death.
- About half of all HIV infections so far have occurred in young people younger than age 25. Since the start of the pandemic, at least six million youth have been infected with HIV.

Health is considered as a fundamental human right and a worldwide social goal. It is essential to the satisfaction of basic human needs and improves the quality of life. From time immemorial, emphasis has been laid on achievement and maintenance of health. A modern, precise and yet comprehensive definition of health takes into account mental and emotional aspects too, besides physical fitness.

The "enjoyment of the highest standard of health is one of fundamental rights of every human being". This modern concept of health places stress not only on the individual but his relationship with the family and community. "The goal of health now calls for not only the cure or alleviation of diseases. Rather it looks beyond to strive for maximum physical, mental and social efficiency for the individual, his family and for the community.

Health as a Social Issue

The provision of this basic right is the responsibility of national government. International agencies, medical establishments, drug industry, non-governmental organization and community organization, self-help group and media. There are several other forces in society, which influence our health. The attainment and maintenance of health depends upon one's access to health goods and services. One cannot remain healthy if the environment around us is unhealthy. There are many forces acting on our household, work place and social level, which determine our health. Apart from, the individual body differences and habits, the government policies, commercial interests, state of environment, quality of medical care rural-urban and economic class are all determinants of health. Improvement in the health status of women in India, in general, since independence, due to various public health initiatives and interventions, but there is still scope for lot of improvement.

The UN Report observed that there is lot of commendable improvement in the health of Indian population during last decade, the two main parameters being:

- Improvement in life expectancy at birth.
- Women's overall life expectancy showing upward trend.

Inspite of these improvements and positive diversions, there are some glaring negative dimensions, which are very disturbing, because they take the monstrous shape of population explosion. The women do not and cannot enjoy and achieve a good standard of health in general, inspite of many efforts undertaken by the government of India and voluntary organizations to improve the health status of women. The following several factors hinder the improvement of health status of women.

Coupled with this there is the fact of inefficient functioning of the primary factors such as community prescription of medicines and costly medical services. All these have given rise to air/water/land and noise pollution related diseases and unhealthy conditions to an epidemic proportion. However, the advances in medical science are not able to provide a cure to many factors to control health damages as people are all illiterate, less aware, less concerned about the various preventive, promotive and creative dimensions of healthy practices. Health, therefore, remains an insufficiently tackled social issue. The lack of primary survival needs like clean drinking water, adequately available nutritious food, healthy and safe housing effects women more, causing a number of health problems mostly physical and psychological. Women work for longer hours at routine tasks such as fetching of water and fuel for cooking, child care and working in the household production or wage employment. Girls start helping their mothers at a very young age in household chores and also have heavy family responsibilities that interfere with their education.

Three-fourths of the 50 million children who are not involved in any school are girls. It is estimated that 30 per cent of the total work of fuel gathering or fetching water and farm works is done by girls aged of 6 years to 11 years. Almost the entire burden of sibling care is on the girl child.

Education influences mortality, morbidity and fertility of women and thus also their social status. Education is considered as a gift given to children by their parents.

The Health Issues

Wife assault has a profound effect on womens' health and well-being. It can result in physical injuries, psychological and emotional trauma:

1. Assaults on women with disabilities can trigger severe physical reactions. A woman with epilepsy may have a seizure. A woman with cerebral palsy may develop even more unclear speech, staggering gait or spasms. A woman with diabetes may go into coma and require insulin.
2. The effects of domestic health on women's mental health and well being can be just as serious as physical injuries. Assaulted women report a higher level of anxiety, physical complaints and depression than women who are not assaulted.
3. A study by the additional Research Foundation found that women who are assaulted by their male partners are seventy - four per cent more likely to rely on sedation and forty per cent more likely to take sleeping pills than women who are not assaulted.
4. In a recent study, eighty-three per cent of female psychiatric patients reported at least one severe incident of physical or sexual abuse by male partners.

5. Physical assault and emotional abuse tend to become more frequent and severe over time. Injuries sustained by assaulted women include bruises, warts, burns, dislocated bones, internal bleeding and more serious problems.
6. Assaulted women may be more likely to attempt suicide than women who are not assaulted.

The Impact on Children

1. Children who witness assault on their mothers can also be seriously affected. They are at the risk of being assaulted themselves and develop adjustment problems during childhood and adolescence.
2. Emery (1989) had listed the following difficulties that have been observed in empirical research–increased aggression, troubled peer relationships, impaired social performance and cognitions, lack of empathy, depressions and cognition tasks.
3. Children of assaulted women are significantly lower than their peers in several areas.
4. Children of assaulted women show a number of common characteristics including:
   (a) Blaming themselves for the violence.
   (b) Physical complaints such as stomach aches, headaches etc.
   (c) Sleep disturbances
   (d) Eating problems
   (e) Rigid gender role
   - Girls–withdrawn, passive, complain and acting as "mother's little helper".
   - Boys–Aggressive, bullying and self-destructive behaviour.

Amniocentesis and Sex Discrimination

The foetal fluid is extracted from a pregnant woman to determine the health of the foetus or the unborn child. Some birth related defects are more common in girls and others in boys. Thus, the purpose of this test is to determine the sex of the child so as to establish the presence of girl child or the defects. The aim of the test is not to assert the sex determination. Most women who go in for the tests, are lead to committing abortion of the female foetus. These women are mostly from middle class families and some even have good educational background.

In cases of accidental pregnancy, abortion following amniocentesis are normally practiced, particularly if the foetus is that of a female. The argument of course remains the same that a girl is less wanted than a boy. It can be hypothesized that irrespective of the sex of the first child, it is unlikely that the second foetus, if it is that of a boy will be aborted, even if the parents want only two children and that too preferably one of each sex. On the other hand, a female foetus is likely to be aborted more readily. Hospital records show mothers who have given birth to daughters, run away from their hospital staff reveal that the babies are killed by women desperate to survive themselves. A daughter is unwanted as she would mean long-term problems for her poverty stricken parents. As woman have become more and more conscious about their identity, their very 'self' has persuaded them to show their mettle in a male dominated society. Women's domain has become larger and their roles have expanded and in some ways become more complicated.

If social status of women is to be uplifted, education should be viewed "as an agent of basic change for the status of women". If a man is educated, only an individual is educated, but if a woman is educated, the entire family is educated.

Female Infanticide

It is defined as 'to kill infants at birth'. The financial burden of marrying off a daughter and the social stigma of having a daughter, have forced people to kill infant girls at birth. There are also some superstitious beliefs, which have led credence to increase in the prevalence of female infanticides. A common belief that they hold is that if you kill a female child, the next one is sure to be male. Another belief they have is that female children bring ill luck to the family. A woman who gives birth only to female children is looked down upon by the members of her husband's family. In order to avoid the wrath of the in-laws, the mother is forced to do away with daughter's since the destruction of a female infant is viewed psychologically in the same light as abortion.

Female Foeticide

It is defined as an act to kill the female foetus in the mother's womb. It is always considered better to kill the female foetus than to give birth to an unwanted female child. Abuse of amniocentesis for female foeticide is prevalent among all communities. As soon as the parents are told that it is a girl, they start making arrangements for abortion. It is a question of women's own choice whether these women enthusiastically go for the test of their own free will or are forced to. Are these choices made in a social vacuum? These women are socially conditioned to accept that unless they produce one or more male children, there is no social worth attached to them. They can be taunted, harassed or even deserted by their husband and in-laws, if they fail to do so. Thus, their choices depend on the fear of the society.

The high status given to male children in India and the increasing demand of at least one male–child has increased female foeticide. A son is considered as an asset whereas the daughter is considered as a liability. There exists a common belief that 'bringing up the girl' is like watering the neighbour's plant. A great deal of pressure is brought on the mother to abort the female foetus. This is double violence on the female sex–on the mother who must make the painful and often guilty decision and the female child that is destroyed.

Factors Responsible for Female Foeticide

1. Increasing dowry demands in daughter's marriage and harassment by in-laws are mainly responsible for female foeticide.
2. Prevalent unhealthy social environment and social pressure are affecting women's thinking against women dignity.
3. Women's biological structure and a feeling of insecurity for daughter's are also responsible for not welcoming their birth.
4. Faith, that a son is essential for salvation (*moksh*) for parent's care, for continuity of family lineage and for the inheritance of property gives strong incentives for sons.

Cycle of Health Problems

Old Age	*Infancy*
– Vitamin, mineral deficiency – Diseases – Social features – Poverty, education of – Health care, level education, lack of education, early marriage and pregnancy, family planning measures, measures low social status	– Low birth weight – Growth retardation – Late weakening 
Pregnancy	*Adolescence*
– Iron, vitamin A deficiency – Birth complex – Abortion – Less weight gain during pregnancy (disease)/decreases	Lack of nutrition Early pregnancy/lactating Nutrition deficiency

The flow chart depicts the milestone phases/stages in a woman's life, the cause of medical or socio-cultural dimensions and the consequent effect on the women's health or life or well being.

Stage	*Causes*	*Results*
1. Conception	Sex determination test	Death or damage
2. Birth	Female infanticide	Death
3. Infancy	* inadequate breast feeding and food or	Death or morbidity * neglect of food
4. Childhood	-No play -Domestic responsibility -Lack of education -Insufficient or low quality of food	Death or illness or less resistance
5. Puberty	-More restrictions -Less mobility -Inadequate food	Death, anaemia Depression Other health hazards
6. (a) Marriage (b) Motherhood	-early pregnancy -repeated delivery abortions, sex determination test, anaemia more weakness no control over sexuality, STD, HIV AIDS.	Death, severe anaemia Psychological problems Impaired reproductive health.
7. Old age	-Continued household -Nutritional deficiencies -Lack of medical care	Anaemia Other deficiency diseases

Again, lack of food and inequitable distribution of food for women in the household, inadequate access to safe water, sanitation facilities and fuel supplies particularly in the rural and poor urban areas and deficient housing conditions all have a negative influence on the women's health.

Reproductive Health

In simple worlds reproductive health means a satisfying, safe sex life, free from the fear of disease and free from coercion and violence. The capability to reproduce, and the freedom to decide, if when and how often to do so; that is women and men have the right to be informed and have access to effective, affordable and acceptable methods of family planning of their choice and access to infertility services.

The ability to go safely through pregnancy and child birth and have the best chance of having a healthy infant, and the right of access to appropriate health care services.

The Component of Reproductive Health are :

1. Family Planning and Abortion
2. Menstruation and Menopause
3. HIV / AIDS and STD's
4. Nutrition during Pregnancy and Lactation.
5. Nutrition during Adolescence
6. Nutrition for Expectant Mother.

1. Family Planning and Abortion

Family is a social unit where relation among members develops and leads to sense of belongingness. Planning means thinking ahead and making intelligent use of resources available to one for achieving one's purpose, and family planning means to plan a family in such a fashion so as to keep up the family needs and resources in balance which lead to a happy, healthy and better life. Family planning is defined as, "Planned regulation by a married couple from the pregnancies which are liable to result from their conjugal union, through the adoption of precautions".

Family planning implies the ability of individuals and couples to anticipate and attain their desired number of children and the spacing and timing of their births. It is achieved through use of contraceptive methods and the treatment of involuntary infertility.

Induced abortion is one of the oldest and most widely practiced methods of avoiding an unwanted birth. When women are determined not to have a child and if other means of preventing birth are not available or have failed, they do resort to abortion, regardless of the risks.

2. Menstruation and Menopause

Menstruation is the monthly shedding of the uterine lining, the blood and tissues that leave the body through the vagina. Menstruation is a normal, natural process that occurs in all healthy adult women who have not reached menopause. Girls can begin to menstruate at any time between eight and fifteen years and women might reach menopause anywhere between forty and sixty years. Women normally have their menstrual cycle of 20 to 28 days. Some may even have it of 36 days. Some women bleed for two or three days, some for seven or eight. All these and everything in between are normal.

Menopause is understood as a lengthy period of transition known as the 'change' of life. But in fact it is the brief time of women's last menstrual bleeding. The long period of several years that women suffer, first from irregular menstruation, which includes distressing symptoms like perspiration and 'hot flushing, and eventually to a complete end to menstruation. Menopause may be physically uncomfortable and emotionally stressful, even when it is a natural process.

3. HIV / AIDS

AIDS is the acronym for Acquired Immune Deficiency Syndrome. It is a syndrome or a condition, not a disease proper. In this condition the body loses the resistance to fight disease-producing organisms, because the virus destroys the very foundation of the defence mechanism of the body. AIDS mostly attacks the productive age group between 15–45 years, since it is usually acquired due to sexual behaviour. Acquired immune deficiency syndrome is not one disease but a combination of conditions, which occur due to damage to the immune system by the human immuno virus.

Acquired immuno deficiency syndrome is caused by a virus called HIV (Human Immuno Virus). It is not a single virus, but a family of many viruses called retro viruses. When a person is infected with human immuno virus, nothing is visible initially. He may be perfectly healthy in the beginning, but eventually the symptoms starts showing. A person with HIV is said to be having AIDS, only when his immune system is totally broken down and does not respond to treatment.

4. Nutrition during Pregnancy and Lactation

Life cannot be sustained without adequate nourishment. Man needs adequate food for growth, development and to lead an active and healthy life.

The world produces enough to feed everyone today in theory. Yet, in fact malnutrition affects more than 500 million people.

Numerous studies indicate that malnutrition is another serious health concern that Indian women face. It threatens their survival as well as that of their children. The negative effects of malnutrition among women are compounded by heavy work demands, by poverty, by child bearing and rearing, and by special nutritional needs of women, resulting in increased susceptibility to illness and consequent high mortality.

5. Nutrition during Adolescence

Adolescence is the period of transition from childhood to adulthood, with accelerated physical, biochemical and emotional development. It is during this period that the final growth spurt occurs. There are many body changes, which result due to the influence of hormones. With the profound growth of adolescence there is increased demands for energy, proteins, minerals and vitamins. Nutrient demand increases with the metabolic demands of growth of energy expenditure and the pubertal changes. The girls needs adequate intake of iron as they lose 0.5 mg/day by way of menstruation. The daily menstrual loss of iron is computed from the iron content of blood lost during the menstrual period averaged over a month. If this lost iron is not replaced, it predisposes to iron deficiency anemia. So in the end we can say that adolescence period is the period of lot of changes, which increase the demand of nutrients.

6. Nutrition for Expectant Mothers

Adequate nutrition before and during pregnancy has greater potential for a long-term health impact than it does at any other time. Maternal health is a complex, influenced by various genetic, social and economic factors, infections and environmental conditions, many of which may affect the foetal growth. Nutrition requirement of the expectant mother's increases because of the additional nutrients required for the following :

- The growth and physical activity of the foetus.
- The growth of the placenta.

Health and family welfare are becoming very important aspects of human life. The right to health has been accepted in all international treaties as a social right. Although there is a lot of improvement in the health status of women in India, in general, since independence, due to various public health initiatives and interventions, but there is still scope for lot of improvement about our partners in sexual life, i.e., men. It is here that the importance of developing awareness regarding reproductive health in adolescent girls and boys belonging to low SES and communities is considered of upmost importance.

- So, an effort is made to develop an extensive and exhaustive curriculum for the very essential areas of reproductive health.

When we talk about reproductive health we cannot be neglecting or even forgetting :

Factors influencing women's health :

1. ***Economic Factors :*** More than one billion people most of them women, live in extreme poverty. Women are more likely to be poor than men are and to be poorest of the poor. Households headed by women, estimated to be one-third of the total world-wide, are many times likely to be poorer than those headed by men.

It would be hard to exaggerate the influence that poverty has on people's health, because poverty restricts choice on so many areas that are basic to good health. Being very poor usually means :

- Not having enough food or the right kinds of food.
- Not having decent housing, sanitation and water supply.
- Not able to get health care when needed/if the care is free, the cost of transport of medicine can put it out of reach or a women may not be able to take time off from work without depriving her family of income.

2. ***Son Preference :*** Recent research on 'Son preference' reveals the dynamic by which the status of women can have a profound, even fatal, impact on the health of women and girls. The low health status of women in most parts of the world, is characterized by low life expectancy, high rates of mortality and chronic low-grade morbidity.

The reasons for Son Preference vary with the cultures and customs of different societies. In some religions, son is needed to carry out ceremonies for deceased parents, where the family name is preserved only through male descendents that can be one reason for the preference. Girls, on the other hand, may be looked upon as an additional expense with the little return, especially in the societies where a wife goes to live with her husband's family and society.

Studies in different areas where son preference is strong confirm that in these societies :

- Girls get a smaller percentage of their food needs satisfied than do boys and boys tend to get the more nutritious food.
- Boys are breast fed longer (when the baby is a girl, they may interrupt breast feeding in order to become pregnant again and try for a boy).
- Boys are more often taken for medical care when they are sick, and more money is spent on doctors fees and medicine for them.

3. ***Education :*** Education is the starting point for women's advancement in many different fields, 'whether we are talking about new farming methods, confidence-building, learning how to handle the budget.

A women who has been to school for a few years is more likely to marry at a later age four years later than an uneducated woman on average.

To have smaller family and to use modern family planning methods.

To seek pre-natal care and have a trained attendant at child birth.
To have healthy children and less likely to have children who die in infancy and early childhood.
To make use of health services generally.
To have larger earning capacity.

4. ***Dietary Intake :*** Lower nutritional status among females is due to both, the greater morbidity they experience and to more inadequate dietary intakes. Within households, food is distributed more in accordance with an individual's status than with nutritional requirements. Throughout their life cycle, females receive less food than do males, and also "inferior quality" foods. At her mother's breast a young girl receives less milk, less frequently and for a shorter period.

This is especially detrimental to girl child, born into families who already have a surviving child, particularly among low socio-economic groups.

5. ***Occupation of Women :*** One reason that work can be hazardous to the health of women is that they do over work. The international labour organization estimates that women put in two-thirds of the worlds' working hours, or in paid labour force or both, leave women with little time for sleep or relaxation. This may lead to chronic fatigue and contribute to malnutrition, stress, and premature aging and other health problems.

Women's work and health-care related in a number of ways. First, the energy costs of work have implications for the nutritional status of workers. Secondly, women's work may effect the health of other household members, particularly children. Heavy work demands on pregnant women affect the birth weights and viability of their infants. A busy, working mother may feed her infant or young child less, or be unable to give children the care they require during illness.

Mental Health

There are numerous mental health problems that effect women world-wide.

Depression

Major depression is the most common serious mental disorder. Women also appear to be more prone to anxiety states. In industrialized countries women are twice as likely as men to suffer from depression.

Several studies suggest that anxiety in women leads to increase with age and with decrease in socio-economic status. Depression is described as a reaction to perceived fear of loss of esteem, respect, status, love, income, attachment to others in the family and rejection.

Different demands are made on women to play several sometime-conflicting roles. The discrimination they faces in various situation may make their problems worse or make them feel less able to cope with them. Every woman's health is affected by the way her society regards and treats unmarried or married women, childless women, mother, poor women, divorced women, minority women, disabled women, widowed and aged women.

Why Women Suffer More Psychologically than Men?

- Stress and strain of the added burden of work.
- Frustration with sex role, socialization and expectations.
- Increasing awareness of rights and choices which affects adjustment within the family and marriage.

Other factors that have been found to put women at risk of depression include:

- Infertility
- An unhappy marriage
- Physical or sexual abuse
- Poverty and isolation in old age
- In industrial countries full time housewives are more likely to show signs of depression than, women working outside the home, especially women with young children.

Occupational Health

One reason, work can be hazardous to the health of the women is they do so much of it. International labour organization estimated that: women put; in two-thirds of world's working hours. Such long hours of force, whether at home or in paid labour force or both, leave women with little time for sleep or relaxation. This may lead to chronic fatigue and contribute to malnutrition, stress, premature aging and other health problems.

A study in India found that there was a high incidence of still births, premature births and death during the peak rice cultivation season. At this time when the rice is being transplanted, every one including whose pregnancy is almost full-term, are in the fields the whole day. The work involved squatting and bending for hours. Such physical strain and pressure in the uterus can lead to premature labour as well as still birth.

Women farm workers, usually poor, uneducated and in desperate need of work, are not in a good position to protest against dangerous conditions even when accidents occur or they suspect that their health is being affected. Urban women face other types of health risks associated with their work, especially women at the lowest socio-economic levels. Typically they have few qualification and few choices as to where they can work. They must take what they can get. Desperate not to lose their jobs once they have them, they put up with working conditions that expose them to variety of changes.

Women's work and health care related in number of ways :

1. Energy costs of work have implications for the nutritional status of workers.
2. Women's work may effect the health of other household members, particularly children.
3. Heavy work demands, on pregnant women affect the birth weights and viability of their infants.

A busy working mother may feed her infant or young child less or be unable to give children the care they require during illness. The largest proportion of women work in agriculture, primarily as labourers, where they are exposed to health hazards, such as poisoning from pesticides and chemical fertilizers which can cause diseases of the liver or birth defects and growth retardation of infants.

Cooking, which occupies a substantial proportion of women's time has its specific hazards. Wood smoke causes lung problems, which in turn place a strain on the heart. Carrying water, in one of the most demanding tasks undertaken by rural women. Heavy loads carried on heads, shoulders or hips require muscular strength and skill. Growth deformities may occur among children who carry heavy loads from a young age.

General Health Problems among Women

1. Reproductive tract infection (RTIs) specially among poor rural women.
2. Maternal mortality accounts for the largest or near largest proportion of death among women of reproductive age in most of the developing countries. Almost 500,000 women die of pregnancy related causes each year.
3. Malnutrition, including anaemia is a serious health problem, specially in women who have too many pregnancies too closely spaced. The women's nutritional status in turn influence her chance of having a normal delivery and child with an adequate birth weight.

4. Nutritional anaemia widespread among women of child bearing and contributes significantly to maternal mortality.
5. Closely connected with malnutrition and anaemia during pregnancy are the hazards of diseases and infection including intestinal parasites and malaria. In area, where malaria is endemic, women lose their immunity during their first pregnancy and malaria of placenta increase the risk of low birth weight.
6. There are also serious occupational health hazards for women. Studies clearly show that women engaged in heavy labour during pregnancy have a mean pregnancy weight gain several kilograms less than other women who have similar food intake.
7. Breast cancer, the main form of cancer affecting women globally is one of the commonest causes of death in many developed countries.

Bottlenecks in Accessibility of Health Services

1. Lack of separate provision of budget for MCH.
2. Knowledge about family planning methods is low despite the huge amount of money being spent on propaganda.
3. The high rates of abortion show the desire and need of the women for family planning and the failure of the family planning information and services to reach them in time.
4. Consequent problems tend to create apprehension among people.
5. The health of women and that too reproductive health has received inadequate attention in rural India.
6. Doctors of the primary health centres do not have adequate training to handle reproductive health problems.
7. Lack of 24 hour crèche facility for women patients with children in every hospital and PHC.
8. Lack of trained ANM's (Auxiliary Nurse Midwive's).
9. Ignorance and lack of awareness among women.
10. Poverty stricken families so women's health does not get the priority.
11. Women do not understand the importance of health.
12. Those who are aware do not reach to the persons concerned because of social and economical reasons.
13. Superstitions among low socio-economic status family.
14. Rigidity–cannot change their behaviour and habits due to which they fail to accept the services.

15. High illiteracy amongst women.
16. One who is providing health service is corrupt and wolfish and he/she utilizes much of the part of the money allotted for health services for himself i.e., money sanctioned for health services are not properly utilized.
17. Women do not give importance to their health. Their first priority is the family members i.e., husband and children.
18. Careless attitude of women towards health in particular as they have been socialized to think that way.
19. Customs and traditions–Midwives required for delivering during pregnancies, are usually not trained.
20. Health services are too far from their residence or houses, physical distance discourages them to take medical help.
21. Increasing dowry demands in daughter's marriage and harassment by in-laws are mainly responsible for female foeticide.
22. Prevalent unhealthy social environment and social pressure are affecting women's thinking against womens' dignity.
23. Womens' biological structure and a feeling of insecurity for daughter's are also responsible for not welcoming their birth.
24. Faith, that a son is essential for salvation (*moksh*) for parent's care, for continuity of family lineage and for the inheritance of property gives strong incentives for sons.
25. The girl child is the most deprived where access to health care is concerned. She is discriminated against not only in nutrition, health and upbringing but also in the right to be born.
26. Less care during sickness.

As pointed out earlier, women are the most deprived group as far as access to health services is concerned. Parents are prepared to spend money on sons, but not on daughters. They are willing to immunize sons, not daughters; are willing to rush to medical care for the sickness of the son, but reach much later and much less for their girls.

Recommendations and Suggestions for Optimising the Facilities Available and Attitudinal Change for Better Health of Women

1. Welcome the birth of a girl child and provide care and support to the mother.
2. Provide timely health care, immunisation, teaching the importance of breast milk, weaning foods to the mother.
3. Enroll the girl in school at the correct age and provide opportunities and support to education by reducing her household burden and child care.

4. Provide an opportunity to articulate her voice about marriage.
5. Discourage that only girls should fast during festivals and such occasions.
6. Provide an opportunity to articulate their voice, regarding family planning 'use of contraceptives' etc.
7. Provide encouragement and love to the girls for their development.
8. Do not discriminate between boys and girls during their upbringing.
9. Bring awareness among females about their rights for health.
10. Explaining the consequences of not looking after their health, for example, explaining the importance of each food groups for proper health growth and diseases due to deficiencies of nutrients.
11. Bringing understanding about their calorific needs specially in conditions like pregnancy, lactation etc.
12. Motivate and encourage them by schemes, e.g., giving food packets, free mid-day meals to their children, e.g., Applied Nutrition Programme and Mid-day meal programme.
13. By putting attractive banners of health at public places like water tanks, playgrounds, meetings grounds, theatre, restaurants, cinema halls.
14. By providing areawise health services so that women can just visit the health centres at their own leisure time as it would be near to their places.
15. Providing for transport facilities if health centre is far from their places.
16. By giving incentives in terms of promotion in jobs, if they have small family.
17. Dissuade parents who are stopping the girls education and dissuade child marriages, old and harmful religious rites.
18. Enact and implement stringent laws and policies to stop misuse of sex determination tests.
19. Provide appropriate activities like play and hobby centres for the development of girls.
20. Facilities for early detection of pregnancy, with low cost pregnancy detection kits.
21. Screening of high risk cases and providing treatment.
22. Advocacy of adequate rest, health and nutrition education.

23. Since women are severally restricted in their mobility, basic health care services must be made available to them as close as possible to their homes.
24. There should be proper publicity about various programmes meant for health. Awareness camps should be organised in order to make women aware about the various schemes and programmes by voluntary and government organisations.
25. Educating the community plays a pivotal role in improving the quality of life and sustains as well as complements the programmes for women and children. The beneficiaries should have a say in decision making so that the programme can be designed according to their needs and aspirations.
26. Reproductive health of women being a global concern, more awareness can be brought about by providing knowledge at the public places like cinema halls, hotels and by non-government organisations.
27. Post-graduate and under-graduate students can take up assignments and projects for developing Information Education and Communication (IEC), materials related to Reproductive Health of women as people in rural areas are quite ignorant about such knowledge.
28. Efforts should be made to revive and uphold the indigenous health system to extend health services to rural women which is at a comparative cost. Mobile health services can also cater to the needs of the rural areas.
29. There is a need to go beyond women's reproductive health aspects and address other priority concerns like sanitation, drinking water, etc.
30. Government policies must reflect health as a basic human right.
31. Health protection measures should be extended to the informal sector.
32. The materials developed can be used in future for giving awareness to people in public places like
    - Cinema halls
    - Hotels
    - Restaurants
    - Cable network and so on.
33. Programmes giving knowledge regarding Reproductive Health through Bhavai, role-plays and dramas could also be transmitted on television and cable networks to make masses aware regarding Reproductive Health.

34. Programmes of such nature could also be taken up with the collaboration of voluntary organisations.

Suggestion for Improving Women's Health

1. The undergraduate curriculum in the medical colleges for teaching maternal and child health should be reviewed and modified suitably particularly to deal with health problems of women and children in the rural areas.
2. From time to time refresher training on
   - Health education
   - Preventive health care like ante-natal care, immunization of children, promoting use of preventive equipment like gloves and mask.
   - Referral to large hospitals.
3. Improving women's nutrition through "Shakti Packets".
4. The real challenge before us is to tackle the careless attitude which most women have towards their health needs and nutrition. Too often, especially in rural areas, females eat last and least. This neglect of health needs of women leads to serious problems and further undermines their position and their capacities. So, there is a need that this practice must be
5. Access to information through participatory planning, participatory learning sessions with the adolescent boys and girls as focus need to be organised.
6. Organising Urban 'Slum Melas' and Exhibitions, focusing on the theme of reproductive health awareness, could be planned.
7. Multipronged strategy wherein involvement of various print, electronic and folk media can be planned to spread awareness for this area.
8. Networking with NGO's and GO's will help in establishing strong linkages for efficient delivery systems of the information packages.
9. Students can write articles in popular magazines, newspapers to reach to these boys and girls.
10. Regular meetings of CV's local leader, paramedical and health personnels with these groups can establish strong data base.
11. Academicians, including students can take up topics related to reproductive health and generate materials for masses, e.g., slides small documentaries, scripts for dramas, role-plays and so on.

12. Academic Institutions can organise exhibitions and workshop on this theme, which can be open to public especially interactive sessions for adolescent boys and girls to answer their quarries or doubts.
13. The extension component of Home Science Colleges and Institutions can take up reproductive health as a thrust area– we are already working for this in both urban as well as rural extension programmes.

The Role of Home Scientists–What Home Scientists can do?

The job of the Home Scientist is not only to gain knowledge but also disseminate this knowledge to the people who require it. Home Scientist has a greater chance to implement and use the knowledge in the field work actually.

- Women's health is neglected not only by the society but by herself, since awareness regarding importance is not known. Home Scientist is required to make them aware about different health conditions and its dangers.
- Home Scientist can use more health related topics and issues for their community work. They can use good amount of teaching aids to promote their work.
- They can organise some camps on health issues such as irradiation, polio, maternal health and its care, family planning, normal as well as pre-pregnancy and post-pregnancy diet, first aid information, etc.
- To make people aware regarding women's health rights and its legal applicability.
- To contribute towards change in some social attitudes and beliefs related to the women's health such as son preference, non-use of health services, use of smoke chullas.
- To provide people adequate information about public health services, policies and programmes run by the government.
- Communicate with people regarding health related issues.
- More emphasis on health related issues and researches on women's health can provide good amount of data regarding health conditions and practices which can help to step further towards this issue.
- To impart awareness among girls of Home Science, special lectures or sessions on health conditions should be planned in which experts can provide information knowledge.

Need to take part in such camps, workshops which give full amount of health education and motivate people including community people to attend such programmes and get information.

Conclusion

To improve women's health status there is no doubt, that the general health services need to respond to women's specific problems. A strategy for improving the health of women in the reproductive age group to reduce the risk of death and illness associated with pregnancy as well as to reduce the exposure to pregnancy itself. Comprehensive minimal care during pregnancy, child birth and there after steps to ameliorate malnutrition as well as decrease the work load of women, and improve access to health services, particularly family planning services, should be the salient instruments for improving the health of women. Facilities for early detection of pregnancy, with low cost pregnancy detection kits should be made easily available.

Thus, to conclude, we would like to say that women's health has become an issue which is almost like lost wealth. Women themselves do not seem very keen to utilize the health facilities. They feel their personal health problems are of least priority and importance in comparison to men, who may be their brothers, husbands or fathers. They also like to spend on their children's education, health and development, rather than their own health.

So to sum up, there is a great need for bringing about attitudinal change in women themselves, rather than the health facilities. The guiding principles for the first time and a half decade of planned development in health in India included measures to :

(i) Make health services more accessible to the women.
(ii) Developing the needed human resources.
(iii) Provision of services for health including maternal and child health and family planning.

Over time, the need to interact more closely with women, has been felt. Obstacles or bottlenecks which do not let women participate fully need to be identified and removed. Often structures and social norms are barriers, and stem from social conditioning which inhibits or prevents women from aspiring to decision making process in this area of concern. Government and non-governmental interventions and assistance should facilitate and promote women's participation for better health.

References

Adams Dianne L, *Health Issues for Women of Colour,* University of Maryland, Eastern Shore, 1995.

Bang, R.A., Bang, A. et al. "High Prevalence of Gynecological Diseases in Rural Indian Women *Lancet–1* (8629) 1989 : 85–88.

Baroda M.S. University of Baroda WOHTRAC and WSRC "Workshop Report on Qualitative Research Approaches and Women Centred Health Care" Baroda : Centre for Operation Research and Training 1997.

Bhaduria Mridula, Some Issues of Women's Health *Social Welfare,* Vol. 46 No. 1 April 1999.

Bhatnagar Suman Rani. Knowledge and practices in household sanitation as reported by Patidar and Baria housewives of village Asoj in Gujarat, M.S. University, Baroda, 1968.

Bora Malaya Madhuri. The study of health habits and sanitary practices of Girl students of Ninth and Tenth classes of three selected high schools is Jorhat Assam, M.S. University, Baroda, 1974.

Bummer E. (1990). *May you be the mother of a hundred sons; a journey among the women of India*, New York, Ballantine Books.

Chatterjee Meera, *Indian Women–Their Health and Economic Productivity*, The World Bank, Washington D.C.

Chetna News, Centre for Health Education, Training and Nutrition Awareness, Jan-Mar., 1998.

CHETNA. 'Women's Health Mela : An Innovative Training Approach for Women' 5–7 April, 1990. Ahmedabad. Chetna, 1990.

Dan Alice, *Reframing Women's Health. Multidisciplinary Research and Practice*, University of Illinois, Chicago, 1994.

Dr. Agnihothri, V.K. (1998). Reaching Health to the poor, Source Book on District Health Management. VHAI Publication.

Dr. Mira Siva (1997). Freedom from illness; Health Status of Women, *Social Welfare*, Vol. 44 No. 28-32.

Feed, R.S., Feed, S.A. (1989). Beliefs and Practices resulting in female deaths and fewer females than males in India. *Population and Environment*. 10(3) : 144–61.

Fogel Catherine Ingam, *Woods Nanacy Fugate University of North Carolina at Chapel Hill*, University of Washington, Seattle, 1995.

Government of India, Ministry of Health and Family Welfare (1992). *Family Health Survey*–Madhya Pradesh and India.

Kapoor Ranjana. Value preference of rural homemakers regarding general sanitation and cleanliness of the home, M.S. University, Baroda, 1977.

Klonoff Elizabeth A., Landrine Hope, Preventing Misdiagnosis of Women, Women's Mental Health and Development, Vol. 1, 1996.

Kolblinsky Mange, Timyan Judith and Gay Jill, *The Health of Women–A Global Perspective,* West View Press, Boulde, San Francisco and Oxford.

Kynch, J. and Sen, A. (1983). Indian Women, well being and Survival *Cambridge Journal of Economics*, 7: 363-80.

Lankester, Ted, Setting Up Community Health Programmes–a practical manual for use in developing countries, MacMillan India Limited, 1992.

Lee Christina, Women's Health, Psychological and Social Perspectives, University of New Castle, Behaviour and Health, 1998.

Levin Bruce Lubotsky Levin, Blan Andrea K., Jennings Ann, Women's Mental Health Services, University of South Florida, 1998.

Lorber Judith, Gender and Social Construction of Illness, New York, 1997.

Mahajan P. Mani and Siby, K. Joseph. "Human Resource Utilization" Musing on an Alternative Development Paradigm Kurukshetra Dec. 1996.

Parrot Roxanne Loniselle, Condit Celeste, Evaluating Women's Health messages, University of Georgia, Athens, 1996.

Pence Donna, Wilson Charles, The team Investigation of Child Sexual Abuse–The Uneasy Alliance, Interpersonal Violence : The Practice Series, Vol. 6, 1994.

Pendse Sunanda. Knowledge and practices in household sanitation and two areas of public health as reported by housewives of two selected localities of Baroda city. M.S. University, Baroda, 1969.

Rana Ansuya, Knowledge and practices regarding personal health and sanitation of the eighth standard students of village Asoj, M.S. University, Baroda, 1971.

Rao, K.V. (2003). Health Planning and Development in Reproductive Health, Gender and Development–an International Perspective, B.R. Publishing Corporation, Delhi.

Rao, T.V. Human Resources Development–Experiences, Interventions, Strategies.

Rodin, J. and Ickovics, J.R. (1990). Women's health : Review and Research agenda as we approach the 21st Century. *American Psychologists* 45, 1018–34.

Rosenfeld Ann, Handbook of Womens' Health, Cambridge University Press, 2001.

Sharma Purnima. Personal Hygiene and Environmental Sanitation of Selected Pupils and their Mothers of Sevasi Village, M.S. University, Baroda, 1978.

Shiva, M. (2002). Freedom from Illness : Health Status of Women. *Social Welfare* Vol. 48(8) pp. 28–30.

Shiva, M., Freedom from Illness–Health status of women, *Social Welfare*, Aug.-Sept., 1997, Vol. 44, No. 5-6.

3

Women and Media

Anuradha Mathu, Rameshwari Pandya

Abstract

The status of women in media in the world generally and in developing countries like India, has been poor and not upto the mark. Women can and are contributing a lot in the areas of social development vis-à-vis gender development.

Our media, especially television films and folk media including dramas, role-plays–'Bhavai's' can take up the challenges of reaching the masses, especially the rural women as we all are aware that 80 per cent of our population lives in villages.

Further, our general masses seem to have developed a kind of lethargy and have thus become passive receivers from the various 'media'. To add insult to injury, the media by and large either does not represent the women genuinely or shows pathetic under representation. Women are also represented as sex-objects in many advertisements/commercials or soaps–popular T.V. serials.

This situation can be improved if we have well-informed women, who in turn can lead media towards more healthy development. The future of media and women are inter-dependent. Women on the one hand will have to fight for their rightful place in media. The media on the other hand will have to take up developmental issues related to women more seriously.

Also, the role of universities and academicians in representating women would be of paramount importance. Wherein, workshops, seminars, symposia and conferences need to focus on issues related to women in and women and media. NGO's and GO's can also play a very crucial role for awareness building and sensitisation.

We need to take this issue seriously as media can be a large industry to provide multifarious kinds of jobs to millions of our women as—news readers, actors, producers, directors, media designers, editors, freelancers, and so on.

Introduction

Media has been the reflector of dominant values and work as an active agency, among reinforcing and strengthening dominant value structure. A platform where various interests can be brought together, exists in the form of media in today's democratic society. While the role of media in early liberal thought was defined mainly in terms of a watchdog, the expectations from this medium widened with development of mass society.

Media is a "power resource", in terms of exerting influence in society, they are played out, they are 'source' of varied definitions of social reality, changing culture and values and most important, they are a source of the "public meaning system". Media is the carrier of public opinion and plays a crucial role in giving voice to the people. All the content of the media is important to our national life, not just what frankly and directly relate to public affairs. To some extent, it sounds true that the T.V. reflects the reality, somehow, it does not stop at the depiction of reality but tries to step forward. It serves as an indicator of what is believed to be desirable and undesirable. It constantly evaluates the reality and points out the ideal picture of the world (Murphy, 1977).

Unfortunately, the definition of the real world is different for various segments of the society. The group of people controlling any media constantly try to influence the reality by presenting their own ideal situations. There is enough evidences and researches to suggest that any medium is a powerful medium which can have positive as well as negative effects. The impact of media on our lives is a point, which does not have to be laboured any longer. Radio, television, films and print world, reach all of us in this age of information and each shines to perfect its modes of communication to become more effective as a medium.

The contents of media are reflective of the values of society, which are further nurtured and sustained through these media. The treatment meted to women and girls are mirrors of the present value of a particular society. For example in India, the very strong stereotype images of women and girls are that of :

(i) Less competent people.

(ii) They can be used for commercialization purpose like any product.

(iii) They are weaker sex.

At present, the whole country is on move and we all can feel the communication revolution of which satellite, computer, television and video are major manifestations. This is the reason the present age is also known as "information age".

Inspite of this boom of media the reach of mass media to the women is still restricted mainly because of low literacy, low purchasing power and lack of relevant information (in-case the main aim is of development and not only recreation).

It is important for national development that half of its population does not become "wasted assets" instead they should be well-informed about all development plans and programmes including those relating to education, health and small family.

In general, films, advertisements, songs, T.V. signboards and drama they do not do justice as all of them portray women in a negative image. Women are portrayed as self-sacrificing persons with no self-respect or as jealous cats. They are shown as inferior, dependent or symbols of sex.

Most of the films and T.V. show women as a weaker sex, second class roles, and most of the time females are shown as sex objects.

- It is very important to break the vicious cycle of "undesirable" images and there is an urgent need to change the complete content of existing communication messages.

A mass medium, says Wilbur Schramm, is essentially a working group organized around some device for circulating the same message, at about the same time, to a large number of people. Such a definition excludes the folk media, group media and natural communication such as in rumour, education and preaching. As generally interpreted the mass media are the press, cinema, radio and television. But books, magazines, journals also need to be included in the label.

Further, media have been playing major roles in our daily lives. In its various forms, the media informs us, seduces us, confuses us and programmes everything from what we should think, feel, smell, see, taste and hear.

Mainstream media, controlled by only a handful of men, more and more western in its perspective and increasingly merging with corporate interests, presents to the world many contradictions. Gerbers sees the effect of mass media in their capacity to take over the cultivation of images, ideas and consciousness. The truly revolutionary significance of modern mass communication is the ability to form historical news based for collective thought and action, quickly, continuously and pervasively across the previous boundaries of time, space and status. Thus, mass media like TV and films are cultural forces which do not simply reflect, but subtly and indirectly help in shaping social reality. Such attitudes and behaviour are adopted through a complex process of imitation and comparison with the attitudes and behaviour presented by mass media.

Several research studies have revealed that the media have been ineffective in discharging their duty of informing and preparing society about women's new role in national development. There are several reasons for this failure, even if we put them one by one the first one could be limited reach of mass media among women this is specially true for remote tribal and rural India. Even those who are exposed to media have only limited exposure that mainly films and film based programmes. Chances for women to display superiority, except in traditionally accepted female areas of knowledge. All the studies report that women depend on men for advice and assistance in the purchase and use of products.

Status of Women in Media

In the battle for equal status and fair treatment of women an important role is generally attributed to the mass media, and in particular to television, because it has become a significant part of life, in a developing country like ours. The presentation of women and men in films and television is contradictory to reality. It misrepresents the real proportion of men versus women in the population or in the workforce of the extent to which social class, age, occupational status are ascribed to the two sexes. It is generally observed that consistently and systematically women are being exploited to the advantage of man's self-esteem. One important reason, one can assume, is that its production, direction and other facets are controlled by men. Apart from that, for majority of women who control it, the decision making level is dominated by men.

A number of studies made in different countries lead to the conclusion that the image of women as it is shown in the films and television is either of a housewife, a mother or as a sexual object. Women are shown as dependent, foolishly indecisive, deceitful, incompetent and so on.

In contrast, to the fast growing body of research into the question of woman's portrayal by the film, television and other mass media, available from almost all parts of the world, relatively little is known about the extent and nature of women's participation in the industries of films and television. The data available are often based on subjective impressions rather than on objective facts. Broadly speaking, the situation of women working within television or films reflect the fact that the world of work is male dominated. This is both in terms of overall number and of distribution across and within specific occupations, women workers are at a distinct disadvantage when compared to their male counterparts. It has been estimated that there are approximately twenty-eight per cent of women in broadcasting in India.

Women are generally concentrated at the lower levels of particular job categories. They are also found in areas, which are overwhelmingly female. At the managerial level, women generally hold not more than ten per cent of the jobs. Despite the fact very few women are found at the top, in any category, there is a noticeable concentration of women in certain areas, where promotion or career development is negligible. However, men not only dominate the scene as producers, but as consumers too, readers of newspapers and magazines are mostly men.

The reason for distortion of a woman's image in media, is that women find their identity with stereotype images outside the film and television too. It is the marginality of women in cultural and social activities generally which contributes to their subordination in life.

All these facts are hardly recognized and whenever women as a group or an individual have tried to protest, against the studied facts, they have had to face the argument which is often raised from all levels of society that women themselves willingly participate in such films, plays and television. Therefore, it can be said that to some extent women themselves are responsible for their distorted picture in media.

Media being one of the traditional strongholds upholding status quo in a conservative society like India, it is only natural that women get a raw deal at their hands both in the media and their portrayal of women in the media.

Media also demonstrates the position of women through the advertisements. A 1984 study stated that seventy-one per cent of the TV commercials in India were on 'grooming advertisements for women. In almost all the cases of media exposure, women continue to be featured as victims of social injustice or pawns in religious power games. In short, they remain ineffective as a force, weak and dependent, helpless and sacrificing and at the same time, the concern of some media critics has been that by repeatedly and consistently depicting women and men in stereotyped roles and by tending to portray any deviations from these roles in a negative rather than positive way, the media may actually work against the potentially transforming effects of those encounters with counter-stereotypes which women and men may experience in ordinary social life.

Passivity, Dependence, Indecisiveness

Consistent findings are that passivity and emotional dependence are rewarded in women while in general, characteristics which are defined as 'good' in men decisiveness, independence, forcefulness, tenacity are defined as 'bad' in women. According to the fictional reality of media, women are actually rewarded for ineffectuality rather than for actively controlling their own lives.

Women in Advertisements

Advertising has been a prime target of attack and scrutiny. The basic explanation for the critical focus on sex role portrayal in advertising lies in the close relationship, which exists between advertising, the consumer goods industry and the crucial economic role of women as consumers. Since women are perceived as the major consumers, advertising manipulates the female image in order to persuade women to buy. Compared to the actual female employment status, working women are under represented in both print and broadcast advertisements. Generally it is shown in advertisement, a woman's goal in life is to attract and attain a man :

- Women are shown in advertising as always young and attractive.
- They are frequently depicted as sexual objects.
- Women in advertisements are restricted to the home and isolated from other women. Outside the home, man is her favourite companion.

Women in advertising seldom appear as competent or intelligent people. Intelligence is presented as a masculine trait. Intelligent women are therefore 'unfeminine' and disliked by men.

Emphasis on women's physical appearance pervades advertisements directed at both male and female consumers. Male oriented advertisements feature beautiful, sexy women as the ultimate reward for using the advertised products. In exchange for beauty and youth, women are rewarded with security and status, love and romance. This, however does not imply that female beauty has lost significance for the concept of femininity as defined in advertising. On the contrary, emphasis on the attractive female physique is actually increasing. The auto-erotic women represents the commercial version of the liberated women. Investigation into the relationship between the visual and textual advertising language in their persuasive process revealed that the three key words associated with sex role portrayal were naturalness, beauty and uniqueness.

Domesticity is the second role of two dimensional image of femininity in advertising. A woman is essentially a domestic person and is expressed in various ways :

1. Women do not work outside the home.
2. Women are not successful in world outside the home: they do not do male jobs.
3. Men and women have strictly delineated sex roles and household tasks.
4. Women like housework, it is fulfilling.
5. Little girls grow up to be housekeepers, wives and mothers.

Recently, women have strongly objected to the way their body is exploited to promote products when hardly any body exposure is warranted. Pretty girls and voluptuous women posing with products make up many ad copies. Indian culture is far different from the Western culture. In the Indian marketing environment therefore such appeals do not cut much ice. Often they are ridiculous. In one of the cigarette advertisement the zip fastener of a woman's bra is shown coming down so gradually to correspond to the price reduction which the organization has introduced. The advertisement is certainly in bad taste.

While selecting a model, advertising agencies look for a good figure, features, complexion and for a person who has photogenic face, or she has to impress the audience and to convince it that she is a at home with the product, particularly where demonstration is required. They are considered to be the images of the products. But nowadays the percentage of advertisements covering a positive image of women are increasing. Women can be seen as performing business tasks and working on computers as well.

Women in TV Programmes

Television is probably the most popular and powerful medium of communication in the world today. Its influence in shaping attitude and concept is unquestionable. The image of women presented on TV screens may have a positive or negative impact in the fight against sexism and discrimination. At present, this impact is predominantly negative.

Television programmes at present are dominated by feature films and film based programmes that exploit the female form and through their socially insensitive approach simply trivialize ane debase the image of womanhood. The vulgarity and violence of these commercial films are to be strongly condemned. It continues to project women in subordinate and exploited roles and ignores their contribution towards economic activity. Most of the programmes present social reality which as a presentation may not be totally wrong. This ignores the new and desirable trends until they become quite established and thus it merely fulfills basically a reinforcing role to traditional pattern rather than leading role.

There has been considerable criticism regarding the treatment of women in Television programme.

- Women as equal companion of the man is never stressed.
- Even *Doordarshan* which aims at education and development along with entertainment does not take programme on women's issue like :
  - Dissemination of information regarding education.
  - Health services and employment opportunities.
  - Knowledge regarding their legal right and responsibility, where to go when they are in trouble.

The committee on Portrayal of women, formed in 1983 noted the following characteristics of the images of women projected in media:

1. A woman's place is in the home only.
2. Most important and valuable assets of a woman is her physical beauty.
3. Women are dependent, submissive they stay quiet even to the physical violence inflicted on them.
4. Good woman is the traditional housewife, where as modern woman who assets herself and her independence is undesirable.
5. Women are women's worst enemies.

It is very commonly seen that fer is used to product sale means selling products. This kind of portrayal of female are responsible in lowering the image of women gender bias is also very dominant on T.V. even if it is for men.

Women in Newspapers and Magazines

Newspaper portrayal of women deals with the treatment of women in pictorial, textual and linguistic content of various newspaper sections. Although, these have been criticized for perpetuating traditional perspectives, they represent an important institutionalized vehicle for information about or relating to women. As for female roles, women were primarily portrayed as spouses, socialities and entertainers. The photo coverage of women as sports figures, professionals, activists and politicians is negligible compared to their portrayal in aforementioned roles.

Women's magazines are distinguished from other media mainly by the fact that they are directed specially to and read primarily by women. Women's magazines are highly valued advertising vehicles. They focus mostly on food, fashion and beauty, thus reinforcing traditional roles of women. Information about relevant socio-economic issues, including the status of women, is largely lacking. The dependence on advertising, which is often bluntly sexist in its depiction of sex roles, is indicated as one of the major reasons for the perpetuation of traditional female images. In India, only upper and middle class women, presented to be primarily housewives, have easy access to both consumer products and the press which promotes the consumer goods industry to women. As a result majority of women, who are always economically active and increasingly work in unskilled labour, are ignored by the press. While the report defines the education function of women's magazines as broadening their audience's horizon by exposing the social conditions of the mass of Indian women, it fails to indicate whether and how they can promote the education of majority of women and particularly of women living in rural areas where illiteracy rates are high.

Images of Women in Mass Media

The presentation of concise and accurate picture of how the media portrays women around the world poses enormous problems of compression and synthesis. Overall, media treatment of women can best be described as narrow. In films, in the press and the broadcast media, women's activities and interests typically go no further than the confines of home and family. Both as characters in fictional media material and as newsmakers in the press and broadcasting, women are numerically under-represented, an absence which underlines their marginal and inferior status in many spheres of social, economic and cultural life. Prevalent news values define most women's problems, as unworthy, admitting women to coverage primarily as the wives, mothers or daughters of men in the news, in their own right, they make the headlines usually only as fashionable or entertainment figures. Mass media advertising directed at women as consumers is condescending in tone and manipulative. In products that are advertised, women are exploited in terms of their sexuality and physical appearance.

Under Representation of Women

Various researches reveal that in all media categories, but particularly on broadcast television and radio and in newspapers, women are grossly under represented and occupy less central roles than men.

Wife and Mother : The Home Orientation of Women

The fact that women are commonly portrayed within the confines of the home, while men tend to be seen more often in the outside world of work, is well documented and one can easily detect differing emphases between countries reflecting somewhat varied social perceptions of what the female role is or should be. Thus, for example, research indicates some emphasis on the role of the long, suffering, self-sacrificing mother or the role of women in the home as housewives and good housekeepers reflecting material and consumer values. So, it is clear that marital status is a more crucial factor in identifying women than in identifying men and that parenthood is more frequently associated with women than with men women as sex object.

One of the most deeply reactionary and yet insidiously flattering images, which the media present of women to themselves and to men is that of beautiful sophisticate, or of the sexually alluring siren. These images are most clearly associated with the visual media television, film, and magazines and are the frequent recourse of the advertising industry, working through these media. The use of women as "bait", in the sale of products ranging from cosmetics to liquor or cars. Complicating this basic picture is the fact that the last five years has seen the growth of a relatively new emphasis on women's sexuality as an element in their liberation from dependence on men.

The Virgin–Whore Dichotomy

Underlying these images of the women as housewife/mother and as a sexual object, runs a strain noted in studies in numerous countries. This points to a fundamental paradox in female imagery and inability to cope with women's real sexuality. The good-bad, virgin whore distinction is a dichotomous strand in an enormous amount of the imagery, which the media ascribes to women. Each side, of the dichotomy can be expressed through a number of variations. The "Virgin" image may be vested in the abandoned wife, sacrificing herself for her children, the sister or daughter or parents. The 'whore' may be seductive secretary eventually abandoned by the faithless husband in favour of wife at home; the siren who incites the crime; the irresistible artiste who torments here lover; here the imagery is concerned with cruelty, inhumanity, insensitivity and unscrupulousness. These roles are propagated by the notion of rewards and punishments; if the woman behaves well she will be given the love of her man, if she behaves badly, she will be alone, unloved or castigated.

The Working Woman : Power and Authority

Various researches indicate that, in relation to women's actual participation in the work force, all media under-represent women workers. For instance, although in reality almost half of the labour force is female, studies show percentages of working women in television portrayals, which vary from thirty per cent to as low as twelve per cent. Studies world wide also show a concentration of women portrayed as employed in a limited number of jobs and in predominantly female fields and roles. This is significant because the question of power and status of men viz-à-viz women in media portrayals relates in part to the kinds of occupational role to which sex is predominantly assigned. Since women are rarely seen in authoritative roles as lawyers, doctors, judges, scientists, they are rarely in a position to exercise direct authority over an adult male. In a study of pattern of advising and ordering in male-female interactions, it was found that dramatic characters on television were selected, occupations were assigned and plots developed in such a way as to minimise the status of women.

Several studies have proved that there is a direct correlation between backwardness and deprivation of communication resources.

The mass media in India are essentially 'class' media, as it is a very effective tool it can be an effective vehicle for social change as well.

Almost every section of the Plan and Policies urged "vigorous" campaigns of education and action; so that plan could come within the reach of women everywhere. Media can be an important tool for women empowerment.

It is important to recognize the power of media in empowering women. Print and non-print material should be devised in terms of content and approach reflecting the crucial role women can play social transformation. Concepts such as 'empowerment' and autonomy in decision making, especially in legal and economic matters are derived in action based terms.

There are disadvantages like:

1. Lack of scientific research in mass media.
2. Monotony of the programme.
3. Twelfth hour decisions of governments in planning, funding and implementing the programmes.
4. Lack of motivation on the part of policy makers.
5. Lack of needed support from higher authorities.

(I) Future Directions to Enhance the Status of Women in Media

Universities can be used for promotion of status of women in media as universities and colleges have certain strengths in using media. These are as follows–

Universities have availability of knowledge, experience infra-structural facilities, course and curriculum development skill and students strength.

Secondly they also have requisite skills for coordination with departments and others linkages with GOs and NGOs.

1. Encouragement of M.Phil. and Ph.D. students to undertake their dissertation related to topic on "Women and Media" :
   - Media Monitoring by women
   - Portrayal of women
   - Status of women
   - Employment of women in media
   - Women's issues
   - Advocacy Research
2. Inter disciplinary research–appreciation
3. Working with media to sensitise the public in the following :
   - Adolescence needs
   - Sexual behaviour
   - Gender equality
4. Research on women and media needs to be strengthened.
5. Conducting indepth researches on the impact of media and its utilization.
6. Seeking from government some kind of concession or rebate on women oriented programmes on electronic media.
7. Impressing on media to maintain a panel of scholars and specialists for specific programmes on women and women's issues.
8. Department of Home Science Extension and Communication, Faculty of Home Science can collaborate with Journalism.
9. Social Work Sociology and Department of Adult Education and develop programmes which are gender sensitive.
10. Universities can conduct training programmes on :
    (a) Script Writings
    (b) Media Research
11. Interacting with media to increased utilization of research fundings this will help in enhancing interest in Media Research and utilization.
12. Research and analysis should be undertaken to assess the ways in which the various communication channels reach.
13. Text books in use in formal and non-formal education system and training should be carefully assessed for removing negative images and reference to women.
14. Research and analysis should be undertaken to assess the ways in which the various communication channels reach and affect women and girls.

15. The outreach of different media by age, sex can be assessed.
16. Reasons for the very low exposure of women to mass media must be identified.
17. Feedback information should be actively encouraged in universities and other research institutions. Besides it should be a compulsory component of the syllabi of mass communication and journalism training institutions.
18. There should be "Resource Centres" at the centre and state levels for identification, collection, dissemination and documentation of materials related to women's issues.

(II) Research on Women and Media Workshops

1. Skills learnt in the workshop for preparing brief summary for policy maker.
2. Disseminating research findings to Media and sponsor agencies.
3. Dissemination and utilisation of Media findings as objective of research.
4. Packaging of research findings into messages.
5. Sessions of workshops will be useful for strengthening presentation skills.
6. Taking a more pro-active role in enhancing the utilisation of media research.

(III) Different mechanisms to elicit active support of media are as follows

1. Directory of media persons should be proped to mobilise. Active support of media persons.
2. Separate media all, fully equipped with modern technology and facilities should be created so that video films can be prepared for publicity campaign.
3. More and frequent interaction with media persons in the form of "Meet the Press", press releases and press conferences could help enhance wide publicity of the women programmes.
4. Preparation of low cost, software on developmental issues.
5. Securing help of NGOs and encouraging them to work in this field.
6. Creation of information bank.
7. Setting up of relevant need based web sites.
8. Enlisting and enrolling volunteers to act as "into-mediaries".
9. The content of media and the production should be educational but still attractive for common men and women.

10. Well thought of programmes for T.V. can be a great instrument for social transformation.
11. Appropriate strategies should be evolved for improving interaction between journalists and women / girls students.
12. Journalists need to be oriented towards a better comprehension of importance of media in imbibing values of equality among men and women.
13. Important / sensitive news and reports should be whetted by female journalists also before publication, this can help in removing bias if any.
14. Programmes on television and radio can be focussed on and made to generate awareness regarding issues of girl child and discrimination and solution to combat such problems.
15. Films are very popular medium of communication especially in India, where the largest number of film are produced, films revolving round women's status, women's issues and discrimination could be made even with small budget films. This would help in generating awareness amongst general masses.

Career Opportunities in Media for Women

- Script Writers
- Journalism
- Advertisements
- Media Education
- Free Lancing
- Film Production
- Columnists
- News readers in Radio, T.V.
- Photographers / Video-graphers
- Media Producers, Directors
- Graphic Designers
- Media Designers
- Editors
- Story Writers
- Animators

Recommendations for Future Action

The role of all agencies is very important and effective in uplifting the images of women presented by media. Improvement can be brought by using following guidelines:

1. Developing mass media material which portray women in a positive and constructive manner and in a wide variety of roles.
2. The adoption of non-sexist guidelines by advertisers, broadcasters, film makers, journalists and publishers.
3. Creating positive attitude among mass communicators towards the integration of women in the mainstream of social life.
4. Allowing for their increased commitment to bringing information for and about women to the public's attention.
5. Making those who control media, aware of the need for a balanced workforce for both sexes.
6. Publicity campaign sponsored by these organizations to expose discrimination against women in the media, to notify women about their legal rights and highlight the public awareness of media images which are insulting and demeaning to women.
7. Spontaneous as well as organized action on the part of consumers to protest against sex-stereotyped portrayals in mass media via letter writing, campaigns, product boycotts, etc.
8. The content of women's programme on radio, television or articles in print media on women should project their multiplicity of roles, life style, problems and struggles.
9. Promotion of Media Literacy : Media literacy teaches people to analyze message conveyed by the media, consider the commercial or political purpose of the image or message and who is responsible for it, and other ideas that it implies. It increases our ability to react to and appreciate (or not) media images and message in a genuine and conscious way. It provides information and statistics on media and culture and provides a set of tools for critical thinking which can be applied to any media "product" or setting.
10. Women should be portrayed in positive roles in media to create transformation of women's images.
11. Women issues awareness advertisement should be encouraged in both print and electronic media.
12. Media organisation should keep contract with the NGO's and other social organisation and act as a watchdog.
13. Women should be shown natural and realistic in the advertisement.

Conclusion

The employment status of women in print media compares favourably with that in other media sectors in terms of numerical representation only. The evidences presented in the currently available literature of women and media indicates that media images tend to define women within the narrow confines of traditional domestic roles and sexual appeal to men.

Women who are half the population are often half the audience. The success or failure of development plans in education, family planning, community development, health and nutrition depends upon the involvement and participation of women. Incidental studies on the impact of mass media indicate that women's exposure to media is often marginal and unsatisfactory.

In any case, films and film based programmes are loaded with derogatory images of women and usually explicitly or implicitly sexist. They play a significant role in reinforcing negative stereotypes.

What are these stereotypes? Basically drawn from a middle class vision of woman that sees her and glorifies her solely in the role of wife, mother and homemaker not only is this a travesty of the vast reality, but equally a gross injustice that denies–and therefore serves to kill rather than help blossom–the richness of a woman's total dimension and her critical larger role within the community and the country. There have been several studies of media with regard to women, which have found the media guilty of sexism, distortion of the images of women and propagation of sex stereotypes and as dependent passive persons. The other side of such misrepresentation is that in most popular media women are seldom shown as working women, capable professionals, labourers, farmers, rather the predominant image is that of the self-sufficient housewife. Thus, the media is always perpetuating the view that the male is in every way superior to the female.

It is clear that women have a long way to go if they are to make any meaningful impact on society through the control of key management and policy-making positions. Women should think first what would lead them towards empowerment and then move forward. Media people should also encourage programmes, which have strong images of the women.

As a Home Science Extension and Communication students work for illiterate and semi-literate masses they can make use of audio-visual aids, games, puppets, cartoons, scripts, songs, objects etc. It is through proper networking that the women's movement will foster a better understanding.

As Faculty of Home Science is dealing with issue related to women as well as with media so they can always conduct special programmes where women can come together and discusses different issues with the experts and also media can give coverage to such programmes. Increasing grants for Research will help increasing research capacity for media research related to women.

Women must become active participants in all the fields to fulfill the all round development of women directly and indirectly only through their involvement in media they will be able to speak for themselves and for the issues relevant to them.

References

Bathia, Sonia. *Women, Democracy and the Media,* Sage Publications, New Delhi 1998.

Binod, C. Agrawal, "Towards equality women in Indian Television" *Media Asia,* Vol. 9, Nov. 3, 1982.

Business @ Gujarat, "Empowered Women", Vol. 1 No. 9, July 2001.

Chatterji, A. and Shoma, A. *Subject: Cinema, Object: Woman*, Parumita Publications, Calcutta. 1998.

Creedon, P. (1987). Women in Mass Communication - Challenging gender values, Ohio University, Sage Publication, New Delhi.

D'Souza., *Electronic Media and the Internet*, Dominant Publishers and Distributors, 1999.

Eashman, L. (1994). Impact of New Communication Technology on Women as Users and producers of the Means of Communication. Media Asia. Vol. 21(1). pp. 32-38.

French, D. and Richards, M. *Contemporary Television, Eastern Perspectives*, Sage Publication, New Delhi. 1996.

Ganesh, S. *Lectures on Mass Communication*, Indian Publisher Distributors, New Delhi. 1995.

Jha, R. *Women and the Indian Print Media*, Chanakya Publications, New Delhi. 1992.

Joshi, I. *Women Dimension on Television (Policy, Personnel and Programme*). Concept Publishing Company, New Delhi. 1991.

Joshi, U. *Textbook of Mass Communication and Media*, Anmol Publications (P) Ltd., New Delhi. 1999.

Kamlesh Mahajan, *Television and Women's Development*, Classical Publishing Company, New Delhi, 1990.

Kumar, K.J. Mass Communication in India, Jaico Publishing House, Bangalore, 1981.

Mehra, M. *Broadcasting and the People*, National Book Trust, New Delhi 1985.

Mukta Gupta, *Role of Women in the Twenty First Century*, Anmol Publications Pvt. Ltd. 1996, pp. 8, 79-89. Call No. HQ 1742 R 658.

Rabi N. Acharya, *Communication Revolution and Society*, Indian Publication Distributors, Delhi.

Rao, N. and Raghvan, G. (1996). Social Effects of Mass Media in India, Gyan Publishing House, New Delhi.

Subramanium, K., Crusading Role of Media. Vidura. Vol. 26, No. 3 May-June 1989 : 9-10.

V.S. Gupta, *Third Revolution in Indian Perspective Contemporary Issues and Themes in Communication*, Concept Publishing Company, 1995, pp. 155-169.

4

Women and Law

Rameshwari Pandya

Abstract

Human rights terminology embodies the demand that the unequal status of women be addressed as a violation of their rights as a breach of the obligation of government to guarantee equal right to all. A variety of laws framed from time to time seeks to ensure that women are not discriminated against and exploited just because they are women. However in practice it seems that it has eluded women. Problems in enforcement of laws is difficult because of low awareness men's attitude towards women's equality and inadequacies of legal provisions Legal Education can go long way in changing the status of women. Legal education will equip her to cope up with the factors of denial of rights to women such as individual, Demographic, economic social and cultural. This will ensure equal rights, still as a society government should guarantee enforcement of laws safeguarding women's equality. There are several NGO's working in this direction of making "New Women" who is aware of her rights and duties.

Introduction

The Constitution of India guarantees equality of opportunity and status to men and women. It directs that women shall not only have equal rights and privileges as men but also that the state shall make provisions both general and special for the welfare of women. Despite the above constitutional guarantee, women have been subjected to deprivation, brutality, and extortion.

Salient Features of Laws Relating to Women

Hindu Marriage Act, 1955

The Hindu Marriage Act applies to all the Hindus by religion which includes Vaishnavas, Lingayats and members of the Brahmo, Prarthana and Arya Samaj. It also applies to the Buddhists, Sikhs and Arya Samaj and Jains to legitimate and illegitimate children of parents who belong to the above religions and sects. All 'Hindus' who do not marry under the Special Marriage Act are governed by this Act, Under Hindu Marriage Act the conditions for marriage are :

- Either spouse should not have an earlier living spouse.
- Should not have mental problem, mental illness.
- The boys or the men should be 21 years complete and girls 18 years complete.
- The parties are not within the degree of prohibited relationship, unless the custom of usage governing each of them permits a marriage between the two.
- The parties should not be *sapinda* to each other unless the custom or usage governing them permits such marriage.

A Hindu cannot contract a second marriage with another till the first marriage is dissolved by divorce or decree. If this is done he/she can be prosecuted by law. A report given to the police by the near relative is entertained. If such a second marriage is proved he/she can be imprisoned and also fined. Under the Act, certain types of marriages are void and fraudulent.

When the spouses find it difficult to continue to live with each other, either of the spouse can apply for divorce under the law. For the dissolution of the marriage, the law has provided certain conditions only on which a decree for divorce can be granted by the court. However, the dissolution of a marriage can be applied for not before the expiry of one year of marriage or of passing of the decree of judicial separation unless permitted by the court under special circumstances. The grounds on which the dissolution of the marriage can be granted by the court are cruelty, adultery, unsoundness of mind, desertion, not being alive, suffering from disease and mutual consent.

Hindu Succession Act, 1956

The Act confers the right of absolute ownership over property and the women can make 'will' leaving her share of property to the heirs. Section 10 of the Act provides for the property of an intestate being divided among the heirs in accordance with certain prescribed rules.

Hindu Adoption and Maintenance Act, 1956

Any Hindu man of sound mind can take a son or daughter in adoption provided that, he has a living wife and he gets the consent of his wife to do so, unless the wife has completely renounced the world, is of unsound mind and has ceased to be a Hindu.

A Hindu woman can take a child in adoption if she is unmarried or is a widow, her marriage has been dissolved, her husband has renounced the world, has changed his religion and he is declared to be of unsound mind.

Under Section 9, the consent of father and mother is necessary for giving the child in adoption unless : (i) they or one of them is dead or (ii) the father or mother has completely and finally renounced the world or (iii) has ceased to be Hindu or (iv) has been declared by a court of competent jurisdiction to be of unsound mind.

The Child Marriage Restraint (Amendment) Act, 1976

The Act raises the age of marriage for girls from 15 to 18 years and boys 18 to 21 years. The offences under this Act have been made cognizable.

The Factories Act, 1948, Mines Act, 1952 and Plantation Labour Act, 1951

They prohibit the employment of women between 7 p.m. and 6 a.m. in factories, mines and plantations, regulate the working hours and contain provision for their safety and welfare. The government is authorised to fix the maximum load that may be lifted by women and to open crèches, etc.

The Employees' State Insurance Act, 1948

The benefits provided under this Act include sickness benefit, maternity benefit, disablement benefit, dependent benefit, medical and funeral benefit.

The Maternity Benefits Act, 1961

This Act is applicable to every establishment, plantation, mine or factory and provides for payment of maternity benefit at the rate of average daily wage for the period of women's actual absence. It has been amended in April, 1976 to cover women, who do not fall within the purview of the Employees State Insurance Act, 1948. A proposal to further amend the Act is under consideration of the Labour Ministry.

The Factories (Amendment) Act, 1976

The Act provides for establishment of crèches where 30 women are employed (including casual labourers or contact labourers) as against one for every 50 hitherto.

The Equal Remuneration Act, 1976

The Act provides for (a) the payment of equal remuneration to men and women workers and (b) prevention of discrimination on the ground of sex against women in the matter of employment and for matters connected therewith or identical thereto. There is a proposal under consideration of Labour Ministry for amendment of the Act with a view to further liberalising its provisions in favour of women.

The Contract Labour (Regulation and Abolition) Act, 1978

The Act regulates the working conditions of contract labour (which includes women), payment of wages and provides for welfare facilities and crèches for the children of working women engaged in construction work.

The Medical Termination of Pregnancy Act, 1971

The Act legalises induced abortion by qualified doctor on humanitarian and medical grounds. This is primarily a welfare measure to protect the health of women though it has also a family planning aspect. Women can now have induced abortion through qualified people. The service is free in public hospitals. All the documents are kept confidential. Before undergoing surgery, if the patient is a minor or of unsound mind, written consent of the guardian is necessary. Since the inception of the programme in April, 1972, 10 million terminations were done upto September, 2003.

The Dowry Prohibition Act, 1961

The Dowry Prohibition was first legislated in 1961. The Act was amended in 1984 to make the offence cognizable, to enhance the penalty both fine and imprisonment and to widen the scope of the Act to make it more effective. The Act was further amended in 1986 to make the penal provisions more effective and stringent. The minimum punishment for taking or abetting taking of dowry has been raised to 5 years and a fine of Rs. 15,000. The advertisements in newspapers, periodicals etc. offering a share of property as consideration for marriage is punishable. The amendment proposes appointment of Dowry Prohibition officers by the State Governments. Offences under the Act have been made non-bailable. A new Offence of 'Dowry Death' has been included in the Indian Penal Code consequential to the amendment in the Act.

A variety of laws framed from time to time seeks to ensure that women are not discriminated against and exploited just because they are women.

The Suppression of Immoral Traffic in Women and Girls Act, 1956

The Suppression of Immoral Traffic Act prohibits trafficking in women and girls for purposes of prostitution as an organised means of living. The Act which was amended in 1978 was further amended in September, 1986, with the objective of making the penal provisions in the Act more stringent and effective. The amended Act is retitled is "The Immoral Traffic (Prevention) Act, 1986" and the salient features are– widening the scope of the Act to cover all persons, whether male or female who are sexually exploited for commercial purposes; enhancement of the period of imprisonment where offences are committed against minors and children; appointment of Trafficking Police Officers, who will have the powers to investigate inter-state offences; prescribing punishment as laid down for rape under the Indian Penal Code or the seduction of victims of trafficking while in custody; interrogations of women and girls removed from the brothels to be held by women police officers or in their absence in the presence of women social workers and setting up of Special Courts for settling offences, which have inter-state ramifications.

Amendment to the Criminal Laws

The Indian Evidence Act, the Indian Penal Code and the Criminal Procedure Code were amended in 1983 to make the offence of rape and such crimes against women much more stringent and effective and also to make a new provision to the Indian Penal Code to make cruelty against women by the husband and other relations punishable. The onus of proof of innocence would rest on the accused of such offences.

Family Courts

An Act was passed in 1984 for the setting up of Family Courts in the country with a view to promoting reconciliation in, and securing speedy settlement of disputes relating to marriage and family affairs and for matters connected therewith.

Indecent Representation of Women (Prohibition) Act, 1986

The Indecent Representation of Women (Prohibition) Act, 1986 was passed in Parliament in December 1986 with the objective of having separate legislation to effectively prohibit the indecent representation of women through advertisements, books, pamphlets etc. The indecent representation of women has been defined to mean the depiction of the figure of a woman in such a way as to have the effect of being indecent or of being derogatory to women or is likely to deprive, corrupt of injure the public morality to prohibit all advertisements, publications, etc., which contain indecent representation of women in any form; to prohibit selling, distribution, circulation of any books, pamphlets etc. containing indecent representation of women. Offences under this Act are made punishable with imprisonment of either description for a term extending to two years and fine extending to two thousand rupees on first conviction.

The Commission of Sati (Prevention) Act, 1987

The Commission of Sati (Prevention) Act, 1987 was passed by the Parliament in December 1987 to provide for more effective prevention of the commission of Sati and its glorification and matters connected therewith or incidental thereto. The Act defines Sati comprehensively to include not only the burning or burial alive of a wife widow with a deceased husband but also of a widow or women with the body of any other relative or any article associated with the husband or relative; anyone who abets the commitment of Sati by inducement, encouragement, participation in processions, preventing the widow from saving herself etc. would be punishable by the maximum penalty, i.e., death or imprisonment for life; the abetment of an attempt to commit Sati would be punishable with imprisonment for life; in the case of persons prosecuted under these offences, the burden of proof that he had not committed the offence shall be on him; those convicted for such offences shall be disqualified from inheriting the property of the person committing Sati; persons convicted under such offences shall be disqualified under the Representation of the People's Act 1951 from the date of such conviction and shall continue to be disqualified for a further period of five years after release; glorification of Sati has been defined in details. The Act of glorification includes observance of ceremonies, collection of funds and construction of temples, punishment by imprisonment which may extend to seven years for the glorification of Sati has been prescribed; while the provisions of the Act necessarily have to be prospective, acts of glorification carried out in further would be covered; the propagation of the practice of the commission of Sati or its glorification by a candidate or his agent shall be deemed a corrupt practice under the Representation of People's Act; powers have been specifically provided to the Collector/State Government that, if satisfied that in any temple or structure any ceremony is carried out with a view to perpetuating the mutilated concept as dealt with in this Act, the State Government in the case of structures and the Collector in other cases, can direct the removal or such temple of structure and the Collector can also seize properties collected for the glorification of Sati.

The preamble to the Constitution of India speaks of securing to all citizens of India equality of status and of opportunity as well as justice–

social, economic and political. Women in India suffer from a variety of social and economic disabilities which prevent them from exercising their human rights and freedom in society. Child marriage, especially of the female infant was common, widow remarriage was prohibited. Even if she succeeded in escaping from the funeral pyre of her deceased husband where she was expected to be burnt alive, a divorce was generally looked down upon and her remarriage was socially disapproved. During the last few decades, a number of legalization have been passed with a view to ensure equality of status and opportunity for women. In practice, however it seems that it has eluded women.

Contribution of Law to Women's Development

This issue can be seen in two parts–The women as they are and the law which have to support them or protect them. Why are women in such a bad condition? Their whole economic contribution is invisible by the census. We need to consider who makes it invisible. Most of the time, the service generated by the census department or the way the data is being collected is erroneous. It does not show what their real contributions are and always show an extremely low participation in state labour force. According to the census of the year 1981, only 14 per cent of the women have been shown as wage earning workers as against 51 per cent of the males. If you want to make them visible, you have to modify it and show what they are actually contributing.

Eighty to ninety per cent of the women are employed in the unorganized sector. The moment you talk about the unorganized sector, they are out from most of the laws, which are there to support and protect the women. The major matters, which concern the males and females both, is what is happening due to mechanization. Who is being replaced? It is the woman; for example, 80 per cent of the women work in agricultural labour. You mechanize it and from the labour force, the women are being replaced now. The policy of the government and technology and science policy also need to suggest whatever innovations are being made, at a particular stage if women will be absorbed.

Where credit facilities are concerned, the banks are supposed to give credit facilities. Most of the bank managers are still male and they are biased in favour of men. They too believe that males are the ones who will repay the loans, but the statistics have clearly shown that repayment of the loans to the banks is by the females, rather than by the males. When banks ask for social security, most of the times, the property is in the name of a male. So even if a female wants to apply, she cannot give security. Even though the government has made the law that families below the poverty line are not required to give social security, banks are not accepting this and we have enough evidence that banks still insist on social security and as a result there is total denial of the bank loan facility for women.

When labour laws are concerned, law is one thing and implementation is another. Our implementation machineries are unfortunately very weak, irrespective of males or females, but because the females are more victimized, it naturally applies to women more. When there is a conflict between the workers and the management, the management allows it to go to the tribunal, because it buys time. At least it takes two to three months and in some cases, it takes 3 to 4 years. After tribunals, it goes to the court. Going to court is time consuming and nobody has the courage to fight the powerful management. In case of women, they are less represented in the unions and their case has been taken much less by themselves as submissiveness is already there.

There should be a law that if you are working for a particular industry for 8 to 9 months, remaining next month should be provided with retriever allowance, if it is a small amount. This is applicable to both males as well as females but unfortunately what is happening is that bulk of women are working in the unorganized sector, and so they are suffering more in this case.

Women and Law

If one compares the condition of Indian women in the early decades of the 19th century with the position in society today, one becomes aware of the silent social revolution that has taken place in their situation. In the early 19th century, social customs and practices like *purdah*, *sati* and child marriages and the deep-seated prejudices against-education of women prevented them from playing their proper role in society. They were confined to their hearths and homes. Today they are not only occupying responsible positions in the society but are making their own meaningful contribution to practically every field of national development. This transformation is mainly due to the spread of education amongst them.

There is still a large gap between the legal rights and the social attitudes and beliefs, which come in the way of actual emancipation of women. Though, theoretically a woman is recognized as the social equal of men, the institutions of caste and the patriarchal family, religious modes and the dominant value systems are still surcharged with the spirit of male dominance. The 'work role' of women on the one hand brings the wife out of the limited sphere of the home and on the other hand, it makes continuous demands on her time and energies.

Social Laws

Legislation Related to Marriage
Special Marriage Act of 1954

The only condition necessary for a valid marriage under this Act is that the man must be over 21 years of age and the woman over eighteen and neither has spouse living at the time of marriage. The marriage has to be registered by a marriage officer and a certificate issued.

In India, the Hindu Marriage Act 1955, amended in the year 1975, and the year 1981 provides for judicial separation divorce and nullity of marriage. It is only when 2 years have elapsed since the date of marriage that a petition for divorce may be made. The grounds for the dissolution of marriage are: adultery, conversion to other religion, unsound mind for not less than 3 years, leprosy, venereal disease and ever bigamy.

The year 1976 amendment permits divorce by mutual consent also after showing that husband and wife had been living apart for 1 year and could not reconcile. After getting divorce husband may be required to pay alimony to his wife for her maintenance. The Dowry Prohibition Bill was passed on May 20, in the year 1961. The Act permits presents in the form of ornaments, clothes and other articles not exceeding Rs. 2,000 in value. The penalty provided in the Act for the offender is imprisonment for 6 months or a fine up to Rs. 5,000 or both.

Economic Laws

The issues pertaining to economic laws include right to property or inheritance, equal wages, working conditions, maternity benefits and job security. According to Hindu Succession Act 1956, not only a daughter is given a right in her father's property equal to her brothers, but a widow also gets a share in her deceased husband's property equal to her sons and daughters. As regards to equal wages, the Equal Permit Act 1976 does not permit wage discrimination between male and female workers.

Political Laws

The two important rights in the political field sanctioned to women by the Indian Constitution are : female enfranchisement and eligibility for legislature. The Government of India Act, 1935 granted female enfranchisement and eligibility for legislature. The Government of India Act, 1935 granted female enfranchisement on the basis of educational qualifications.

Violence against Women

The problem of crime against women is not new. Women in Indian society have been victims of humiliation, torture and exploitation for as long as we have written records of social organization and family life. There are many records of episodes like abduction, rape, murder, and so forth, of woman. But significantly, female victims of violence have not been given much attention in the literature of social problems, criminal violence, or public, and the scientific communities alike ignored for so long the varied evidence that women were being greatly exploited in our society.

The attitude of indifference and negligence can be attributed to three factors, i.e., lack of awareness over women because of which violence acts against women were not viewed as violent or their religious values and social attitudes. As the causes of wife battering, rapes, kidnappings and abduction intra since the late 1960s and early 1970, the issue of violence towards women has been transformed from a private issue to a public problem.

Sociologists in the West have started talking about female exploitation ever since they shifted their perspectives in order to consolidate their appreciation of social dynamics. Likewise, criminologist, particularly radical crime scientists, have started taking an interest in problems such as criminal violence against women ever since they started a reappraisal of the old assumptions underlying ever crucially problematic behaviour this shift has had a profound consequence in research and theory building. It has become increasingly difficult to sustain the notion that criminality, specifically male criminality, is a behavioural quality monopolised by a narrow section of the lower class. However, in India both sociologists and criminologists have yet to develop an interest in this crucial problem of deviant behaviour. They have yet to realize their academic responsibility, in fact they have easily avoided the evaluation of social and legal norms and the underlying morality of society that criminalizes activates which have developed out of the contradictions in social values and sub-system.

Defining Violence against Women

Gender violence lie all other historical manifestations of violence is embedded in the socio-economic and political context of power relations. It is produced within class, caste and patriarchal social relations in which male power dominates. A narrow view of violence may define it as an act of criminal use of physical force. But this is an incomplete concept and violence also includes creation of an atmosphere of terror (threats and reprisals, exploitation, determination, unequal economic and social structures like the creation of an atmosphere of terror) threats and reprisals and other forms of religious cultural and political violence. While violence against women is part of the way the state controls people, it also encompasses aspects of structure violence and from control and coercion exercised thorough hierarchical and patriarchal gender relationships in the family and society.

1. Women's Harassment

Though it is that the incidence of violence by men towards women is not identical in all groups and communities, and that moral and socials beliefs and family arrangements differ from group to group, yet instead of examining these group differences and analyzing the sub-cultural and socio-ethical beliefs of these groups, we should concentrate on violence against women as perceived in general terms.

There is no women who has not suffered at one time or another the harassment, humiliation, exploitation and violence that shadows her sex. In daily life, women are routinely defined by sex, and even if all men are not potential kidnappers, rapists, batterers and murderers of women but all women are potential victims.

At home, they are often worse off, reduced to slavish drudges and maltreated in a hundred different ways. Constantly derided and mocked at, frequently bullied, sometimes associated and occasionally burnt to death, they remain victims in every vole Indian women, thus, can be described as the underdogs of a society. Where through in theory, the law of equality is practiced and women are considered to beat par with their male counterparts, in reality, the men remain powerful and thrive at the expense of the women. Whereas in Western countries, the women's question is mostly one of identity, job equality and sexual roles. In India, the question is simply one of stark survival.

In recent years, the incidents of aggressive crimes against women are reported to be escalating alarmingly in our country, and this in itself is a sufficient cause for increased concern. On the other hand, the awareness of rights among women has increased leading to the rise of the feminist movement, bringing with it a new sensitivity to all forms of subjugation women by men.

Similar increase is found in other crimes too. The number of registered cases has also spiraled alarmingly in the past few years. Besides, the actual number of cases reported as estimated to be many times more than the number recorded.

2. Bride Burning

So far, we have been concerned with some of the personal and social characteristics of the victims and the offenders, which give a background to the crime of bride-burning. The separation between the criminal situation and the participants personalities (victim, her husband, and husband's (parents and siblings) is arbitrary and analytical. Also, the crime really cannot be abstracted from the situation of the burning itself, that is, from the constellation of circumstances existing immediately prior to and during the commission and preparation of bride burning criminal etc.). In other words, the problem of dowry death is not and cannot be a uncaused problem; it is the product of a complex multi-dimensional process. It has to be analyzed both in terms of the murderer's and the victim's personality traits as well as the situation in which the murder was caused. Let us, therefore, try to understand the background of the situation in which brides are burnt.

Our main thesis is that the economic situation in a woman's husband's family contributes much to her adjustment soon after her marriage as well as to her humiliation and cruel treatment. In a materialistic society, there are constant pressures on individuals and families for having more and more money not only to provide more comforts to themselves and family members, but also to have some future security. However, there are individual and situational difference for achieving such economic aspirations, for instance, in the alternatives available for earning more money, one's educational achievement, the money available for investing in business and so forth.

Dowry deaths are found more in the middle classes and educated groups. We do not have statistics to show how many males and females are of marriageable age in these groups but on a rough estimate, it could be said that the number of males in relationship to females is not low in these groups, and in the normal course there should be no need to pay and get a husband. But every parent and his daughter want a boy with a job and or economic security. The boys postpone their marriages, till they get jobs. Since the problems of educational unemployment exists in our country, in many cases, the boys have to spend money in getting their sons admitted to good institution, in completing their education in getting daughters married, and so forth. Therefore, parents accepts money in their son's marriage out of economic necessity. The problem of dowry is thus basically a problem of demand and supply.

There are many cases in which the fathers of brides have to incur heavy debts or even sell their property to meet the dowry demands of the eligible bridegrooms and their parents. In several cases, they continue to fulfill the demands of their daughter's in-laws forgetting that a woman cannot buy peace, not to speak of affection, by meeting the monetary demands of her in-laws. The demand may lead to constant ragging and bullying which is even more damaging to human spirit.

Psychologists have maintained that most of our women suffer from a martyr complex. A large number are more suicide prone in the age-group of 18-30 years because in this age, rapid hormonal changes in her body make a woman expendable, depressive and vulnerable. And when they experience tension after marriage instead of love and affection from the husband and the family, they take their own lives, often on flimsy pretexts.

Earlier also, there were suicide and murder due to conflicts, but not they are reported in the newspaper due to the awakening of women's rights.

3. Violence of Women in the Family-Wife Beating

There have been few attempt to deal with and understand the problems of male violence in the family. Most of the violence in the family is due to some natural occurrence and seek to reconcile their marriage by making the women more understanding and more adaptable. The women's movement has to take up the issue of violence in the family both physical and mental–from a different perspective of women's role in the society and in the family. The reluctance to do so can only serve to maintain the current status quo of women within the family.

The study by Flavia D'mello of a very small number of battered women and the survey result are :

1. The age of women who reported being beaten was from 16 to 65.
2. The educational background of women–illiterate to post-graduates.
3. The women living in nuclear families–60 per cent, the women living in joint family–40 per cent the family structure did not have much effect on marital violence.
4. 10 per cent of women were beaten within the first 6 months of marriage.
5. 10 per cent women had children. Thus the presence of children did not lead to decreases in violence.
6. The monthly income of the family ranged from Rs. 150 to Rs. 5000.
7. 60 per cent of the men from middle class did not touch alcohol while in the working class, a large percentage were habitual drinkers. But not all of them beat their wives while they were drunk.

8. The women from the middle class backgrounds had husbands who were lawyers, journalists, public prosecutors, executives and successful businessman.
9. The immediate cause of violence as reported by the women:
   (a) Arguments over money.
   (b) Jealousy and suspicion of the women's character.
   (c) Instigation by in-laws.
   (d) Housework.
   (e) Alcohol.
   (f) Women's desire to work outside the home or women's high esteem.
   (g) Dispute over children.
   (h) Extra marital affairs on the part of the husband.
10. The violence encountered include :
    (a) Beating with hand and blows.
    (b) Beating with sticks and iron rod.
    (c) Sitting on the stomach while the women were pregnant.
    (d) Beating with utensils or knives and ladles.
    (e) Throwing women against objects or bashing their heads against the wall.
    (f) Burning breasts, vagina, etc.
    (g) Excessive sexual demands and sexual perversions.
11. The injuries suffered were :
    (a) Deep cuts requiring stitches.
    (b) Broken bones.
    (c) Miscarriages.
    (d) Nervous breakdown.
12. Most women had tried to find some assistance at home by :
    (a) Going home to the family.
    (b) Staying with friends.
    (c) Staying alone.
    (d) Seeking advice of counsellors.
    (e) Seeking advice of religious heads.
    (f) Complaining rescue homes.

About 50 per cent of the women had jobs. In this study the dowry factor did not emerge as the major factor contributing to wife beating. At best it served as an excuse as any other. When the middle class women interviewed when beaten for the first time, they were numb with shock. Every women interviewed said, "I did a not know that educated men beat their wives". They had not seen wife beating in their families. The initial reaction was to deny it even to themselves. They said that the shame and humiliation of the first beating had left a permanent scar on their psyche. They did not tell anyone this reluctance to confess ranged from a few weeks to five years. After the initial shock that began to question their worth. They began to wonder whether there was something wrong with their behaviour, their actions and their mode of dressing in order to please their husbands and in-law. But soon they began to realize the fact that they got beaten, no matter what response. The repeated assaults threatened their physical safety and survival become a major issue. It is at this stage that the women sought help. But wherever they went, they were sent back.

Myths regarding wife beating in our society.

1. The first myth is that Middle Class Women do not get beaten :

The women come from all section of the society, belonging to different religious, educational levels and from all socio-economic classes. About 20 per cent of women from the middle classes were working. So wife beating in slums is prominent, it is because these women have less privacy. These women were more hesitant to talk about it, more embarrassed. However, once they began to talk about it, it was evident that the violence has greatly scarred them psychologically, making them withdrawn, less confident, etc. This could be because working class women accept the violence, and thus do not see it as something being related to them as individuals. The middle class women begin to question and doubt themselves.

2. Another myth is that the victims of violence is a small fragile helpless women belonging to the working class.

But in actual fact women handling responsible jobs as doctors, lecturers, journalists and models get beaten by their husbands. Many of the women we interviewed were big people and many a times active feminist themselves ask, 'why do women continue to live in a situation where they are eventually murdered or are driven to suicide? Why don't they seek a way out? The theory of learned helplessness gives an insight into the mental state of passive resignation experienced by those women.

4. Prostitution

Prostitution has existed in one form or another in all class based patriarchal societies. In ancient homes, female prostitution in several societies were linked to religious practices. By contrast, in modern times, it tends to be associated with promiscuity, crime and social condemnation.

She should do so for payment. It penalized the victim, and provided the prostitution needs to be contained within certain areas only. By penalizing her, the act subjected her to further exploitation and forced her to live like a criminal under constant fear of police harassment. Even the pimps and touts went scot-free. The SITA was penal status and welfare provisions were alien to it. There was only one provision by which an application could by a woman or a girl to be placed in a protection home or care, i.e., an opportunity to get out of prostitution.

As a result of pressure from progressive sections of the society the scope of the definition of prostitution was broadened by amendment act of 1986 and the act was renamed as Immoral Traffic Prevention Act.

5. Abduction and Kidnapping

All kidnappings are not the same, to speak then of kidnapping does not mean that we are dealing with a homogeneous collection of human situations and activities. Kidnapping has different motivations–political, economic and individualistic. Political kidnappings and hostage taking in recent years have increasingly attracted world wide attention. Kidnapping with and economic motive has two manifestations–ransom and sale for prostitution. For ransom, the kidnapping is considered very profitable. Sometimes, even though ransom is obtained, the victims are killed to eliminate witnesses. Kidnapping of women for marriage, sex satisfaction or for prostitution is done with individualistic motives.

6. Molestation of Women and eve teasing

Women are subjected to various forms of molestation, physical and mental torture and eve-teasing at home, in streets and public places, places of entertainment, campus of educational institutions, prisons, rescue homes, crowded places like markets, meals, festivals, railway platforms and bus stands, running trains and buses, workplace etc. the cases are grossly under reported because the victims and their parents and guardians avoid to report cases to the police.

7. Lock-ups a Nightmare for Women

Molestation of women by the police and their stripping by policemen is common. The [CrPc] Criminal procedure code was amended after independence in this regard. Section 160 lays down that no woman or female of any age can be called to the police station even for interrogation in any case by a police officer of any rank. In case a women is to be questioned, she has to be interrogated "at her place only".

Problems in Enforcement of Laws

1. Absence of Awareness

It has been found that even after several decades of the introduction of social legislation, it appears that bulk of rural and many urban women have not heard of the existence of various laws. Very few of them know the right and are able to enumerate provisions incorporated in these rights.

2. Sources of Knowledge

Sources through which women could gather information seem to be weak. Sources of knowledge include mass media channels like newspapers, books and periodicals and personal contact between various agents, e.g., office where females work. The formal sources like books, periodicals and newspapers have played a secondary role and have not been effective in making people aware of legal rights.

3. Men's Attitude towards Women's Equality

Another problem which inhibits enforcement of social legislature concerns the attitude of men. Since men continue to head the family and do not approve of granting equality to women, the idea of granting legal rights would continue to remain a far cry.

4. Inadequacies of Legal Provisions

The laws relating to women in India require drastic alteration. Though there has been considerable legislature in regard to women after the enactment of the constitution the actual position of women today is not very different from the earlier period. The equality clause in the constitution has made little or no impact on the social and economic life of women in India.

Legal Awareness among Women an Educational Issue

The status of women in a country can be judged from their freedom, decision making power, opportunities for self-development, security and their participation in the social, economic and political issues. The women especially from the rural and the poor sections, by and large are denied most of these.

Since marriage and motherhood are the only respectable choices left for women, under the male domination, right from birth, the girls and women are denied every sort of freedom. They are treated as the property of their fathers and husbands. Ramdas (1986) says, "the textbooks, the media, all conspire and combine to prop up the stereotypes of women as being either as submissive, self-effacing, non-aggressive daughter, and obedient, dutiful and faithful wife or a self-sacrificing mother goddess". She is made out to be inferior, weak and defenseless. All women are considered less intelligent and uninformed. This concept regarding women, prevents them from having any opportunities for self-development and thereby prevent them also from intelligent, noteworthy participation in the economic, social and political matters.

The social and cultural inhibitions against a woman are profound. These inhibitions have prompted low levels of literacy among women, especially rural and poor, which in turn has resulted in low level of participation in outside affairs. This kind of environment, not only helps to maintain status-quo for the women regarding their pitiful condition but is also instrumental in further degradation and escalation of crimes and violence against women and injustice to them.

There has been a constant rise in dowry deaths, bride burning and other crimes against women such as molestation, assault, rape and kidnapping in the country. Scores of women suffer injustice both at home and outside, in matters of inequality in status, pay, property, opportunities for self-development, marital adjustment and independent living.

Factors Responsible for Crimes against Women

There are many reasons why crimes against women and injustice to them continue to increase. It is a general belief in India that good women are those who do not complain and accept all injustice wholeheartedly. Most victims do not report family or outside violence to the police either out of fear or humiliation or because of further harassment. There is hardly any deterrent and the culprits feel they can easily get away with any crime. Long delays in court proceedings also encourage rise in crimes.

Public response to violence against women is of indifference. It is not very uncommon to find public holding the view that since they are women, their lives are of no consequence. There may not be much sympathy for the victims of injustice as society mostly blames them for the crimes of which they are the victims.

Low levels of literacy and education make women ignorant and therefore reluctant to avail legal help. Lack of information about legal procedures and lack of resources–such as money and time for availing legal help, discourage even the educated women from resorting to any legal course for the injustice caused to them.

Many women are not even conscious of everyday exploitation such as:

- Lack of basic rights–food, rest, privacy, etc.

- Lack of opportunities for self development–education, training, economic independence, decision making freedom regarding both minor and major personal matters.
- Lack of enjoyment inside or outside home.

Women fighting for their basic rights are shown having masculine qualities to act decisively like men. This also distances them from taking any legal help in a traditional society, like ours.

Both formal and non-formal education systems at present, more or less describe women as kind, simple and obedient persons with no self-respect and tendency for defense against any type of injustice. Traditional media such as books and modern media such as films and television, both present acts of crime and injustice to women in such a brazen manner, that a feeling is created that these acts are simple and even legitimate.

Menfolk at home, male heads of various religious, educational and occupational institutions–all discourage women from taking any legal measures for the injustice and crimes against women by pointing out the imaginary or even real dangers in legal suits.

Many traditional women's magazines and organizations are also guilty of women's degradation since they also portray women in the second class roles, virtuous and totally self-sacrificing, unintelligent and incapable of resorting to any legal defense for the injustice showed to them. So families, societies, religions and media are some of the big obstacles in stopping women from hitting back the insulting society and refusing to be bullied.

Need for Legal Awareness among Women

Society cannot progress, if women are left behind. Since most men fear loss of control over women, they are not likely to free women and treat them with equality and justice on their own. The unjust treatment to women must be questioned by the women themselves. From the dreary, suicidally depressed housewives, trapped in lifeless marriages or inferior second class workers or timid, defenseless members in a society, they can be saved to become vital, strong and questioning all forms of injustice. The essential steps are to help women to discover their lack of power of independent decision-making and to discover their strength. It is possible to change the status of women and thereby their plights.

A number of measures both in form of actual help and education can be suggested to help women fight against injustice and crimes against them. These can be women's organizations, vigilant groups, family courts, women lawyers, feminist movements, free or subsidized legal help, stringent laws, sensitive judiciary and effective law enforcement machinery.

However, these measures may not check injustice and crime against women, if women themselves do not develop awareness about them and avail of legal help.

Education Helps in Creating Legal Awareness

Can all the formal and non-formal education processes be geared up to develop much needed legal awareness among the women? A number of women's studies centres have been established at the university level in our country. Based on their research findings, courses, such as "Women and Law" for college girls can be introduced in their core study programmes.

The content can include :

- Awareness about vital women's issues.
- Social constraints–female foeticide, infanticide child marriage dowry.
- Women's multiple role's burden.
- Invisibility of women's social and economic contribution.
- Subservience pertaining to decision making, property, etc.
- Marginalization of women's due to mechanization.
- Negative images of women in media.
- Family violence to women.
- Women's lack of control over their own bodies.
  - Actual motivation for availing legal help.
  - Familiarity with legal procedures, law courts and women's cells.
  - Expenditure on legal suits.
  - Laws and the latest amendments pertaining to welfare to women.
  - Agencies involved in helping women to avail legal help.

There is a need to go deep into women's issues and stop being concerned only with a few narrowly defined issues like changing women's titles from Miss and Mrs. To Ms., smoking and swearing by women and dress for women. The larger issues like stopping atrocities and crimes against women, removal of all forms of inequality, reducing male domination and oppression and creation of just social and economic orders. Women need to fight for physical freedom as well as freedom of expression and of choice and representation.

To reach the school dropouts and illiterate girls and women in rural and urban poor areas, the non-formal educational media will have to be to employed to develop legal awareness among them. They can be pictorial posters and folders, films, tele-films, serials, sports, video tapes, plays, puppet plays, street plays and songs. The non-formal media for literate women can include books, magazines and newspaper articles besides the above mentioned media. All regional and national papers can devote regular columns to women, highlighting women's legal rights. Media can play an important role in propagating and perpetuating values of equality between sexes and can encourage more women to become familiar with legal protection available to them.

Women can be helped by media and women's organizations and programmes like "Mahila Samkhya" to question their present plights by coming in contact with other women. Who in similar situations have successfully reasoned and fought against injustice through their write-ups and first hand interviews. What is needed more is a free dialogue with greater involvement of women. The message of all these should be that women, at present are deprived of power of independent decision making and opportunities and it is possible to change the status of women if not voluntarily, through legal help.

Education can be an effective instrument of change only if it can help liberate women from oppressions and exploitations because of their traditional submissive roles. We need formal and non-formal education to educate women and others about women's plights and the role legal awareness can play in emancipation of women.

Legal literacy or para legal training, is of paramount importance. The government, as well as non-governmental organisations, have prepared and disseminated material on legal-literacy on a large scale is the last few years. One leading example is set of 10 booklets, entitled 'Our Laws' published by the Department of Women and Child Development highlighting salient features of the rights available to women.

Legal literacy is imparted through several awareness programmes, training-cum-orientation modules, literature dissemination, sensitization workshops and multi-media campaigns involving films, plays, songs posters and so on.

This present effort presented here is a Ph.D. research study summary to streamline all efforts towards legal literacy amongst adolescent girls who are at a threshold of their lives to decide for marriage, job, and other such decisions. This study was conducted by Pandya in 1990. This study is a systematic and scientific experiment to impart legal education.

This is the result of the investigation conducted to assess the legal awareness of the students and also their opinions towards legal education. The sample consisted of sixty first year women students of Home Science of M.S. University of Baroda. Four test materials were used to collect data. They were :

(1) Personal Information Schedule, (2) Questionnaire relating to legal information, (3) an Opinion Questionnaire on legal education, and (4) a

Questionnaire on legal awareness. The students were personally met by the investigator in the classroom situation and the Questionnaires were administered and the data was collected.

Methodology

Sample : The sample for the study consisted of sixty first year B.Sc. Home Science women students, studying in the M.S. University of Baroda. It was a stratified random sampling, twenty students were selected from each area of Arts, Commerce and Science groups at school level. They were all between the age of 18 and 20 years and all of them were women students.

Test Materials : Four test materials were used to collect data.

1. The first one was a personal information schedule. This included questions relating to the respondent's age, subject at higher secondary school, medium of instruction, class secured in 12th standard, father's occupation, mother's occupation and their religion. This was in the pattern of a check list with structured responses.
2. This questionnaire was related to the source of legal information of the respondents.
3. This questionnaire assessed the opinions of the subjects regarding legal education.
4. This questionnaire was regarding the legal awareness of the students and consisted of questions concerning the laws related to women. It included true and false type of responses and also multiple choice questions.

Since the attainment of independence several measures have been taken to improve the status of women. These laws have been intended to bring the legal status of women in equality with men. The unfortunate part is that many women in India are quite ignorant of the laws and not much trouble is taken by the authorities to make women aware of them. Many laws are thrust aside by orthodox priests or the people themselves, deriving excuses from traditions and customs. In order to remove the social inequality in the field of legal provision, it is necessary that laws are implemented adequately and people are educated to follow them. There are many laws which have been bought out for women's equal status, but in the absence of translating them into practice, they have remained only in papers. To make this a reality and a movement, an awakening in necessary, this would rouse the social conscience of people.

Legal education in Home Science should be considered more seriously than anything else because in recent years crime against women has assumed giant shape. Even facts related to figures on crime serve as an eye opener for Home Scientists whose activities are geared towards betterment of family, community and nation, keeping the women as their focus.

The aim of the present study was to assess the characteristics of the first year Home Science students, their source of information about the laws pertaining to women and also to know their opinions towards legal education for women and their level of legal awareness.

Procedure : The investigator personally met the students in a classroom situation. On establishing good rapport by explaining the purpose of this study, the printed questionnaires were distributed among them. The venue selected for this study was the M.S. University of Baroda, Baroda. They had taken about an hour to complete the questionnaire.

Method of Scoring : The Opinion Questionnaire on legal education was scored according to the procedure. Items having positive opinion regarding legal education were given the score of 1, and the items with negative opinion were given the score of 0 (zero). The total score in this was 6. Percentages were calculated for responses and the scores were rated. Scores from 0 to 50 per cent were favourable to legal education. Scores from 51 per cent and above were favourable to legal education.

The level of awareness of women regarding law, was obtained by giving weightage to the items. The correct responses were given a score of 1, and the incorrect responses were given the score of 0 (zero). The total score in this was 15. The percentages scores were rated as follows:

Score (%)	*Level of Awareness*
61% and above	Good
36 to 60%	Average
0 to 35%	Poor

The following statistical treatments were given to the various types of responses.

Percentages were calculated to the responses of the Questionnaire one, relating the background information, for the 2nd questionnaire, relating the source of information for law and for the 3rd questionnaire, regarding option about legal education. The Chi-square test was applied to the 4th questionnaire, on the level of legal awareness of the respondents, in the selected variable.

Results and Discussion

(a) Characteristics of Respondents

The findings showed that the most of the respondents were aged between 18 and 19 years (Table 1). Age of the respondents was likely to have direct bearing upon their values and attitudes as well as their outlook. Such findings suggests that students from same class do not vary significantly in terms of age, as is ordinarily known. The percentage of respondents who had offered Arts, Commerce/Science at school did not differ. Similarly respondents from English medium at higher secondary education and those from Gujarati medium were more or less equal in percentage. The smallest percentage had Hindi for the medium of instruction.

Less than 50 per cent of the respondents had obtained second class in 12th standard. Little more than one fifth of the respondents only had obtained first class in 12th standard as seen in Table 1. The mothers of 65 per cent of the respondents were housewives bank, running own business, working as LIC agents, lecturers, etc. An almost equal number of respondents had fathers who were in service or doing their own business. An overwhelming majority of the respondents were Hindus, only two respondents were found to be non-Hindus, one was a Sikh and the other a Christian.

(b) Source of Information for Legal Education

Among the sources of dissemination of knowledge of legal rights, the most important one has been the T.V. The sources through which First Year Home Science students could gather legal information included mass-media like T.V., newspaper, books, periodicals. Besides, these people with whom they had informal contacts also acted as a source in dissemination of information.

It may be said that persuasive communication affects behaviour and thought process of individuals and as such informal agents of communication and dissemination knowledge exert direct impact upon people. This is clear in the present investigation. Informal sources like family members, friends and neighbours play prominent role in making people aware of provision of legal rights. The largest section of respondents has known the rights through informal sources.

As Table 2 depicts, among the formal sources radio, magazines and newspapers, have played a secondary role. This role is subsidiary in imparting legal education whereas T.V. is most popular medium which respondents reported as the source of information of law. Most negligible has been the part played by the schools and the voluntary agencies in imparting legal education.

Table 1 : Percentage Distribution of the respondents according to their Characteristics

(N=60)

Sources	*F*	%
Age (Years)		
18	28	47.00
19	28	47.00
20	4	6.00
Stream		
Science	20	33.33
Arts	15	24.90
Commerce	20	33.33
Home Science	5	8.33
Medium of Instruction		
English	27	45.00
Gujarati	30	50.00
Hindi	3	5.00
Class obtained		
Ist	17	28.00
IInd	25	42.00
IIIrd	18	30.00
Father's Occupation		
Business	31	51.66
Service	28	46.66
Special case (Father expired)	1	1.66
Mother's Occupation		
Employed	21	35.00
Housewife	39	66.00
Religion		
Hindu	58	96.66
Non-Hindu (Sikh, Christian)	2	3.44

Table 2 : Percentage Distribution of the Respondents according to the sources of Information Regarding Law

(N=60)

Sources	*F*	*%*
Informal		
Family	51	85.00
Friends	31	52.00
Neighbours	6	10.00
Formal		
School/College	5	8.00
Magazine	30	50.00
Newspaper	32	53.00
Radio	7	11.00
T.V.	54	90.00
Films	34	90.00
Courses taken at		
School	5	8.00
Outside school (by other agency)	4	7.00
Course not taken	51	85.00

(c) Opinions about Legal Education

The largest percentage of respondents have favoured legal education as desirable for Home Science students. They opined that publicity of women's right is necessary ane legal education is necessary for equality of both the sexes. Table 3, further shows that majority of the respondents believed that society would progress when men and women are given equal status ane legal education would help the women in solving their problems faster. Similarly majority of respondents had found it desirable to continue present trend of equality between husband and wife. Majority of the respondents were of the opinion that legal education was very desirable for Home Science students as they were mostly female students. A mere enactment of social legislations would not better the condition of women unless they were given legal education.

Table 3 : Percentage Distribution of the respondents according to their Opinions about Legal Education

(N = 60)

Sr. No.	*Sources*	*f*	%
1.	Legal education is desirable for Home Science students	51	85.00
2.	Publicity of women's right is necessary	47	78.33
3.	Legal education is necessary for equality of sexes	45	75.00
4.	Society will progress when men and women are given equal status	43	71.66
5.	Legal education will help the women in solving their problems	45	75.00
6.	Present trend of equality between husband and wife is desirable	46	76.66

(d) Awareness Regarding Laws

Since the attainment of independence, several measures have been taken to improve the status of women. These legal measures are (1) Property rights (2) Legislations related to marriage (3) Rights related to divorce (4) Prohibition of dowry (5) Law regarding abortion (6) Law against rape (7) Law against eve teasing (8) Law against polygamous marriage.

Table 4 shows that 44.9 per cent respondents had correct knowledge about the laws that sons as well as daughters can legally inherit the property of their parents. Rest of the respondents had no knowledge about the can that a man can not have legally more than one wife. Surprisingly, majority of respondents were not aware of the fact that an eve-teaser can be legally punished.

About existence of law against rape, only 46.6 per cent of the respondents were aware and rest of the respondents were unaware about this law. Table 4 further shows that a very large number of respondents, 61.0 per cent did not know about existence of other laws related to women.

Table 4 : Percentage Distribution of the Respondents According to their Awareness Regarding Law

(N=60)

Sr. No.	Sources	f	%
1.	Correct age of marriage (a) Boys 21 yrs. (b) Girls 18 yrs.	40	67.00
2.	Right of marriage same for men and women	9	15.00
3.	Law can help a wife, when husband beats her	20	33.00
4.	Law can interfere when there are difference among husbands ane wives	25	42.00
5.	Giving and taking of dowry is illegal	50	83.00
6.	Divorce is permitted by law	48	80.00
7.	Women are free to dissolve their intolerable married life	29	48.00
8.	MTP is legal in Gujarat	23	38.00
9.	Sons as well as daughters legally inherit the property of their parents	27	45.00
10.	Legally man can have second marriage	35	58.00
11.	Man can have legally more than two wives	33	55.00
12.	Eve-teasers can be legally punished	14	23.00
13.	Is there any law against rape?	28	44.00
14.	Maintenance to be given by husband to his divorced wife ane children.	27	45.00

Opinions and Awareness Regarding Laws Across Student's Variables

The preceding discussion reveals that the Home Science students favoured various legal rights and that some respondents were more favourably inclined towards the women's rights than others. Attitudes and opinions of human beings are shaped by a wide variety of factors. The surroundings social milieu, the back ground like mother's occupation, father's occupation, stream ane medium of study, religion they belong and the extent of media exposure, helped in widening one's mental horizon (Table 5 to Table 18).

Table 5 : Opinions of respondents about Legal Education according to the Age

(N=60)

Opinions about Legal Education	*Age Group*						
	18 years N = 28		*19 years N = 28*		*20 years N = 4*		*Total %*
	f	%	*f*	%	*f*	%	
Favourable	20	71	24	83	2	50	77
Unfavourable	8	28	4	16	2	50	23

X^2 tab = 5.99 X^2 tab > X^2 cal

X^2 cal = 3.39 ∴ it is insignificant at 0.05 d.f.

Table 6 : Opinions of Respondents about Legal Education according to the Stream of Study

(N=60)

Opinions about Legal Education	*Steam in Higher Secondary*						
	Art N = 20		*Science N = 20*		*Commerce N = 20*		*Total %*
	f	%	*f*	%	*f*	%	
Favourable	15	75	15	75	16	80	77
Unfavourable	5	25	5	25	4	20	23

X^2 tab = 5.99 X^2 tab > X^2 cal

X^2 cal = 0.19 ∴ it is insignificant at 0.05 d.f.

Table 7 : Opinions of Respondents about Legal Education according to the Medium of Instruction

(N=60)

Opinions about Legal Education	*Medium of Instruction*						
	English N = 27		*Gujarati N = 30*		*Any other N = 3*		*Total %*
	f	%	*f*	%	*f*	%	
Favourable	23	85	20	67	3	100	77
Unfavourable	4	15	10	33	0	00	23

X^2 tab = 5.99 X^2 tab > X^2 cal

X^2 cal = 3.68 ∴ it is insignificant at 0.05 d.f.

Table 8 : Opinions of Respondents about Legal Education according to the Class in XIIth Standard

(N=60)

Opinions about Legal Education	*Class in XIIth Standard*						
	Ist N = 17		*IInd N = 25*		*IIIrd N = 18*		*Total %*
	f	*%*	*f*	*%*	*f*	*%*	
Favourable	17	100	20	80	9	50	77
Unfavourable	00	00	5	20	9	50	23

X^2 tab = 5.99 X^2 tab > X^2 cal

X^2 cal = 12.50 ∴ it is insignificant at 0.05 d.f.

Table 9 : Opinions of respondents about Legal Education according to Father's Occupation

(N=60)

Opinions about Legal Education	*Father's Occupation*						
	Service N = 28		*Business N = 31*		*Other N = 1*		*Total %*
	f	*%*	*f*	*%*	*f*	*%*	
Favourable	22	79	23	74	1	100	77
Unfavourable	6	21	8	26	0	00	23

X^2 tab = 5.99 X^2 tab > X^2 cal

X^2 cal = 0.99 ∴ it is insignificant at 0.05 d.f.

Table 10 : Opinions of Respondents about Legal Education according to Mother's Occupation

(N=60)

Opinions about Legal Education	*Mother's Occupation*				
	Employed N = 21		*Unemployed N = 39*		*Total*
	f	*%*	*f*	*%*	
Favourable	20	95	26	97	77
Unfavourable	1	5	13	33	23

X^2 tab = 5.99 X^2 tab > X^2 cal

X^2 cal = 4.74 ∴ it is insignificant at 0.05 d.f.

Table 11 : Opinions of respondents about Legal Education according to Religion

(N=60)

Opinions about Legal Education	*Religion*				
	Hindu N = 58		*Non-Hindu* N = 2		*Total* %
	f	%	*f*	%	
Favourable	44	76	2	0	77
Unfavourable	14	24	0	00	23

X^2 tab = 3.84 X^2 tab > X^2 Cal

X^2 cal = 0.006 ∴ it is insignificant at 0.05 d.f.

Table 12 : Level of Awareness of Respondents about Legal Education according to the Age

(N=60)

Level of Awareness	*Age Group*						
	18 years N = 28		*19 years* N = 28		*20 years* N = 4		*Total* %
	f	%	*f*	%	*f*	%	
Good	5	18	3	11	0	00	13
Average	10	36	13	46	0	00	38
Poor	13	46	12	43	4	100	48

X^2 tab = 9.49 X^2 tab > X^2 cal

X^2 cal = 5.52 ∴ it is insignificant at 0.05 d.f.

Table 13 : Level of Awareness of Respondents about Legal Education according to the Stream of Study

(N=60)

Level of Awareness	*Stream of Study*						
	Arts N = 20		*Science* N = 20		*Commerce* N = 20		*Total* %
	f	%	*f*	%	*f*	%	
Good	3	15	3	15	2	10	13
Average	7	35	8	40	8	40	38
Poor	10	50	9	45	10	50	48

X^2 tab = 9.49 X^2 tab > X^2 cal

X^2 cal = 0.40 ∴ it is insignificant at 0.05 d.f.

Table 14 : Level of Awareness of Respondents about Legal Education according to the Medium of Instruction

(N=60)

Level of Awareness	*Medium of Instruction*						
	English N = 27		*Gujarati N = 30*		*Any other N = 3*		*Total %*
	f	*%*	*f*	*%*	*f*	*%*	
Good	6	22	2	7	0	00	13
Average	12	44	11	34	0	00	38
Poor	9	33	17	57	3	100	48

X^2 tab = 9.49 X^2 tab > X^2 cal

X^2 cal = 0.40 ∴ it is insignificant at 0.05 d.f.

Table 15 : Level of Awareness of Respondents about Legal Education according to the Class obtained in XIIth Standard

(N=60)

Level of Awareness	*Medium of Instruction*						
	Ist N = 17		*IInd N = 25*		*IIIrd N=18*		*Total %*
	f	*%*	*f*	*%*	*f*	*%*	
Good	5	29	3	12	0	00	13
Average	9	53	14	56	0	00	38
Poor	3	18	8	32	18	100	48

X^2 tab = 9.49 X^2 tab > X^2 cal

X^2 cal = 30.32 ∴ it is insignificant at 0.05 d.f.

Table 16 : Level of Awareness of Respondents about Legal Education according to their Father's Occupation

(N=60)

Level of Awareness	*Father's Occupation*						
	Service N = 28		*Business N = 31*		* *N=1*		*Total %*
	f	*%*	*f*	*%*	*f*	*%*	
Good	4	14	4	13	0	00	13
Average	15	54	7	22	1	100	38
Poor	9	32	20	65	0	00	48

X^2 tab = 9.49 X^2 tab > X^2 cal

X^2 cal = 8.62 ∴ it is insignificant at 0.05 d.f.

Table 17 : Level of Awareness of Respondents about Legal Education according to the Stream of Study

(N=60)

Level of Awareness	*Mother's Occupation*				
	Employed N = 21		*Housewife* N = 39		*Total* %
	f	%	*f*	%	
Good	4	19	4	10	13
Average	13	62	10	26	38
Poor	4	19	25	64	48

X^2 tab = 5.99 X^2 tab > X^2 Cal

X^2 cal = 11.20 ∴ it is insignificant at 0.05 d.f.

Table 18 : Level of Awareness of Respondents about Legal Education according to their Religion

(N=60)

Level of Awareness	*Mother's Occupation*				
	Hindu N = 58		*Non-Hindu* N = 2		*Total* %
	f	%	*f*	%	
Good	8	14	0	00	13
Average	23	40	0	00	38
Poor	27	46	2	100	48

X^2 tab = 5.99 X^2 tab > X^2 cal

X^2 cal = 2.26 ∴ it is insignificant at 0.05 d.f.

Respondents' study of Arts, Commerce or Science through English, Gujarati or Hindi medium did not seem to affect the opinion as well as awareness of the respondents regarding laws related to women.

Respondents who had secured first class in 12th standard had more favourable opinion towards legal education to be given to the Home Science studies. Same trend is observed in case of the legal awareness.

Significant variation emerged when opinions and legal awareness of the respondents were assessed in relation to the different grades obtained. As regards relationship between religion and the opinion about legal education, no significant relationship was found to exist.

It is generally presumed that occupational status, or in other words, the nature of job that a person undertakes exerts impact on the mental horizon of the person. His or her world view is shaped, to some extent, by his or her mother's and father's occupation. But this assumption did not seem to hold true particularly in case of father's occupation in this study.

Mother's employment status had significant relationship as far as the opinions towards legal education as well as knowledge regarding various laws related to woman, were concerned.

This may be due to the fact that women play a pivotal force in every family. They shape the family and inculcate habits in their children. It has been known that education of mother means education of the family. If a mother is aware of her rights and duties, she will transmit that to other family members more easily.

Implications of the Study

The students of Faculty of Home Science lack awareness about various laws related to women but at the same time have favourable opinions about legal education as a course for Home Science students. This study reveals that there is lack of awareness and that there is scope of learning about different laws related to women.

It gave an insight regarding the different laws which requires more emphasis while planning the course "Women and Law". These laws need more stress than other laws as many of the respondents expressed their unawareness about their existence. It implies that a course dealing with different laws related to women can be developed.

Role as an Extension Communicator Worker to Develop Awareness Regarding Womens Rights

We as extension and communication experts can solve this problem of denial of women's rights can make the women aware of their rights. Through an effective communication, we can use development programmes to fight against these rights. Thus it becomes our utmost duty to increase general awareness regarding Women's Rights amongst women.

The suffering and the denial of rights is mainly because the law has not succeeded in playing its role of social engineering and changing the deep rooted social and religions attitudes. Therefore, women will be free only when they abandon their traditional identities and roles to adopt mal-practices, and when they use equalitarian socialisation. A profound social and cultural transformation is required before sexual equality could be realised. And we know that such change is not easy to bring about in a short time to anticipate a future : "NEW WOMAN". Let us atleast make the beginnings.

Conclusion

Thus, the perspective of feminist groups has to question these and continually stress that a woman's identity is not her family, and to provide supportive structure for those who seek to break out of these oppressive structure. To study the nature and the extent of wife beating in our society, we might be able to provide insight into the dynamics and help to understand the situation of marital violence and why the victims are often deprived of a reasonable solution to opt for, in trying to solve the problem of violence in their marriage. The social bond approach may explain wife-beating, dowry deaths and murder, but it explains rapes and abduction? What are the frustrations of feeling of reactivation, which creates such attitudes towards woman, that individual criminality assault them or abduct them? What are their dimensions and measurement? If frustration or a feeling of relative deprivation is the cause, when does it lead to rape and when does it lead to adduction? Or changing a system of gender stratification is ultimately and empirical question, in the absence of theory that attempts to integrate the various partial theories, it is difficult to frame research that can help to determine relative importance.

From the above discussion it can be concluded that overall the personal, social and educational reasons are most important. The need of the hour is to work out the effective strategies to make women aware of their rights. This can be done through multimedia approach. Women themselves need to change their attitude and come out of their traditional image by taking up unconventional career.

Education develops an individual's personality. Such learning experiences can be provided to girls at school or college, so that they can develop leadership qualities.

There is an indication that in future women's participation will increase exposure to urbanization, higher education, mass media, industrialization and employment. These facts favor modern outlook and rational approach for development which in turn would empower women.

Recommendations for Future Action

1. The various disabilities and constraints on women which emanate from socio-cultural characteristics of Indian Society amply indicate that majority of women are still not enjoying the rights and responsibilities which have been guaranteed to them by the Constitution.
2. Though the changes in social attitudes cannot be changed abruptly, there is necessity to accelerate the process of change by deliberate and planned efforts.
3. The inherent nature of much source legislation is confusing and sometimes contradictory. Legislation requires some alterations.

4. All marriages should be required to be registered with the Registrar. Compulsory registration of marriages will be an effective check of child and bigamous marriages.
5. The Dowry Prohibition Act has miserably failed to achieve its purpose. It is suggested that a ban on making gifts at the time or upto one year after marriage should be proposed.
6. Besides alterations in the gamut of legal provisions, attempt should also be made to involve the selection of population for whom these legal facilities have been extended. But participation from grass root would come only with the help of voluntary organizations which have the necessary feel of the situation area and people.
7. Rural women are an illiterate lot. Illiteracy leads to ignorance. It is therefore advisable to run adult education centres for women where legal provision, their necessity and procedure should be explained to them.

References

Agarwal, B.C. and Chandiram, J. Towards Equality : Women in Indian T.V. Unpublished Paper. Media Asia, 1982.

Antomy, M.J. "Women's Rights". Clorion Books. Robo Printers, Delhi, 1989.

Arya Ram, Rights of Women, Rawat Publ. New Delhi, 1972.

Bhoite, A. Sex ratio and the status of women in India. Ahfad Journal 5(7), 1988.

Chandra, A. Introduction of Home Science. Metropolitan Book Company Pvt. Ltd., New Delhi, 1978.

Chatterji, S.A. The Indian women's search for an identify, Vikas Publishing House, Delhi, 1988.

Ghosh, S.K. (1993) Women and Crime, Ashish Publishing House, New Delhi.

Haksar, N. and Singh. A Demystification of law for women, New Delhi, Lancer Press 1986.

Jaising Indira, (Feb. 1986). The Politics of Personal law. The Lawyers Vol. 1 No. 2.

Jaising Indira, (July/August 1944) The Communal Nature of Personal Laws do we need a Marital Property Law. The Lawyers, Vol. 9, No. 7 & 8.

K. Vasanthi Devi. Women's Education for Social Change. In the University News, Oct. 8, 1985.

Kaushik Vijaya, Sharma Bela Rani, Women's Rights and World Development.

Patwa Subhadra, Directory of Women's Organisations Year of Publication 1990.

Rosemeyer Sunanda Sagar, Women's Rights–Search for an Identity, Dominant Publishers, New Delhi.

Shamsuddin Shams Women, Law and Social Change, Ashish Publishing House, New Delhi, 1991.

Sharma Preeti (1990). Hindu Women's Right to Maintenance Deep and Deep Publications, New Delhi.

Tmasevaski Katarina, Women and Human Rights, Zed Books Ltd. London & New Jersey, 1993.

Women in Action, the book on women, Peace & Justice Nov. 3, 1999.

Web Sites Refereed

(a) www.amnesty-usa.org/women/indiex.html#programme>

(b) www.jca.ax.apc.org./ajwrc/

(c) www.burma.net

(d) www.chair.org

(e) www.women21.org.kr.

5

Women and Education

Anuradha Mathu, Rameshwari Pandya

Abstract

The movement for improving women's status all over the world has always emphasised education as the most significant instrument for changing women's subjugated position in the society. Higher education of girls developed immensely during 1937 when several commissions and committees were appointed. General objectives of girls higher education was integrally related to home and social environment. The fact that education can be used as a tool for development and modernization has been well established. Educated women would be able to utilize their full potential to play constructive roles in the family and community.

Important mile stone in higher education for girls was 1932 when Lady Irwin College was established followed by 1950 starting of Faculty of Home Science in Baroda.

National Policy of Education recommended more colleges, freeships, girls hostels, NGO's efforts for enrolment of girls students, yet economic, familial, educational and social reasons are important causes of school dropout. It is important to tackle these problems and take advantage of education.

Introduction

Education has been regarded both as an end in itself and as means of realizing other desirable ends. It develops the personality and rationality of individuals, qualifies them to fulfil certain economic, political and cultural functions, and thereby improve their socio-economic status. It has been recognised as a major instrument which societies can use to direct the process of change and development towards desired goals.

The movement for improving women's status all over the world has always emphasised education as the most significant instrument for changing women's subjugated position in the society. The aim was to use education to make women more capable of fulfilling their traditional roles as wives and mothers and to make them more efficient and active units in the process of socio-economic or political development.

History of Higher Education for Girls

The landmark in the history of girls' higher education was the establishment of an Indian Women's University in the year 1916 in Bombay, which is now known as SNDT Women's University. This university was established with the following objectives :

1. To make provision for the higher education of women through modern Indian language (mother tongue as the medium of instruction).
2. To regulate pre-university education to start, aid, maintain and affiliate institutions for such education and to formulate courses of studies specially suited to the needs and requirements of women.
3. To make provisions for the training of teachers for primary and secondary schools.
4. To institute and confer, such degree and diplomas, titles, certificates and marks of honours in respect of degrees and examinations as may be prescribed by the regulation.

Some other objectives were also added from time to time. In the year 1921, women's social status had begun to show an upward trend. Girls were encouraged to take advantage of whatever chances for education were available. During the year 1937, higher education of girls developed immensely. Several Educational Commissions and Committees were appointed in different States. Then came post-independence period. Dr. Radhakrishnan was appointed by the Government of India as Chairman to report on Indian University Education and he suggested improvements that would suit the future requirements of the country. The Commission had recommended some special courses for girls in order to enable them to fit themselves well in their social setup. The courses were :

(a) Home economics, i.e., Home Science,
(b) Nursing,
(c) Teaching and
(d) Fine Arts.

There was a prevailing view that it was no longer necessary to give special attention to girls at the level of higher education, since girls are taking advantage of it in increasing numbers, adequate to the needs of the society. The figures of comparative enrolment of boys, and girls, students at higher education stage reveal that the proportion of girl students to the higher total enrolment in Indian universities was about 13 per cent in 1955-56, about 17 per cent in 1960-61 and 21 per cent in 1965-66. Thus, in one decade the proportion has increased from 13 per cent to 21 per cent. So the Education Commission expected the total enrolment of girls in higher education to be 33 per cent during the next decade to meet the requirements for educated girls in different fields. Therefore, the Commission recommended programmes for girls education. They are :

1. A programme of scholarships and financial assistance to girl students in colleges and universities on a liberal scale,
2. A programme of the provision of suitable but economical, hostel accommodation for students with all the necessary amenities on a large scale. Liberal grants should be provided by the Government of India for this purpose as also by the State Governments. Both these programmes are particularly necessary to encourage girls from rural areas to take advantage of higher education.

General Objectives of Girls' Higher Education

Objectives are the most important in an educational system to give it a proper direction. The objectives in the curriculum should provide ample opportunities both to the gifted, as well as the ordinary students and should be a means for an all round development of personality. And the objectives must always be integrally related to the students' home; social environment, the life and the work after the education. The Education Commission observed, that "In modern world the role of women goes much beyond home and bringing up the children. They are now adopting a career of their own and sharing equally with men, the responsibility for the development of society in all its aspects." After considering all necessary points they developed the general objectives of girls' higher education, as :

1. To create right attitude towards life–individual and social.
2. To impart useful knowledge for various aspects of life.
3. To give practical training for running their life.
4. To develop good personal habits.

5. To inculcate a sense of social awareness and a spirit of service to society.
6. To make career for future.

As needs and circumstances changed there was a periodical review of all the courses. Therefore, to fulfil the objectives, it is for the society to provide greater opportunities for the educated girls to be of social use by utilizing their knowledge for social and national development. The national Committee on Women's Education recommended :

1. Development of more employment opportunities particularly of a part time nature.
2. Improvement in employment information and guidance services for women entering higher education.
3. Development of open university system should be expanded extending the facility to all the girls in the rural and backward areas.
4. Correspondence courses and self-study programmes can be specially useful for girls who are unable to do so because of circumstances but desirous of continuing education.

Higher education for women has gained a wider role and responsibility all over the world. Education for women has suffered a lot during the last several centuries. Today, in the twenty-first century, we cannot afford to ignore the importance of higher education for women longer.

The reason for its need and urgency is that there is no biological difference in the system of males and females and the task of higher education for women assumes all the more significance for the Third World countries, where colonialism has remained a great force hindering education for the general masses and the women in particular. The colonial powers dominated every realm of human life. In the colonies the truth stood naked. The native cities took benefit of the colonial rule while the common people remained buried enmasse in ignorance with the overthrowing of colonial domination. The Third World countries have taken up the task of higher education for women.

At the outset, it must be stressed that the intensity of higher education for women is not uniform in all these countries. In fact, there had been heterogeneity in the intensity of the problem. For instance, the situation of higher education for women in the African countries is not similar to that of India. There, in Africa, the tribals look at women education quite differently. The fact is that women's higher education is specific to a country's stratification life style, and national ethos.

While introducing the same in India, contextually we should keep in mind the historical, social and political make-up of our country, but before we do that we should very specifically spell out the objectives of higher education at large. Higher education in India, has witnessed tremendous expansion since independence. There has been an enormous increase in the number of colleges and universities. However, the success story of this impressive growth turns bleak when the question of quality is raised. The standards in higher education have been eroded by the rising tides of mediocrity.

Higher education has been finding it difficult to meet the challenges of knowledge expansion, uneven growth, financial crisis, student unrest, teacher turnout and a number of other problems. The consequence of this failure to meet these challenges is a fall in standards which is a serious threat to developing nation like ours.

The issue of women's higher education came into recent focus in our country largely after independence. Higher education occupies an important place in the process of nation building. India today is also engaged in building the nation right from the grassroots. Out of all the problems, education in particular should be demanded as one of the most powerful factors for development.

The problem of higher education among women is precisely the problem of assigning an equal status to women in a society which is to be egalitarian. It has been our endeavour in the present inquiry to study the higher education for women in non-social and academic situation including the structure of education vis-à-vis the needs of the society, and the social background of the female students.

Higher Education for Women in India

The instruction offered after the twelve years of elementary and secondary school is in the purview of higher education in the US. Higher education in the US include two year community and junior colleges, four year college universities that award undergraduate and graduate study, and graduate and postgraduate study in India.

The term higher education in India embraces graduate course B.A., B.Sc., Agriculture, M.B.B.S. etc. and postgraduate courses are offered at the post-graduate centre, universities and professional institutions. The two year intermediate of (Andhra Pradesh), two year P.U.C. of (Karnataka), Higher Secondary Education of (Tamil Nadu) or such equivalent courses offered after SSC qualification do not come under the purview of higher education. The two year course is taken on by the Board of Secondary Education Intermediate higher education in India.

Academic Courses

Anthropology, Biology, Botany and Zoology, Chemistry, Economics, English, Fine Arts, Foreign Languages, Geography, Geology, History, Journalism, Library Science, Political Administration, Philosophy, Physical Education, Engineering, Computer Science, Institution and food wise management, Business Administration, Visual and Performing Arts, Studio Arts, Population Studies, Adult and Continuing Education.

Financial Support

In respect of financial support, Indian Universities are small in number and they are fully financially supported by the Central Government. The State Universities are large in number and have to depend for their finance mainly on the State Government and the University Grants Commission. The financial condition of most of the State Universities is not sound and they have to depend on the State Government for grants. The colleges in India generally get grant-in-aid from the respective State Governments.

Some private managements have to manage the colleges with their resources till they get financial support from the government. Professional and Technical college by and large get financial support from the Government. But there are some private professional and technical colleges which depend financially on their own resources and they collect donations from the students who seek admission in their colleges.

Accreditation

The colleges and institution of higher education are affiliated to universities. Each university constitutes an affiliated committee usually consisting of a chairman who is Dean of the concerned faculty and two or three members of Academic Council/Senate/Syndicate. This kind of procedure adopted by the universities for giving affiliation to the colleges/ institutions of higher education is being criticised for its subjectivity. In order to maintain standards in higher education, there should be serious thinking at the national level to abandon the present practice of giving affiliation and to have council.

Colleges and Faculties

The affiliated and constituent colleges of the universities generally impart graduate level education and some may impart postgraduation level education too. The technical and professional colleges generally have 4-5 years of graduate courses and generally two years Postgraduate courses.

Many universities in India prepare students for Postgraduate, M.Phil and Ph.D. degrees. Generally university campuses are considered as the centres for creation, preservation and dissemination of knowledge.

For academic leadership, generally university faculty, carrying the constituent colleges of the universities and other colleges are affiliated to one or the other university. Different discipline/departments come under different faculties. The community observed faculties in Indian Universities are :

Faculty of Arts, Faculty of Science and Technology, Faculty of Commerce, Faculty of Education, Faculty of Law, Faculty of Engineering and Faculty of Medicine.

Objectives of Higher Education for Women

Higher Education leads to promote excellence, adventure of ideas, and search for the truth. It is to cultivate new knowledge and interpret old knowledge in the light of new needs and discoveries. It has to provide the right kind of leadership in all walks of life and identify gifted youth and help them to develop their potential to the full by cultivating physical fitness, developing the powers of the mind, right impacts, attitudes and values. According to Singh, Sharma and Ahmed (1986).

To develop the ability in an individual which would help him or her to conceptualise a phenomena or situation and enable him or her to contribute to societal development through his knowledge, skills, as well as by generating new knowledge. Accordingly, the objective of education at the undergraduate and postgraduate level are:

- Imparting in-depth knowledge of the subjects concerned.
- Developing critical and analytical abilities.
- Developing the ability to relate this knowledge in real life situations.
- Developing vocational and professional skills.
- Developing social, cultural and aesthetic value.
- The provision of opportunities for the intellectual aesthetic, ethical and skill development to individual students and the provision of campus environments which can constructively assist students in their more general development of growth.
- The advancement of human capability in society at large.
- The enlargement of education facility for post-secondary age groups.
- The transmission of advancement of learning and wisdom.
- The critical evaluation of society through individual thought and persuasion for the sake of society's self-renewal. In Europe,

the committee on higher education (1961-63) enumerated four objectives of higher education :

1. Instruction in skills suitable to play a part in the general division of labour.
2. The aim should be to produce not mere specialists but rather active women.
3. Advancement of learning and the search for an essential function of institution of higher learning and the process of education in itself is most vital when it partakes of the nature's discovery.
4. The transmission of common culture and common standard of citizenship.

For the education in the context of development and modernization, the objectives are :

- To seek and cultivate new knowledge to engage vigorously and fearlessly in the pursuit of truth and to interpret old knowledge and beliefs in the light of new needs and discoveries.
- To provide the right kind of leadership in all walks of life to identify gifted youth and help them develop their potential to the full by cultivating physical fitness, developing the powers of the mind and cultivating the right interest, attitudes, morals and intellectual values.
- To provide society with competent women trained in Agriculture, Arts, Medicine, Science and Technology and various other social purposes.
- To strive to promote equality and social service and to reduce social and cultural differences through diffusion of education.
- To foster in the teachers and students and through them in society, generally the attitudes and values, need for developing the good life in individuals and society.

Need for Higher Education for Women

Higher education may be viewed in terms of the need of its consumers. The term consumer is very wide and heterogeneous, it includes young and old of both sexes.

Theoretically the need for higher education for both the male and females is the same. But it is sometimes argued that males and females are different in their social and cultural needs.

Surely, there are fields which are suitable to women, for instance, they are more skilled to work on embroidery, kitchen, beauty parlours, but such socio-cultural differences may result in defeating objectives of higher education.

The basic argument which is given for women's higher education is not that higher education for women is different from that of men. Our main thrust is that in the field of higher education women should also be the equal partners. The commission on higher education for women University of Madras, in 1979 rightly observed, "For women and men college education is necessary for character formation, ability to learn creative self-expression and personal development".

Similar feelings were recorded in the report of education commission (1964-66). "For full development of our human resources, the improvement of homes and for moulding the character of children during the most impressionable years of infancy".

The education of women is of even greater importance than that of men because of the following reasons:

- In the modern world the role of women goes much beyond home and the bringing up of children.
- Now women are adopting a career of their own and sharing equally with men the responsibility of the development of society in all its aspects.
- Equal partnership must be allowed to continue in the fight against hunger, poverty, ignorance and health.
- The importance of higher education for women forms the higher steps of the hierarchy ladder on which the lower ones very much depend on and draw inspiration and support for its effectiveness.
- Education would lead to a healthy, social, economic and political changes that are indispensable for improvement of the position of women in the society.
- Women would be able to utilize their full potential to play constructive roles in the family and community.
- In contemporary India, women are both citizens and home-makers and thus they have to perform both these functions efficiently and effectively.

Development of Home Science in Higher Education

Home Science at college level was offered as early as in 1932 at the Lady Irwin College, New Delhi at initiative of all India Women's Conference. This college also offered post-graduate diploma in education and teachers training to produce teachers to take positions in schools as well as newly opening colleges of Home Science.

According to the University Education Commission, the objectives of Home Science at higher education are :

1. To prepare students for home making and for a variety of professional fields such as teaching, dietetics, management, food service, certain business careers, Home Science extension and research.
2. To help people solve problems of food, clothing, shelter and relationships that deal with the development of understanding, skills, and attitudes, essential for the improvement of the ways of living of individuals, families and community groups.

Baroda, became a significant nucleus of Home Science in 1950 when the first faculty of Home Science was established by Ms. Hansaben Mehta. Thus, in the post-independence period, Baroda was the most important landmark. Not only was the Faculty of Home Science able to offer five specializations at the B.Sc. (Home Science) degree level, but by 1980 it offered B.Sc., M.Sc. and Ph.D. degree also in all five specializations. Then in the mid 1960 and 1970s another landmark was made when the Agricultural Universities were established in most of the States. 'Home' being an important unit of production and consumption in an agrarian country like ours, the need of teaching Home Science was recognized in most of the agricultural universities, where Home Science colleges were opened. Thus, Home Science as a professional discipline is gaining a position in the Indian society today.

Progress of Girls' Higher Education

The National Policy of Education recommended the following points:

1. More colleges and universities should be opened for higher education.
2. Incentives like scholarships, freeships, etc., should be provided to enable girls from rural areas to pursue higher education for girls belonging to weaker sections. In addition to freeships and scholarships, burparies should also be provided to meet their requirements, for food and lodging.
3. Girls should be encouraged to enter professional courses.
4. The girls wings of the universities could undertake large scale extension programmes in order to activate girls and women in the surrounding areas to take advantages of educational and occupational facilities of various types.
5. In order to increase the representation of rural girls in higher education, thirty per cent seats, may be reserved for girls.

6. All agencies involved with preparation of curriculum, prescription of textbooks and organisation of educational processes will have to evince awareness towards women's issues. Appropriate voluntary agencies, women's groups etc. should be involved in giving a new perspective to the various issues of content and process of education. As a result of implementation of recommendations of the National Policy on Education and implementation of special programmes for women's education in various five year plans, the higher education for girls in India expanded very rapidly. The following table will show the progress.

Year	*Total Enrolment*	*Number of Colleges for Women*	*Percentage of Women*
1980-81	27,52,437	609	27.2
1981-82	29,52,066	624	27.7
1982-83	31,33,093	647	28.1
1983-84	33,07,649	676	28.4
1984-85	34,04,096	712	29.1
1985-86	36,05,029	741	29.6
1986-87	37,54,409	780	30.6
1987-88	39,10,828	786	31.3
1988-89	40,74,676	824	31.7
1989-90	42,46,878	851	32.2

Source : University Grants Commission, Annual Report, 1989-90.

Thus, there has been tremendous expansion of educational opportunities for girls in the field of higher education both general and technical. Besides this, girls education at the university and college levels has itself been re-oriented in response to the changing requirements of the society and the demands of the public and private sectors.

Studies show that Kerala continued to lead in terms of girls enrolment in higher education with 52.7 per cent followed by Punjab. Bihar remained at the bottom with girls enrolment in higher education with 16.2 per cent in 1989-90. Facultywise distribution of girls enrolment in higher education shows the highest percentage of girls enrolled in the Faculty of Education with 52.9 per cent of its total enrolment in 1989-90, followed by the Faculty of Arts with 43.6 per cent and Faculty of Engineering and Technology having enrolment 7.6 per cent the lowest.

Major Problems in Girls Higher Education

The higher education of girls at present suffers from several weaknesses in institutions, failure to maintain academic calendars, outdated curriculum, disparities in the quality of education and lack of adequate support for research.

The proliferation of colleges and universities by the State Government without prior consultation of the UGC is the principal problem in the maintenance of standards in higher education for girls. The Commission is in no position to control this situation. The only instrument available with the Commission is non-sanctioning of grants to such colleges and universities.

Reasons for Dropout of Girls in Higher Education

Though there is much in common between the education of boys and of girls there is some difference between the way in which the girls' problems and boys' problems have to be tackled. This arises out of the peculiar social and economic conditions prevailing in the country and the existence of an age-long tradition as a result of which although in theory there is equality of educational opportunity between boys and girls there is in practice no such opportunity. There are many reasons for dropout of girls in higher education. The reasons can be categorised as :

(a) Economic, (b) Familial, (c) Educational, and (d) Social.

(a) Economic Reason

Poverty is the predominant factor that hinders girls to get higher education. Parents of middle and lower classes think, it is wise to save money for their dowry rather than for their education. Whenever, the purse of parents gets tight, or light they at first step, strive to stop the expenditure on education of their daughters. Most of them consider it an unnecessary expense as the girl has to go to some other family. The higher education is also so expensive that parents of middle class cannot afford it. In every third family we find girls who are not able to get education due to financial difficulty of the parents.

(b) Familial Reason

There are narrow-minded parents who think that education spoils the character of their daughters if their loving daughter goes to college she will not enter the kitchen; in other words she will not be able to prove herself to be a modest daughter-in-law. In college she will only learn fashion, in co-education she may spoil her character. They argued that when their daughter need not earn, then what is the need of higher education. Instead they will get her married.

(c) Educational Reason

The dearth of good college or university or not getting admission are also serious problems faced by girls for higher education. Absence of proper hostel is also a problem for those who want to go to other places for education. The educational reasons which stand in the way of girls' education, are inadequacy of facilities, particularly distance of college or university, irrelevance of the content of education, curriculum not suited to their requirement etc.

(d) Social Reason

It was felt that higher education for girls resulted in increasing the number of spinsters. So most of the parents wanted their daughters to discontinue higher education. Parents are generally of the opinion that it will be late marriage for their daughters if they continue higher education. Thus, the problems of losing girls' higher education to marriage is very common. According to a survey, on an average 75 per cent of girls lose their education due to marriage. They give up their studies to enter home life.

Free Higher Education for Girls

Higher education is an important phase in the process of educating a country. Several provisions have been made thereby increasing the rate of enrolment and educational status of women at various levels.

In the State of Gujarat, girls education is free at all levels. The free education policy was introduced in schools in 1979 and was extended to colleges in 1986 with the following view :

- Educating women is the first step towards the attainment of the goal of literacy, equality and development.
- Education increases awareness amongst women regarding their social and economic rights and lowers the chances of their oppression and exploitation.
- Education helps women to recognise their own identity and their right to be the dignity of society.
- Higher education opens grounds for various specialised professional fields.
- Free education may act as a facilitator particularly to women belonging to lower socio-economic status for higher education.
- Free higher education seems to have helped to increase the enrolment of girls at higher educational level and also to bring desired gender equality. In the Maharaja Sayajirao University of Baroda, the proportion of girls enrolment to that of boys was 42 per cent in 1990-91, against 33 per cent, in the year 1980-81.

In the absence of this policy, it is feared, the enrolment of girl students would not have risen this fast. The reason being that the parents discriminate between their male and female offsprings in the matter of financing their education. They incur relatively less in the range of one-third to one-fourth expenditure for items such as books, stationery, etc. meant for their daughter's education. It was perceived that the policy of tuition free higher education for girls in Gujarat has not only turned out to be an effective antidote to the observed societal discrimination, but also reflected that educated mothers are better and efficient household producers. Thus, the attainment of the objective of "efficiency in household production" may be more of a social than a personal gain- which lends further to the promotion of free higher education for girls.

National Perspective Plan for Girls' Higher Education

For the acceleration of girls higher education the Kothari Education Commission- remarked :

"As at present, students should have free access to courses in arts, humanities, sciences and technology. It would be wrong to restrict their choice or to compel them to take particular courses. The more academic type of girls with ambitions of pursuing careers in research or teaching at the colleges or universities level or in professions such as medicine, or technology should have all the opportunities and incentives for doing so."

The Commission felt that there is a special need to link up higher education with specific avenues of employment for girls. Girls should also be given opportunities to take up research work under schemes of Indian Council of Medical Research (ICMR), Indian Council of Agricultural Research (ICAR) etc. The Commission also recommended universities should set up research units to deal with girls' education. These should take up follow-up studies to educate girls, consider girls' higher education from the point of view of employment opportunities available for girls.

The University Grants Commission also provided developmental grants to Central Universities and 95 State Universities besides existing more than three thousand (3000) colleges for general development programme. To support educational broadcasts, University Grants Commission (UGC) has set up seven audio-visual research centres and seven research centres for production of software. Besides these, University Grants Commission provided assistance for installation of mini/ micro-computer system to 110 universities and 1216 colleges. The Commission has been assisting the universities since 1986 to promote women's studies programme and setting up of centres/cells for women's studies to undertake research projects, development of curriculum, training and extension. The objectives for incorporating women's studies within the university system are both academic and social.

The Indira Gandhi National Open University (IGNOU) widened the access to higher education by providing opportunities to learners from disadvantaged groups like women, people living in backward regions and hilly areas.

Conclusion

Higher education as a major catalyst of social change is badly lacking for the majority, more so for the lower socio-economic status and rural women in comparison with their counterparts. However, the rate of girls' enrolment in higher education has been increased from the last two to three decades. Besides this, several provisions have been made thereby to increase the number of girls in higher education.

Programme of scholarships and financial assistance to girl students in colleges and universities on a liberal scale and programme of the provision of suitable but economic hostel accommodations for girl students with all the necessary amenities on a large scale, to encourage girls from rural areas to take advantage of higher education. Regarding the course, Home Science, Fine Arts, Nursing and Teaching are the main courses provided for them. There are many problems and constraints for girls in higher education.

Girls enrolment and retention in education can be accelerated by taking different measures like providing suitable infrastructure as lack of availability of higher education institutions near to their residence or homes leads to dropout as there is little security for girls because of increase of incidence of eve-teasing.

Parental perception is also not very positive as majority of the parents have negative perception of higher education, especially for girls. They have a feeling that higher education spoils the girls. They have a fear and strong suspicion of pre-marital sex and bad company in the colleges and universities. Another wrong conception in our society is that the daughter is the property of someone else after marriage. So, why invest on her by sending her to college. It is high time to break this myth. Merely freeship and reservation are too meek a solution for this complicated problem of womens' education. This problem can only be solved by bringing educational awareness and attitudinal changes amongst masses in general and parents of girls in particular.

References

Agarawal, S.P. Women Education in India Present Status, Perspective Plan, Statistical indicators with a global view Vol. 3 1995-98. Concept Publishing Company, New Delhi.

Agarwal, N. (1993). Women, Education and Population in India, Chugh Publication, Allahabad.

Brown and Arkins. (1988). Effective Teaching Higher Education. New York. Methert. pp. 7-17.

Chatterji, J. (1990). Education and Training of Girl Child : Some Suggestions Kurukshetra, p. 27.

Datta, S.C. Education for all : An Alternative Strategy, Indian Journal of Adult Education, Vol. 44 No. 12, December, 1983.

Desai, C. (1976). Girls Education and Social Change. Bombay A.R. Sheth and Co. Education Publishers.

Gupta, N.L. (2000). Women Education through the Ages, Concept Pub. Company, New Delhi.

India, University Grants Commission, hand Book of Indian Universities, New Delhi. 1985-86.

Jain, N. 1985. *A study of policy of higher education for girls in the Faculty of Home Science.*

K. Vasanthi Devi. (1985). Women's Education for Social Change, University News, Oct. 8.

Kalbagh, C. 1985. *Women and Development*, Discovery Publishing House, New Delhi.

NCERT 1991. *Education and National Development*. Report of Educational Commission.

Prasad Janardan, Kaushik Vijay, (1994) Women Education and Development. A New Perspective, Kanishk Publishers. New Delhi.

Rawat, V.B. Will Reservation Emancipate Women ? Legal News and Views. Vol. 13 No. 3, March 1999, 6-7.

Saxena, S. 1996. Higher Education for Women. *University News,* XXXIV(4).

Sen, N.B. (1995) Progress of Women's Education in Free India. New Book Society of India, New Delhi.

Sharma Usha, Sharma B.M. (1990). Women and Higher Education, Commonwealth Publishers, New Delhi.

Sharma, U. 1985. *Women's Education in Modern India*, Commonwealth Publishers, New Delhi.

Siddiqui, M.H. 1993. *Women Education, A Research Approach*, Ashish Publishing House, New Delhi.

Talesara Hemlata, (1999), Higher Education among Women. National Publishing House, New Delhi.

University Grants Commission *Annual Report* for the year 1989-90. U.G.C., New Delhi.

6

Women and Adult Education

Rameshwari Pandya, Richa Kapoor

Abstract

The importance of adult education for human resource development is seriously recognized one and emphasis is given to girls and women's education as 50 to 60 per cent of them could not get the benefit of it. Only through there active participation national development can be possible. As adult education can create consciousness about realities of life, develop skills to help them increase their family income and reduce drudgery of life. Adult education is flexible, diversified and need based so women can take its benefits. It is important while planning care is taken to follow the theories of adult learning and understand that psychology of adult, their concept, role, readiness to learn and motivation are different. But by providing good conditions, providing positive factors and using innovative methods and materials the objective can be achieved using mass media can create more dynamic learning environment in distance education. The diversification of objectives context and form is possible through communication media as it breaks the barriers of space and time.

Introduction

Adult education is an impelling need; the need is so imperative and over-powering that all men and women must be helped to acquire the skills and knowledge that would enable them to properly fit into the society which is fast moving.

An illiterate person will face innumerable hurdles in this scientific and rapidly changing world of cut-throat competition. Literacy is not only a means of liberation but also an instrument of social change. It is a tool for acquiring and sharing information on national development. Economic recession and growing burden of debt have no doubt played a major role in decline of basic education. Literacy increases peoples' capacity to cope with the demands of living and working.

Adult education is a tool to influence human thinking in a right direction. In fact, development of society depends primarily on the quality and effectiveness of its people. The importance of adult education for human resource development is being seriously recognized which is imperative for the economic development as well as for strengthening the base of democracy. The significance of universal literacy as an instrument of galvanizing and mobilizing the people, arousing community consciousness and community participation for bringing about social change.

According to the UNESCO the term adult education denotes the entire body of organized educational processes, whatever the content level and method, whether they prolong or replace initial education in schools, colleges, as well as apprenticeship. Whereby person regarded as a adult by the society to which they belong develop their abilities, enrich their knowledge, improve their technical or behaviour in the two-fold perspectives of full personal development and participation in balanced and independent social, economic and cultural development.

Adult education programme as envisaged in the national adult education programme is meant primarily for women and learners belonging to deprived section of the population. This does not meant that others willing to join adult education programme should be excluded, but emphasis must be given to this section of the population for they constitute about 60 to 70 per cent of India's population which did not have the benefit of any type of education formal or informal.

After 1952, adult education programme became an integral part of the planned programmes. Social education organizers training centres were set up in various parts of the country, and public library movement was given a fillip. Use of radio as medium of education began to be recognized and the Ministry of Information produced a number of educational documentaries.

At the national level, in 1956 an important step in the field of adult education was the establishment of the National Fundamental Education Centre, whose functions include training and orientation of key personnel, experimentation in preparation of materials, conducting research and evaluation in the field of adult education.

Yet, another effort in the field of adult education has been the launching of non-formal education programme during 1975-76 in the country and out-of school youth and adults. A significant step in the field of adult education in the country has been the launching of National Adult Education Programme all over the country on October 2, 1978 with the uphill task of covering ten crore illiterates in the age group of 15 to 35. Also in 1978 the universities were involved in a substantial way in the national adult education programme of Government of India.

In 1983, the UGC converted the centre for adult education into full-fledged university departments for adult and continuing education. To implement the recommendations of the review committee on role of university towards the community, the UGC, in 1989, instructed that all extension programme must be conducted in area or community adopted by a university department or an affiliated college. This helped ensure development of a relationship between university, college and the community. Colleges were provided with grants to open a community education centre in the community. This centre was to function as the extension centre of the college. In 1992, the university extension departments were asked to ensure that the communities adopted colleges for eradication of illiteracy and conducting continuing and adult education courses on a regular basis.

Today, universities in the country are involved in nation-wide extension programme through Departments/centres set up and funded by UGC. These institutions are involved in programmes like literacy, post-literacy, continuing education, and science for people, environmental education, legal literacy and technology transfer through involving students and teacher.

Active participation of women in national development, as envisaged in our Five-Year Plans since independence, is not possible as long as majority of our women are illiterate and ignorant. Half of our population comprises women and the grim reality is that not just their problems, but their very existence has been ignored despite the fact that majority of our labour force consists of women who produce a little less than 50 per cent of our food. Their cases are overlooked whenever there is opportunity for being trained for skilled jobs. In general the position of women in our country is not a happy one as they are illiterate, and are ignorant of political, legal, social and economic issues.

Considering the position of women in our society and the responsibility they shoulder, it is a known fact that they are not well-equipped to discharge these obligations.

A large number of women are outside the reach of formal education and they could be educated through adult education programme. The adult education programme should be such that they motivate the illiterate women to join functional literacy classes and sustain their motivation to continue with the programme. Thus, it can help in creating social awareness of the importance of education in improving the quality of life.

Adult education programme can create consciousness about realities of life, develop skills to help them increase their family income and reduce drudgery of life and make them literate so that they can help in development.

Vital National Resource

Women constitute an important part of human resources of the country. For a developing country like ours, the contribution of women is as indispensable as that of men. It is widely recognised that the success of national development very much depends upon the active and useful participation of women in all developmental programmes. But when we cast our glance over the existing status of literacy among women of our country, we are greatly disappointed. It is because of inadequate expansion of education among women in India that they feel themselves unable to shoulder their responsibilities in different walks of life, and this has an adverse effect on their own development and the development of the society as well. The equal partnership between men and women is a must to fight against hunger, poverty, ignorance and ill health.

We, in India, have accelerated the pace of educational expansion after independence, but due to rapid increase in population and for several reasons social, economic and political—we have not been able to extend the benefits of education to the entire population of the country. Hence the huge number of illiterates among whom the number of women is much higher than that cf men.

For full development of our human resources, for the improvement of our homes and for moulding the character of children during the most impressionable years of infancy, the education of women is of even greater importance than that of men. So, keeping these points in view, our government has decided to impart education to women so as to equip them in performing their duties and for shouldering heavy responsibilities at home as well as outside. For the very purpose, the government has started adult education programme for adult illiterates from October 2,

1978 all over the country. Now it is the duty of all the people to make efforts for the success of this programme.

The essential pre-conditions for the success of adult education for illiterate women is that it is quite useful and effective from the point of view of fulfilling their immediate needs. Women would be interested in adult education if it assures them economic benefits. This is possible only by giving a practical bias to their education.

National Adult Education Programme

The National Adult Education Programme, launched in 1978, while emphasising acquisition of literacy skills was to be :

- relevant to learner's need
- flexible regarding duration, time, location, instructional arrangements, etc.
- diversified in regard to curriculum, teaching and learning materials and methods.

The outline of NAEP suggested the following types of programme to be organised under the scheme :

- Literacy with assured follow-up.
- Conventional functional literacy in association with a dominant development programmes.
- Literacy with learning-cum-action groups.
- Literacy for awareness and formation of organisations of the poor.

The programme was to cover by 1984 the entire illiterate population in the 15-35 age group. The programme consisting of literacy, functionality and awareness, with literacy comprising reading, writing and numeracy; functionality aiming at improvement in the learner's skills and capabilities in the discharge of his function as wage earner as a member of the family and as a citizen; and awareness seeking to arouse a sense of social obligation and consciousness about the manner in which the poor are deprived of the benefits of the various laws, policies and facilities designed for them. A programme of 19 months was to be followed by post-literacy and follow up activities.

It was also intended to link up the programme with other development programmes of the government. There should be 30 illiterate adults in each centre. In each centre there will be one instructor, three supervisors and a project officer.

According to the 1981 census, 243 districts out of 402 have literacy rates below the national average. The literacy rate is also very low amongst women, scheduled castes, scheduled tribes, migrant labourers and other weaker sections of the society. As contemplated in the Sixth Five-Year Plan document, it was to be endeavour of the government to take steps for covering 100 per cent adult illiterates in the age group of 15-35 by the year 1990.

Functional Literacy for Adult Women

The programme of functional literacy for women has been provided in the Fifth Five-Year Plan to endow them with necessary knowledge and skills to perform the functions of a good housewife, efficient mother and a useful citizen.

The scheme is a programme seeking to deliver a package of services to illiterate women in the country. Attention is confined to adult women in the productive age group of 15-45 years and special attention is given to women in the age group of 15-35, since the latter group is likely to be more receptive to the requirements of attitudinal change.

A change in the outlook of women is very important and this can be brought about by drawing their attention to the socio-economic, political and cultural changes and developments taking place around them, in society, in the country and in the world.

Adult education plays an important role in Women's Development in India in the following ways :

- Increase the rate of literacy among women.
- Improve the general level of health and nutrition.
- Enable women to raise their family income.
- Improve the quality of local skills by providing vocational training in tailoring and embroidery, textile design and printing and machine knitting, etc.
- Make them aware of new simple household techniques.
- Inform them about new governmental policies and privileges offered to farmers for loans, seeds, etc.
- Encourage them to lead a more hygienic and healthy life simply through cleanliness and other preventive methods.

Besides imparting instruction in simple but useful art and crafts, there are many other significant areas of which adult women can be imparted adequate knowledge. India is making sincere efforts to raise the standard of living of every citizen through planned development. For the immediate solution of the problem of rapidly increasing population, it is essential that the illiterate adult women are acquainted with the problems and know the need and importance of family planning and family welfare programmes. It would not only enhance their own happy lives but also the lives of their children who would be healthy and happy indeed.

Another factor relating to women's development is that they are able to know and understand their fundamental rights and duties in the existing social structure. It is seen that most of illiterate women often come to grips with superstitions and many other social evils of which there is an adverse effect upon their individual development. Such women cannot be expected to make their children's growth in the desired direction. With the spread of right education these women may get rid of superstitions, caste feelings and inferiority complex, etc.

Adult education programme tries to make use of leisure time of adult women. For this purpose, Mahila Mandals are organised where women take part in *bhajan*, *kirtan*, folk music and songs, stories and talks on different useful matters. Our movement relating to the development of women through adult education is required to be designed in such a way that all those people, institutions and organisations, interested in women's advancement, come forward voluntarily with their helping hands and cordial cooperation. By this way national objectives can be achieved.

Theories of Adult Learning

The body of knowledge relating to the art and science of teaching and learning is known as "Andragogy".

According to Simpson's adult learning, theories most commonly emphasized the experimental dimension of life and stressed the self-directness of adults. Self-directness is seen both as an empirically observable trait and as a property that should be encouraged.

Adults learn through their lives, with the negotiations of the transitional stages in the life-span being the immediate causes and motives for much of their learning. They exhibit diverse learning styles-strategies for coding information, cognitive procedures, mental sets and learn in different ways, at different times, for different purposes. They live their life situation and they want the learning outcomes to have some immediacy of application. Adults use experience as a resource in learning so the learning content and process must bear a perceived and meaningful relationship to past experience what is to be learned should be related to the individual's developmental changes and it may help us to understand more clearly how to structure our own learning opportunities for Adults life tasks. But it affects them sometimes serving as an enhancement and sometimes as a hindrance.

There are four main characteristics about adult learning activities :

1. They are usually episode in character, not continuous.
2. The goal that is set is usually some concrete task, some immediate problem that seems to be important.

3. Each adult adopts his or her own learning style in relation to the needs of these learning episodes.
4. Since most of these learning episodes are directed towards specific goals, there is relatively little interest in overall principles.

Adults throughout their lives engage in rather more systematic learning in order to achieve a particular goal or solve a specific problem.

Understanding Adult Psychology

- The adults learn in adult ways.
- Their ways differ significantly from child learning because adults have much accumulated experience, skills, knowledge opinions and prejudices. For them learning is best done by building outwards from these foundations, rather than in items presented separately and memorized.
- Accumulation of experience makes adults differ more from each other than children and young people. This needs to be borne in mind in devising learning opportunities for them.
- The education of Adults is concerned with helping mature and experienced people to accept changes in the light of critical thinking/new knowledge that challenges their previous assumptions.
- Because of their existing knowledge and experience adults are also resistant to change. New learning and new attitudes may be uncomfortable or painful experience for them.

Methods of Motivating Adults to Learn

Without adequate motivation learning cannot be effective. Thus, these are the methods of motivating adults towards learning.

Rewards : To give prizes motivate adults to work harder and do better in learning. Such rewards may be in the shape of money or kinds. Even to thank an individual doing well can motivate him to learn. Although artificial goals thus set up for achievement, work as incentives. These are of secondary importance. Hence, to give such prizes is not regarded as the best technique.

Punishment : It is called negative reward in the sense that to give unpleasant experience to an individual for not doing a certain work creates an interest to work hard and achieve the target. Thus, creates an interest to work avoiding the unpleasant consequences try to learn better. But such technique is not always taken as a desirable step of motivation.

Games and Sports : There are some simple games and sports which can be utilized for promoting adults learning. Some of these are indigenous or traditional and others are modern, printed or manufactured devices. But the use of carefully selected games and plays create immense interest and joy in learning and helps motivating adults to learn better. This is regarded as a desirable and positive method of adults motivation.

Competition : To create competitive spirit among adults to learn better is a good technique of motivation. But sometimes it leads to rivalry and undesirable consequences. It is however, necessary that some healthy competition be encouraged among adult learners so that they can improve their achievements and learn better.

Examination : Tests are administered for evaluating the achievement of performance of adult learners. These are also intended to work as incentives for promoting learning. Some times, examinations acts as regards for good learners for boosting up their morale and slow learners for spurring their efforts. Occasionally, tension tends to act as negative motivation for adult learning.

Respect and Liking : Regard and liking of learners for teacher's love and affection of instructors, for pupils contribute a lot to adult learning. Such mutual concern and exchange of ideas act as powerful motivation to learn more and better.

Liking for Subject : When the subjects or learning materials are liked by adult learners, learning not only becomes easy, but is also facilitated. To create such interest is the best kind of motivation and can be enhanced if the material or subject matter is relevant to the needs and conditions of life and aspiration.

Both Intrinsic and Extrinsic Interests : Motivation may be intrinsic or extrinsic. If interest is inherent in the subject matter and self-directed or self motivated, it is intrinsic. When it is imposed from above or there is fear of punishment or insult, motivation becomes extrinsic. The former is positive, creative and permanent in nature whereas the latter is negative and temporary in character. Attempts should therefore be made to provide more and more intrinsic motivation and less and less extrinsic one, so that learning will be more effective and expeditious. Both positive and negative motivation should be hand in hand for bringing and about the best type of learning.

Good Conditions for Adult Learning

1. Adults generally learn best in an atmosphere that is non-threatening. Experiments and different learning styles should be recognized, supported and encouraged by adult educations.

2. The learning environment should be physically as well as psychologically comfortable. Long lectures and tasks should be avoided as far as possible.
3. Since experiences of an adult differ from that of another, mere heterogeneity is evident among adult than among student. This factor is to be taken into consideration for effective teaching as well as preparation of materials.
4. Suitable materials should be made available to them for the purpose.
5. Practical activities for adult learners prove more effective learning.
6. Demonstration and use of audio-visual media materials are necessary for ensuring better learning outcomes.
7. Adult seems to learn when they do not have to rely on memorizing but can learn through activity at their own pace with material that seems relevant to their daily lives and use their own experiences finding "RIGHT" answers at the first attempt seems important. Generous practice will enforce new skills. Adults who have been out of touch with learning can often improve their educational performance grammatically if they are helped by "Learning to Learn".

Positive and Negative Factors Associated with Adult Learning

Positive Factors	*Negative Factors*
1. More and more examples from life should be taken in Adult education programme.	1. Less practical life examples are used for explaining about the topic concerned.
2. Open sessions should be conducted for more direct communication and debates should be conducted to satisfy the quench for knowledge amongst adults.	2. Lack of interaction and time among the teachers and students resulting in communication gap between the Teachers and Students.
3. Education should be kept away from politics and the politicians. No one should interfere with the Education system. The Special Grants should be sanctioned from the Ministry of Education. It should be devoid of political immunity.	3. Illiteracy is largely a result of political and social factors. Ruling parties hold back the right of the people to their own self-determination. The non-implementation of the policies and programmes are vested interests of the prevailing Government hinder the success of Adult Education in India.
4. Education can bring awareness of low population. Only the educated can make	4. Rapid population growth has been an obstacle to the attainment of

(Contd.)

(Contd.)

Positive Factors	*Negative Factors*
the uneducated understand the problem of over population. Then and then only the further steps for Adult education can begin. For which dramas and cultural programmes are conducted periodically in rural and urban regions to bring social awareness.	much desired goals, while a slower rate of population growth would have ensured or facilitated the achievement of adult education.
5. The times have changed when a grandfather can sit with his grandchild to learn what he was unable to. Age is no barrier for Education or Learning. Various types of classes are conducted just like yoga classes where all age group people come to learn and practice.	5. People feel inferiority complex and an insult to learn at a later age. They feel shy to attend the Adult education classes.
6. Specially designed courses and training programmes should be conducted with easy to understand lectures with lots of practical examples to teach should be implemented in the education system.	6. Various Models of learning methods are enforced as per the industrialized countries resulting in dissatisfaction on the part of state of education system.

Difference between Adult and Child Learning

The organized body of knowledge relating to the art and science of teaching young children is called Pedagogy, whereas the body of knowledge relating to the art and science of teaching adults is known as Andragogy. The former is generally teacher directed and the latter is self-directed.

1. Concept of the Learner

The personality of the younger learner is not yet properly developed and taken the final shape whereas the adult personality is adequately developed.

2. Role of the Learner's Experience

In case of young learners, learning experience is gradually developed and cannot be used as a resource. On the other hand, in case of adults, experience is a rich source of learning.

3. Readiness to Learn

Among the young learners readiness to learn is almost uniform whereas among the adults counterparts is developed variously according to the background of life problems and life tasks.

4. Orientation to Learning

In case of young learners learning is subject or curriculum centred, but adults learn through their life tasks or problems encountered from time to time.

5. Motivation

Young learners are motivated according to their external rewards and punishments whereas adult learners are influence by their internal urge and drive.

The psychology of the learners varies according to their age, education and socio-economic status. Children and youth can be motivated to work for their future goals through active learning, whereas, adults want the welfare of their families and present life. They want immediate gains from learning. The gains may not be just intellectual, but may also be in a physical form.

Difference between Child Education and Adult Education

Sr. No.	*Variable*	*Adult Education*	*Child Education*
1.	Structure	Problem-oriented	Highly organized with specific learning goals
2.	Content	Skill-oriented related to participants need	Academic knowledge oriented generally reinforcing dominant values and concepts
3.	Time	Short in duration and flexible in presentation	Set-time developed by organization i.e., terms, semester, quarter
4.	Control	Uncoordinated and fragmented	Highly organized
5.	Locate	Depends on local condition and facilities	Building with special facilities i.e. classrooms etc.
6.	Functions	Emphasis on groups skill required to meet community needs	Certification and meeting greater social and political objective of organization or political entity
7.	Rewards	Related to community or individual betterment immediate gratification, improving specific economic or social well being of participant	Oriented towards degree or certificates
8.	Methods	Methodology based on target group needs and local resources	Structured curriculum
9.	Cost	Inexpensive, local people, materials and facilities	Based on specific allocation per participant or programme

Role of Media in Adult Education

In recent years, the inadequacy of the formal system to cater to the varied education needs in the society, has come to be recognised. A large section of people do not enter the fold of formal education due to various reasons. Many of those who are in jobs might like to pursue education in some form which may be beneficial to them. This they could pursue, if only the restrictions of the formal institutions with respect of time, place and other requirements are not strictly imposed. Some of them may even prefer a course of study with a greater practical base in their own occupations, than pure academic pursuits. Obviously to cater to the needs of such a clientele, education has to be more flexible and available to them wherever they are. Over the years attempts have been made to provide such a system of education which marks the initiation of distance education in this country.

As we know, in adult education there is a great reliance on the motivation of the learner as he is a willing adult who has voluntarily chosen to be a student. Distance education is gaining ground in India in recent years as an alternative channel of education along with the formal one. Several agencies have come up with more specific skills and knowledge, training through postal tuition. Most of them are private agencies offering courses for very definite aspects, such as, interior decoration and language learning. Besides these some courses under what is popularly known as 'Continuing Education Programme' also fall under distance education in the sense that they provide it to learners at a distance.

1. *Correspondence education.* In India, this scheme has not been able to develop as an independent system of education and it has yet to respond to the challenge of designing and offering newer and more courses which would cater to the educational needs of a larger clientele.
2. *Open University Scheme.* This scheme offers several courses in humanities and social science through correspondence-cum-personal contact programmes to any willing learner irrespective of his educational background. The only criteria for entry is that the learner should be of a particular age limit and should be literate.

The open universities are trying to provide opportunities for higher education to adults studying part time while in full employment through multi-media system. The innumerable possibilities of communication through the adoption of mechanized ways and mass media are being tapped. Thus what is lost through the minimization of teacher-pupil interaction will be made up through the use of several media. This would need additional facilities such as full-fledged libraries of books, audio-visual aids and video cassettes.

To be relevant, acceptable and long lasting, alternative system of the formal education has to be well designed, effective and affordable. Moreover, its speed has to be accelerated to provide education to the students all over the country through an effective communication network.

Mass media can help to adopt education to complex individual needs, wishes and conditions. It can improve the quality of education at a comparative lower cost than that of the formal system. Mass media creates a more dynamic learning environment in distance education. The diversification of objectives, content and form is possible through communication media. It breaks the barriers of space and time. Adult education can employ both small media and advanced media for educating the adult.

Advantages of using Mass Media

1. *Access.* Mass media can provide educational opportunities to large number of people who had previously been denied such opportunities and that it would be done in a cost-effective manner. It is an inexpensive method of teaching. It has provided access for learning to many people, as mass media can take education to a large number of the population.
2. *People from all age groups.* Mass media can be used to teach courses from a wide range of discipline areas, both vocational and non-vocational. The basic necessities are that the student be motivated to learn and the instructional materials be well designed. If radio is the only teaching medium available in the country because of poor ground communication, it can be developed as a most effective teaching medium. The provisions are that the teaching sessions be well structured and soundly based, from an instructional perspective, and that the students be well motivated. Of course, the problem is that not all students are highly motivated. Thus it will always be better if a range of mass-media are used to educate people.
3. *Effectiveness.* If mass media are used to educate people, then it will be more effective than just one media for educating adults. Mass media is most cost-effective when large number of students are involved. The larger the number, the smaller the preparation cost per student. It can be a highly cost-effective way of teaching to those who are isolated geographically. And both developed

and underdeveloped nations have found mass media as a means of taking education to the socially isolated.

4. *Geographical Isolation.* People in India are isolated because of distance, because of terrain. The country consists of a number of modes with the sea on one side and high mountains on the other side. Mass media can be used as a technique to take learning to all locations.
5. *Social Isolation.* People can be isolated for any number of reasons. Mostly, it is because they are disadvantaged in some way, be it financial, physical, emotional or because of family circumstances. Most of all, mass media can help in taking education to the masses.
6. *Disadvantaged Groups.* Taking education to disadvantaged groups is no easy task. People in such groups lack confidence in their ability to learn. Mass Media can introduce education as well as importance of education to the disadvantaged groups of people.

Constraints in the use of new communication media for Adult Education in India :

1. Language-wise complexity of the audience, especially in the absence of multi-channel facility; for example the students from villages who have subsidised TV sets to watch but cannot understand either English or Hindi adequately as there is inadequate and difficult production of language free TV programmes.
2. Inadequate acquaintance with TV or even radio as educational communication technologies on part of the persons In-charge of adult education; inadequate institutional facilities to acquaint them. In India, only six institutes out of thirty relay radio talks for distance education and TV support is almost nil.
3. Less coverage of the contents of education by the radio and TV media. The programmes specially on TV are of very general nature and not student based. In an effort, to make them applicable to the masses, they are reduced to the most elementary levels.
4. Improvised resources for the development and expansion of TV and computer based communication technologies. India at present buys advanced technology from the developed world in the fields of communication technologies and micro-electronics. The maintenance and repair facilities are simply non-existent in small cities, towns and villages.
5. Low socio-economic levels of the Indian students of adult education can not afford audio and video cassettes.

6. Small number of students having regular access to the radio and TV broadcasts.
7. Inability of the educational institutions to meet the financial liabilities for use of the new technologies, specially video production.
8. Technical and expensive process of preparing excellent quality video films. The small audio and video production units in each university may burden already overstrained economy of our country.
9. Large size and complexity of the background of the clientele to be covered under adult education. The masses include decentralized, tribal, rural and illiterate adult persons with apathy towards education and new communication technology.

Suggestions to Overcome the Constraints

Like many innovative approaches, adult education also may not register much success with raising quality of education or coverage of learners, unless such steps are taken :

1. Encouragement to cost production techniques; starting from production of slides films and later transferring them to video cassettes compared to straight video production will be cost effective. The new audio-visual can play a highly significant role in adult education only if the country becomes self reliant and self-supporting regarding the indigenous technologies.
2. Encouragement to community TV viewing and both community and individual listening for larger coverage of clientele.
3. Encouragement to both the students and the teachers who are used to conventional media and methods to master some new skills involved in the use of new communication technologies.

It is hoped that India will soon overcome these problems related to the electronic media to be able to take full advantage of their great audience appeal capacity to record maximum information in the given space and facilities of easy transport storage and long life. Basically, learning in adult education as in other approaches, takes place through various senses and stimuli. No one aid can be recommended for all types of learning and all types of learners.

A variety of both conventional and technology based audio-visual aids will help adult education. The audio-visual aids which cost less are easily available, are easy to prepare, carry, use and store and which bring about the greatest clarity in learning will have to be given the priority in distance education. One has to be realistic as to which is immediately achievable and which can be achieved in many years to come. The despairing situation, arising out of the reduced use of conventional low cost media and unavailability of modern electronic communication technology need to be averted for the genuine growth of adult education. India still being a developing country, a mixture of traditional and sophisticated media can serve the instructional purpose of adult education.

References

Ahmad Nasim, "Benefits of Literacy and Learning", *Literacy Mission*, Vol. XXI (1-4). 1997, pp. 18-22.

Ansari, N. *Adult Education in India*, S. Chand & Co., New Delhi.

Bhatia, S. *Development-oriented Adult Education*, ed. By S.C. Bhatia and M.L. Mehta, 1985.

Census of India (1991).

Chandra, A. and Shah, A. *Non Formal Education for All*, Sterling Publishers Pvt. Ltd., New Delhi. 1987.

Chatterjee Bhaskar, "Strategies for Post-Literacy in the Next Decade" *Indian Journal of Adult Education,* Jan.-March, 1996 pp. 27-45.

Clark, R.E. "Reconsidering research on learning from media", *Review of Educational Research*, 1983, 53 (4) 445–459.

Dighe, Anita and Patel, Illa, "Gender Equality in Literacy in India Some Issues", *Perspectives in Education,* Vol. 9(1), 1993, pp. 3-14.

Evaluation of Literacy Campaign in India–Report of Expert Group, New Delhi. Directorate of Adult Education, 1994.

Garrison, D.R. "The Role of Technology in Continuing Education", *New Directions for Continuing Education,* 1987, 36, 41-53.

Garrison, D.R. and Shale, D., "Mapping the boundaries of distance education : Problems in defining the field", *American Journal of Distance Education*, 1987, 1(1) 7–13.

Ghosh, Avik, "Adult Education : Looking Beyond Literacy Campaign", *Economic and Political Weekly*, Dec. 20, 1997, pp. 3246-48.

Heinich, R., "The proper study of instructional technology", *Educational Communication and Technology*, 1984 32(2) 67-87.

Leagans, P.J. Selected Concepts from Educational Psychology and Adult Education for Extension and Continuing Education.

Mutanya, Hohannes Ntara Sylvery, Training of Teachers for Adult and Non-formal Education : Alternative Approaches used in Tanzanian Colleges, *International Dissertation Abstracts* 43(7), Jan. 1983.

National Policy on Education, New Delhi, Ministry of HRD, Government of India, 1986.

Patel, Ila "Trends in Adult Education Research India", New Delhi, *National Institute of Adult Education*, 1994.

Pillai, Sadasivan, "From Three R's to Empowerment", *Indian Journal of Adult Education*, Vol. 58(3), 1997, pp. 71-76.

Post-Literacy Strategy, *Literacy Mission,* Dec. 1993, pp. 23-26.

Ramabrahmam. *Adult Education–Policy Performance*. New Delhi, Gyan Publishing House, 1988.

Sharma, Inderprabha, *Adult Education in India, A Policy Perspective*, 1985.

Singh, R.P. and Shukla, N. *Non Formal System*, Bahn Publishers, Chandigarh. 1979.

Sudame, G.S. and Goel, D.R. *A Study of School Broadcasts in Baroda District for Advanced Studies in Education,* Baroda: CASE, M.S. University, 1988.

UGC-Guidelines for the Programmes of Literacy and Continuing Education in Universities and Colleges, 1992.

University Grants Commission (1982); Revised Guidelines on Adult and Continuing Education and Extension, New Delhi.

7

Gender and Socialisation

Anuradha Mathu, Rameshwari Pandya

Abstract

The vast economic, social changes round the world due to technological and scientific development, have generated a keener interest in women's status, role of education and development in ensuring quality of life. There are many facets of gender discrimination, the first and foremost is the family, then the school and finally the society. Discrimination against the girl child and gender inequality in the Indian society is associated with the ethos of patriarchy and traditional gender stereotyping. From the very day of her birth, a girl is considered as misfortune for the family.

School rélated factors are responsible in the discontinuance of girls education. Girls are frequently caught in a vicious circle. Their initial socialization and subsequent adoption of home based cultures predisposes them towards certain kinds of school subjects. To make full use of women's potential we need to handle curriculum very carefully in the light of economic, technological changes that are taking place in the society, the whole curriculum needs to be examined, reoriented and revalidated.

Recommendations have been suggested like representation of women in management positions. Immediate action programmes to universalize early education should be taken up as the first and the most challenging assignments in the interest of girls.

In the 'Vedic times' and in History also we have witnessed great women like–'Jhansi Ki Rani', Maitrey, Sarojini Naidu, Indira Gandhi, and many more. The list is endless. However, during Muslim invasions, Moghul empires ruling India and colonial–British Raj–Women in India started becoming a neglected lot–discriminated against and down-trodden and many a times victims to male 'Chavinism' or male dominance.

Women, thus started becoming easy targets for victimization and violence in the form of–rape, bride burning, even teasing, castration of female reproductive organs, gender discrimination in work places, private, public and government.

When it comes to women's rights–they are not usually aware about their rights to property, education, legal rights, political rights, decision making power or even basic human rights. Those of us, who are privileged–fight for our rights. Women in middle and upper-middle and higher socio-economic status may not have to be scared, concerned or bothered because their rights, responsibilities or even position comes to them in easy manner–without any effort.

It is the lower socio-economic status women and women in the rural–far flung areas or in slums in urban areas, who are the worst sufferers of this discrimination because of the following factors or reasons :

- Illiteracy
- Poor economic conditions
- Poor health status
- Lack of awareness regarding their rights
- Lack of support from the family
- Lack of legislations protecting them in unorganised sector.
- Lack of knowledge regarding government programmes and policies for women in the areas of :
  - Education
  - Economic development
  - Social upliftment
  - Water
  - Energy

Thus, it is here with this discussion and background that some solutions can be put forward, being in the area of extension and communication, where we are in constant dialogue, interaction and working with women from sections :

- Do not discriminate with your girl child in your homes, spread awareness that her life is as precious and as important as that of a boy.
- Programmes on television and radio can be focussed on and made to generate awareness regarding issues of girl child and discrimination and solutions to combat such problems.
- Films are a very popular medium of communication especially in India, where the largest number of films are produced.

The Difference between the Concept of Sex and Gender

Over the past year there has been some confusion concerning the words "sex" and "gender". Sex has generally to mean biological differences [at a minimum, chromosomal, hormonal and morphological] between males and females. Gender has come to mean the socio-cultural sex. The term gender is used to distinguish between males and females. By using this term for the theoretical questions. Biology does not constitute a relevant variable, rather it is socio-cultural definition of, and reaction to, biological sex that produce and reinforce inequality between male and females. Biological differences whatever hey may be--are basically constant across historical time and space.

Sex differences are not gender differences. Few people should say that being a female means being womanly or being a male means manly. Sex differences are physiological features related to procreation, to biological reproduction. The sex division of labour in reproduction is well understood. Males produce sperms, females produce eggs, and females bear youngs. Sex differences are found in all mammals. However, human form their very origins have interpreted and reshaped their physical and social environment through symbolizing. Human are self-reflective, culture-creating animals. Human have sex differences but like all other aspects of physical differentiation, they are experienced symbolically. In human societies, sex differences are experienced as gender differences, which is not true.

A woman is regarded as an epitome of sacrifice, love, courage and affection. Her qualities act as the pillars of strength for the building up of mankind. She is the saviour of the nation. Existence of mankind without women is next to impossible hence it is truly said, "A woman is made for a man and not a man for a woman". She has an abundance of love and affection within her, which is why she is considered as a perfect gift of God to mankind. She is born to sacrifice whatever it may be. And she does it rightly despite being in pain. She is a multifaceted personality being a wife, a daughter, a mother, a manager, a teacher and a human at the same time. She represents strength and grace at the same time, is mentally strong yet gentle in behaviour. There is perhaps no stronger metaphor for hope, renewal and pain than the birth of the child.

The vast economic social changes round the world due to technological and scientific development, have generated a keener interest in women's status, role of education and development in ensuring quality of life.

The current interest in women's education, status and development is very different from the earlier feminist movement, which was only a negative social protest, it is positive attempt order, to develop and harness women's potential.

With the fast moving world stepping into the twenty-first century, still are in the same nutshell of the word gender. Right from conception till death, we live with the Gender but discriminating it. Why so? Who are responsible ones? There are many facets of gender discrimination, the first and foremost is the family, where the child is born, then it is the school where he/she is educated and finally the society in which this child grows up. In the family, the female child is discriminated in cases like traditions of the family, household chores, their health and so on. After moving out of the house with hardships, the school too lets them down by not letting them use the educational advantage. And finally the society, which is a web of the gender bias. The norms, customs and traditions of the society made by the people just considered women to be the weaker sex. The status of women needs to be uplifted by the sensitizing people against gender.

The subject of gender justice is very vital, so far as the Indian society is concerned. It is more so important in the present phase that society is passing through, the status of women continues to be pathetic as there is no gender justice. Men do not accept them as their equal and the women themselves have not realized that they are equal to the men.

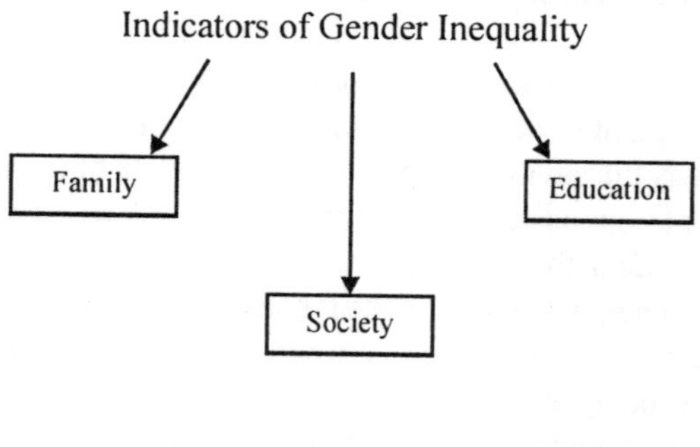

Family

Before independence, the place of girls/women in the Indian society was within the four walls and behind the *purdah*. Also the traditional India has seen a women or a girl child as a member of a family wives or mothers and not as an individual with an identity or right of her own. The main role of the women or girl child is just to cook, look after children and take care for other family members. Women's work was only considered as an extension of their 'natural activities', whereas men's work was seen as conscious human labour. There is no direct relationship between the status of women in society and women's power within the household.

Discrimination against the girl child and gender inequality in the Indian society is associated with the ethos of patriarchy and traditional gender stereotyping. In a traditional Indian society, the role of men and women were not equally balanced and hence the conceptualization of low self-esteem and unequal opportunity of the girl child in every sphere of life. From the very day of her birth a girl is considered as misfortune for the family.

The dominant values in our country are such that women or girl child are perceived primarily as mothers and wives. Such social definition of all gender makes their contribution to the household as well as to the economy of the country negligible. This ideology leads to a devaluation of women's / girl's productive works because it is seen as a mere extension of household work and regarded as subordinate and secondary to men's work. Housework, childcare and subsistence production like collection of fuel, fodder and water, rearing the livestock and working in the farm, all these are regarded as an extension of girl's domestic work and are not recognized as work.

Girls are profoundly affected by environmental degradation because they depend on bio-mass based resources for food, fuel, fodder, water and medicinal needs. Environmental degradation leads to a substantial increase in women's time and energy spent in gathering these resources. Several studies have shown an increase in male migration to the cities, due to the decline in access to land for cultivation, fodder for cattle, minor forest produce for consumption and sale, and so on. Women are left behind to fend for their families, leading to an increase in the physical and mental stress levels among rural and tribal women.

In the urban context, lack of water supply, medical care, access to education and the public distribution system are inadequate or absent. Women and children are thus a vulnerable group, exposed to the deteriorating urban environment. Women's work and the condition for work in the informal sector are oppressive and explorative because of low wages, long hours of work, lack of provision of holidays and maternity leave. The constant tensions and anxiety in these situations result in continuous pressure on women and affect their mental health.

Intra-household allocations that discriminate against women cannot be attributed to particular macro policies. But the prevalence of inequitable gender relation in society definitely determines outcomes. Intended on unintended consequences find their expression in the intensification of children's education (especially for girls), increases in time spent by women on home maintenance, and higher level of the stress and violence in society.

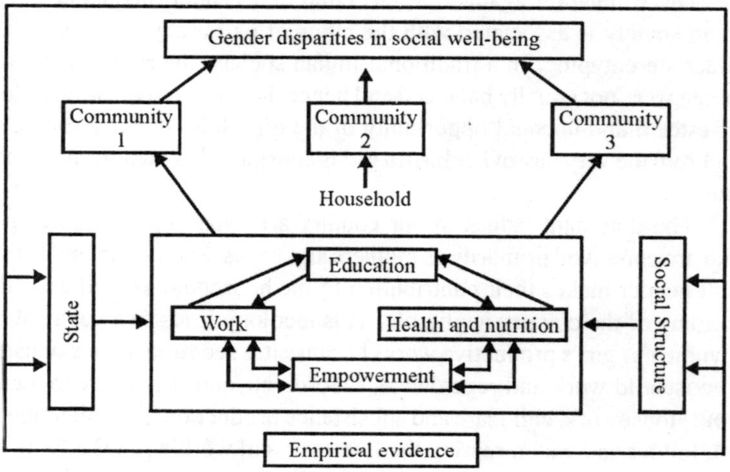

Source : Dutta Anindita & Sinha (1996).

A major shortcoming in the research on gender disparities in social well-being is the relative paucity of empirical studies. Secondly, among the empirical works that do exist, gender has often been considered as an absolute and independent variable isolated from the total social context. Further, the household as the unit of analysis is more often than not forsaken in favour of broad-based and large-scale observations at the micro and macro levels. In such a situation the root of the problem of female marginalization is bypassed. Again, most empirical studies tend to concentrate only on one, or a best two, principal aspects of social well-being thus losing out on important interlinkages between the various aspects of social well-being. Finally, the intra-gender version of the problem is often ignored. Disparities in social well-being also occur within the same gender category due to differences in caste, class, religion, urban and rural background, etc. Such disparities are clearly not primarily based on gender but could occur due to the factors mentioned above. They need careful analysis in order to bring out clearly the disparities that may exist in different spheres of social well-being due to factors other than gender. In the absence of such an indepth analysis, there is likelihood of these other social factors being ignored and the disparity being analyzed only along gender lines. Such an analysis would yield only an incomplete picture of reality.

Sachidanand (1997)

It is evident from this figure that the two main determinants of social well-being are the social structure and the state. Social structure determines the social order from which value systems, customs and traditions of a community emerge. These, in turn, determine the traditional status and position accorded to women in any community. The state, on the other hand, influences the gender disparities in social well-being through various intervention programmes and policies aimed at correcting the gender imbalance in social well-being.

The problem of gender disparities in social well-being must be backed by empirical evidence. Care must be taken to ensure that the household remains the unit of analysis since it is within the household that the root of the problem lies. Again, within the household, the enquiry must not be limited to only one or two aspects but must include all aspects of social well-being in order to bring out clearly the interlinkages between them. Finally, households in different social categories must be studied in order to understand the inter-gender aspects of the problem. A composite picture of such disparities in social well-being will emerge only if the various social categories are considered.

To sum up, the proposed model calls for :

1. A study of gender disparities in social well-being in the total societal context.
2. The use of more empirical evidence, collected through primary source.
3. The designation of the household as the unit of analysis.
4. The inclusion of various social categories in the analysis.
5. The study of all aspects of social well-being.

Education

The concern for girl's education has received a lot of importance from policy planners and educationists, particularly after independence. The constitutional provision of providing compulsory education for all children until they complete the age of 14 years is applicable to both boys and girls. Further, the National Policy on Education (NPE) of 1986, updated in the year 1992 proposes an adult literacy and primary education, with a focus on girls and other disadvantaged groups (Government of India, 1986). It postulates integration of gender perspective in all aspects of planning. Further, it enjoins that the education system would play a positive interventionist role to empower women. Also, the removal of women's illiteracy and obstacles inhibiting their access to and retention in education, are given an overriding priority.

Certain school-related factors are responsible in the discontinuance of girl's education, e.g., schools are at times distantly located and sometimes inaccessible. In such circumstances parents find it extremely difficult to send their daughters to school. Not only it involves loss of time and energy, but has also added security problems which, parents are not prepared to take, particularly in the rural areas. In the north-eastern states of Assam, Manipur and even in the plains of Uttar Pradesh and Rajasthan this phenomenon is commonly observed.

In case the school is located near the habitation, but are co-education schools, the girl's, parents show their reluctance. This is true for Muslim community and also orthodox Hindus who prefer separate schools for girls. Similarly, the absence of women teachers in rural areas discourages parents from sending their daughters to school. One of the reasons being that they do not find it safe for their daughters. Also there is a common feeling that only women teachers can best understand girls and problems related to them in a better way. Through the proportion of female teachers has been increasing gradually (for example, in 1986-87, 40.2 per cent of the primary school teachers were women as compared to 15 per cent in the year 1950-51, the corresponding proportion for the upper primary stage was 30.92 per cent and 15 per cent respectively), the concentration of women teachers in urban areas and inter-state disparities continue to be sharp.

Perhaps one of the reasons of continuing demand for women teachers in rural areas is the most of the girls hardly reach secondary training institutions. The major strength of the Universal Elementary Education (UEE) programme is its sensitivity to local conditions rather than a rigid framework. The approach is tailored to meet local situations and needs. Planning and management are decentralized and the emphasis is on involving local communities.

The goals of the programme include a specific focus on reduction of gender disparities in education, as reflected in low enrolment, retention and achievement of girls, particularly those from socially and economically disadvantaged groups.

Despite the increase in enrolment we find that the drop-out rate of girls continues to be a major problem. During the year 1993-94, little more than one-third (39 per cent) of the number of girls enrolling at the primary stage dropped out before completing primary level and about 57 per cent dropped out before completing upper primary levels. Of the remaining 43 per cent who reached high/higher secondary stage, another 10 per cent dropped out before completing the school stage. Thus, only about 32 per cent of girls entering the primary stage reach the end of schooling. High drop-out rates among girls are embedded in the socio-cultural and economic factors (Government of India, 1995).

In order to strike the goals of a democratic citizenship, to make the pronouncements concerning equality of educational opportunities, real, are not far reaching. To utilize the talent of half of human resources, we need to develop appropriate tools. One such tool is a rightly planned, well structured curriculum. Courses in education can serve the purpose of molding attitudes, equipping young people—men and women with appropriate vales to a great extent.

The need to provide place for "Women's Studies" in the curriculum has been felt since the Second World War, to bring about consciousness among men and women towards their rights and obligations as :

Women have been suppressed under custom and law for which man was responsible in the shaping of which she has no hand. Women has as much right to shape her own destiny as man has to shape his. It is up to men to see that they enable them to realize their status and play their part as equals.

Most educationists and sociologists agree that the causes of educational backwardness among women are economic, social and cultural. Burden of domestic work, lack of consideration from the family, agricultural base are the deterrent effects on women enrolment. Lack of school in near vicinity or distance from home could be said to be some of the other reasons.

Our educational institutions are also charged for their discrimination. Most institutions restrict some subjects to boys only and some subjects to girls. Consequently girls are left with fewer choices for their pre-vocational courses than their counterparts. Science subjects are more popular with male students than female students. A boy is usually excited by the prospect of a science course. He experiences a sense of wonder and a sense of power. The girl may come to the science less with a less eager curiosity than the boy.

Girls are frequently caught in a vicious circle. Their initial socialization and subsequent adoption of home-based cultures predisposes them towards certain heterosexuality, that is, restrict the expression of homosexual and lesbian impulses. In restricting same-sex relationships, the interdependence of the genders and the gender division of labour that undergirds gender stratification are reinforced.

In general, gender ideologies provide for women fewer responsibilities and more restrictions than for men. Their rewards are more symbolic, and their rights protective, while the rewards and rights of men are more "real" and positive. Finally, men face not only fewer restrictions but those they do have often address the potential abuse of their rights and reward advantages.

Gender Socialisation and Some Other Agents

• Peer Group • Literature • Religion • Media etc.

In millions of daily interactions between people, women are repeatedly and systematically disadvantaged and devalued to men, in a wide variety of different contexts. Gender inequality is sustained primarily because men have the wherewithal to do so, regardless of what women may desire. Structured inequality, by which men acquire resources superior to those available to women, allow men to coerce or bribe women into the behaviours they desire. Yet in most times and places people do not perceive such coercion and women do not consciously think that they are more oppressed than men. When the term, "Gender system" is used, it includes systems of gender stratification and differentiation, as well as the gender division of labour, gender social definitions, and power inequities between the genders.

The division of labour places child rearing overwhelmingly in the hands of women. This fact has vastly different ramifications, depending on the sex of the child, especially in terms of the "relational capacities" of each gender. The fact that women "mother" produces daughters, but not sons, who want to be primary child rearers. It does so because females come to value relationships with others as central to their lives; they spend their lives preoccupied with issues of love and symbiosis. Conversely, the fact that women constitute the primary child rearers results in sons who are oriented to individuating themselves and establishing strong ego boundaries. Such sons become men who are fearful of women, misogynistic, and insistent upon male superiority and dominance. The different developmental processes that boys and girls undergo during the preoedipal and oedipal stages of childhood, contingent upon having a female as primary love object. From this perspective, the results occur unconsciously. They result regardless of conscious efforts by adults to teach other behaviours and orientations to their children, simply from the different developmental task girls and boy confront, depending on whether their primary love object is of the same or the other gender. The divisions of labour and gender inequality are, therefore, the automatic results and reinforcement mechanism of the very system that produces them.

The degree of gender stratification is not uniform throughout a complex society. It varies by social class and possibly by race/ ethnicity or religion. Under girding all systems of stratification is inequality of power and authority, which are themselves coerce and valued resources.

Socialisation Theory

Socialization theories concentrate on the more conscious and purposive efforts of especially adults to teach children socially defined, gender appropriate ways of thinking, feeling and acting. This perspective includes both Symbolic Interaction Theory, as developed by sociologists, and Social Learning and Cognitive Development theories, which are primarily the province of psychologists. Although they differ in specifics, these theories focus on how, as children, people internalize socially defined norms for their gender and make gender a fundamental component of their self-concept. The key processes are rewards and punishments (both direct and vicarious) by "significant others" and, especially, modelling the behaviours of people either whom the children identifies. Besides, parents and peers are seen as fundamental to the processes. In addition, media, games, sports, schools, clothing styles, language, and most other social and cultural phenomena are viewed as contributing to it.

The gender socialization approach assumes that adult behaviours, attitudes, priorities, and choices are to be understood largely as direct expressions of internal conceptions of the self. To the extent that the adult generation "successfully" socializes children to socially acceptable conceptions of gender, those children will mature into adults who will make choices consistent with their gendered self-identity. In this way, the gender system is replicated from one generation to the next.

Everyday Life Theory

The gender socialization theory focuses on childhood engenderment processes. Another set of theories, reflecting Symbolic Interactionism. Ethnomethodology, and the Dramaturgical Approach, addresses the processes by which adults seek ongoing confirmation of their gendered self-identity and inadvertently recreate social definitions of gender itself. For instance, Goffman argues that both men and women require members of the other gender to validate their identities. They do this by giving one another opportunities to display those behaviours socially defined as specific to one gender. In general, Goffman argues that people are constantly involved in the work of producing gender differentiation while pursuing affirmation of their own sense of identity. For men, this quest entails demonstrations of weakness, vulnerability, and ineptitude.

Recently, West and Zimmerman extended Goffman's insights. In addition to recognizing that people organize their activities to express gender in normative ways, they argue that people are predisposed to perceive and interpret the behaviours of others as expressions of gender. They assert that virtually all activities can be, and usually are, assessed according to their gender content. Such behaviours and interpretations create and legitimate gender itself.

Gender Differentiation and Engenderment

Adult males and females in most societies differ from one another, on the average, in one or more of many types of traits : cognitive skills and styles, basic personality, emotional expression, self-concept, priorities among various social roles, task competencies, preferences, aspirations, motivations, language usage and so on. This does not mean that there are in fact sharp differences between all or most males, on the one hand and females on the other. "Degree of gender differentiation" refers to the number of traits upon which males and females differ, and the extent to which the genders differ on those traits. Gender differentiation does not conceptually, imply inequality. To say that two categories differ does not logically convey that one is valued or rewarded more highly than the other.

The Gender Division of Labour

Sociologists and anthropologists have long recognized that in almost all societies men and women do at least somewhat different kinds of work. The tasks for which each gender is responsible may overlap or be totally segregated. Moreover, with a few important exceptions, the precise nature of what constitutes men's tasks versus women's varies extensively cross-culturally. Such variability is especially noticeable when comparing societies with fundamentally different forms of technology and economic bases, (e.g., horticultural, agrarian, industrial). For instance, in one society or societal type, (e.g., horticultural) women may be responsible for growing most or all of the food, while in another, (e.g., rice-growing agrarian societies) both are involved in food growing but their specific tasks differ.

The important cross-cultural uniformities in the gender division of labour are two. First, women are uniformly more responsible than men for the work of child rearing, food preparation, and care of the domicile. Men's participation in such tasks ranges from none at all to substantial, while women's participation is uniformly high. Second, men always participate in a variety of extra-domestic tasks of their societies in those realms that in complex societies are differentiated as the economic, political, religious educational and culture-producing spheres of activity. Women's participation in such work varies from practically none to substantial. The following generalization about the gender division of labour can, therefore, be made : Women tend to shoulder the bulk of the responsibilities associated with children and the household, and vary in the extent to which they participate in other types of work; men are universally involved in extra-domestic work tasks, and vary in the extent of their domestic and child-rearing work. In general, the more men monopolize extra-domestic work tasks, the more women monopolize the domestic / child rearing tasks and vice versa. The "gender division of labour" is, therefore, a variable : the extent to which the work activities of men and women in a society– both within and outside the household and family are gender segregated. The general theoretical issues concern how the gender division of labour affects and is affected by gender inequality, and what causes it to change.

Just as gender differentiation does not logically imply inequality, neither does the gender division of labour. That men and women do different kinds of work is not tantamount to saying that the types of work done by one are superior in any fashion to the types done by the other. But again, empirically the two are indeed related.

Power and Authority

"Power" is defined in the Weberian sense as the ability of persons or groups to command compliance from other persons or groups, even in the face of opposition. Power requires resources superior to those controlled by compliers. Power wielders must have at their command something that compliers value and need or want and cannot otherwise get in sufficient quantity. It might be money or material goods, approval or love, services, safety from physical harm, or the like. However, the bases (types of resources) and degree of the power inequity differ from one form of stratification to another, and from one society to another. By definition a system of gender stratification implies superior power for men.

"Authority" is also defined in its Weberian sense as legitimated power. "Legitimacy" refers to a perception on the part of both the power wielder and the complier that the former has the right to make binding decisions or issue commands, and the later, the moral obligation to comply with them. Stable power relations tend to be legitimated over time, but even if legitimacy is withdrawn, most often those in authority also possess superior power resources upon which to fall back. The legitimacy of male power is rooted in gender ideology. The theoretical issues concern both the process by which male power is converted into authority and those that sometimes work to produce widespread rejection of the legitimacy of male power.

Power and authority exist at all levels of analysis. Power exists when husbands, or any individual males, can extract compliance from wives or other women with whom they personally interact. When women feel duty-bound to comply with the requests or demands of male interaction partners, authority exits. Again the main theoretical issues concern the bases for such power and authority. How is that, as individuals, men possess greater power resources than women? How do women come to feel duty-bound to comply with the demands made by make interaction partners? There is also the theoretical question of how males use their power or authority to sustain their advantages, and the conditions under which women gain in their power resources.

Power and authority accrue specifically to those who are incumbent in elite roles, particularly in dominant social institutions. In modern industrial societies, political and economic organizations constitute the dominant social institutions, with religious, educational, and other culture producing organizations constituting secondary but nonetheless important ones. In gender-stratified societies, elite roles are and have been overwhelmingly filled by men. Elite incumbents may have other common attributes in given societies (e.g., racial, religious, class background), but their maleness is historically and cross-culturally nearly uniform.

The Socialization Perspective

The theoretical approaches that constitute the socialization perspective focus on variables that function to teach gender "appropriate" characteristics, especially to children. Children are usually viewed as relatively active agents who are involved in seeking information about who they are and, given that, what forms of behaviour are appropriate for them to exhibit. They are seen as immersed in a linguistic, behavioural, and symbolic gender-sea from the moment of their birth on, as people in their environment constantly both emit gender and react to children on the basis of their gender. Children gradually develop the capacity to sort the world according to gender, to identify self as belonging to one category, and to take on the attributes socially assigned to that gender. Their identity, thus becomes thoroughly gendered.

Their phenomena create this process : modelling, positive sanctions (rewards), and negative sanctions (punishments). Further, sanctions can be experienced directly, or they can be experienced vicariously as children observe responses positive and negative to the behaviour of others. To the extent that children are surrounded by adults who are strongly gender differentiated, modelling and both positive and negative sanctions are likely to induce substantial engenderment in the younger generation.

They will have an ample supply of potential models from which to choose, all exhibiting the same gender-specific traits. In contemporary nations, mass media often heavily expose children to further examples of models whose behaviour is kinds of school subjects particularly those which utilize the verbal skills which develop more quickly in girls than in boys at primary school.

Women are not being trained for excellence. They are viewed as competitors with men in the field of job opportunities, hence educationists feel that prospects for development, raising women's status and career opportunities in developing countries are less. To make full use of women's potential, we need to handle curriculum very carefully. Through the technique of curriculum making along scientific lines has been developed, the controlling purposes of education have not been sufficiently particularized. We have aimed at a vague culture, an ill defined discipline, a nebulous harmonious development of the individual, an indefinite moral character building, and unparticularized social efficiency, or often. Enough nothing more than escapism from work. But the era of contentment with larger undefined exactness and particularly in the light of the economic, ideological and technological changes that are taking place in the society, the whole curriculum needs to be examined, reoriented and revalidated.

Careful analysis of the subject levels that women the most concerned party has remained complacent and uninvolved regarding the introduction of new subjects like Women's Studies and women have accepted the pattern of education available, or have learnt to be satisfied with their lot. Men's apathy is natural as they do not want to increase their competitors in the field or job, education, knowledge and skill. Surprisingly enough our policy makers have not paid any attention towards the inclusion of Women's Studies in the curriculum. The Draft Plan on Education and Draft the Seventh Plan are silent on this point.

The subject of women's studies has not been generated out of our rational needs like that of population education, hence there appears to be a lack of national consciousness to provide it a place in the curriculum. It will not be impertinent to say that society does not foresee dangers from women folk as it sees from the explosion of general population. It is clear that our system of education that has been ignored, neglected and denied educational opportunities to women that constitute of nearly half of the population and play a very vital role in training the young citizens is not only inadequate but socially unjust and biased. Hence our present curriculum as a whole needs to be replanted, recast, modified and revalidated to provide a proper place, emphasis and articulate Women's Studies.

Another important feature of which experts and educationists in the field of curriculum designing are not aware but convinced that course content of various subjects in general highlights the role, place and achievements of man and undermines the role of womenfolk in a very subtle manner. In the curriculum sex basis has become vulnerable like caste, religion or language. It will not be out of place to mention that just as history is being considered to be rewritten from the point of view of national integration, in the same way course content in various subjects needs to be planned with a view to giving equality of treatment to women. Hence, there is a need to scrutinize and review curriculum in all subjects particularly in education, which is a very popular subject for women.

As long as curricular and non-curricular discrimination and differentiation on grounds of sex are not ended, both girls and boys will continue to receive an education, which is incomplete, infallible, and inhibiting to the full development of their potential as human beings.

Society

Social Structure–Status of Women

Status refers to position of a woman as an individual in social structure defined by her designation rights and obligations. In Indian society, boys are encouraged to develop masculine character such as aggression, dominance, independence, sense of adventure and achievement orientedness, whereas, girls are encourage to acquire feminine characteristics of submissiveness, nurturance, dependence and less achievement orientedness. There are different notions of activities for boys and girls and expectation of different behaviour of the two different sexes. This has a direct impact on the socialization process, which passes direct from childhood to adolescence and adulthood. Differential socialization of the two sexes within the family and society is perhaps the single most important contributor to sex stereotyping among children and is often discriminatory towards girls.

The demographic picture of India shows that 40 per cent of the Indian population consisting of children below 14 years and nearly half of these young Indians are girls. According to 1991 census, the total population in India is 843.93 million and the child population (0-14 years) is about 308 million of which fifty per cent are female children.

The discrimination against the girl child is inherent in our traditional social structure, cultural norms and religions value system that springs from patriarchal, patrilineal Indian ethos, which powerfully operates in some Indian states like Rajasthan, Bihar, Uttar Pradesh, Madhya Pradesh, Himachal Pradesh and in some parts of Tamil Nadu. Social traditions have a major bearing in shaping attitudes towards girl child. The neglect and discrimination that the girl child is subjected to are extensive and deep-rooted. Discrimination against the girl child exists everywhere in food, clothing, education, medicine and immunization, even in care and affection. Indian society is a male-oriented society and there is a strange invisibility of the girl-child. Growing up as a female in Indian society is full of constraints and complexities with 'values' varying from male and female children. There is a social acceptance of the neglect of the girl child, which is rooted, in the traditional social structure, institutions and ethos, and this is almost a pan-Indian phenomenon.

Family structures and social values function such a way that girls grow upon looking themselves as inferior and subservient, entitled to much less of everything than sons; less opportunity, less authority, less property, less status, less power and virtually no choice. The duality of values that operates in the patriarchal family is internalized at an early age, as a natural inevitable part of life. She acquires qualities of submissiveness, meekness and self-sacrifice. The socialization process reinforces these stereotypes at all levels in the society moulding her in, and to be a prisoner of her gender, unable to retaliate against the implicit and explicit injustice. In fact, she propagates cultural values, which militate against the interests of the female gender. Customs, rituals, traditional practices frequently make a girl the 'lesser child' who is denied optimum opportunities and means required for growth and development during the various stages of childhood.

Today's girl child is tomorrow's woman. If tomorrow's woman is to become an equal partner with man in bringing about social change and development, this is the time to accord the girl child her rightful share of human dignity and opportunity. This concept has found an appropriate place in the Plan of Action for implementing the World Declaration on Survival Protection and Development of Children in 1990s. The World Summit on Children singled out the urgency the situation of the girl child and called for support for her equitable development, an indispensable step towards achieving equality for women. "Efforts for enhancement of women's status and their role in development must begin with the girl child. Equal opportunities should be proved for the girl child to benefit from the health, nutrition, education and other basic services to enable her to grow to her full potential."

A recently published UNESCO monograph curtailed an unfinished story–gender patterns in media employment by Margaret Gallagher shows that there is much unsaid behind that healthy appearance. From the very onset, women are caught in an environment that heavily favours women to work mainly at the lower level of administration action as a secretary, clerk, junior manager's, receptionists, etc.

Though they constitute almost 50 per cent of the vote-bank, women have a low political profile. The Jayalalitha's and Parvathi's are the exception, not the rule. In the last Parliament there were only 30 women MPs in a House of 543, and in the upcoming elections out of the 16,000 old candidates in a nation-wide field, only three per cent are women. Though they have spear headed large scale grassroots movements like the Chipko crusade and anti-liquor protests, women by and large seem to be below or above conventional politics.

Although launching various schemes for women development is in full swing, the success lies in distant dreams. Government, NGO's and other international organizations are spending colossal sums of rupees every year for the uplift of women. However, it seems to have little impact in their lives. What makes them suffer a lot in silence in this matter, is their utter ignorance as they are uneducated, so the quality of life suffer.

Gender Social Definition and the Maintenance of Gender Inequality

Social definitions are beliefs, values, stereotypes and norms are widely shared by societal members. They arise over time and at any given time reflect historical as well as contemporary phenomena.

"Gender norms" refer to behaviour that is expected of people on the basis of the status to which they are assigned, given their sexual biology. They vary over time and space in two ways : the level of consensus among societal members and the number of behaviours that are defined as gender specific. To the extent that consensus is widespread concerning proper behaviour for people on the basis of biological sex, the violation of gender norms will be perceived by others (of both genders) as deviant behaviour and negatively sanctioned. The likelihood and severity of negative sanctions, in turn, reflect the strength of gender norms. While the specific content of gender norms varies widely over time and space, the underlying themes are relatively constant in gender-stratified societies. Appropriate behaviour for men is defined as that which helps to sustain their commitment to gender specific work tasks and aids in their exercise of power/authority over women. For women, it is also that which helps to sustain commitment to their traditional work as well as their different behaviour towards men.

In addition, in gender-stratified societies, men will want to be sure of the paternity of their offspring, especially their sons. Such assurance requires restrictions on female sexuality. Gender norms for women but not necessarily for men—will, therefore, include behaviours directly and indirectly related to chastity.

Earlier, gender differentiation was defined as real differences, on the average, between men and women. Regardless of the reality of such differences, there usually exists beliefs or perceptions that the genders are fundamentally different on a variety of traits. There beliefs constitute "gender stereotypes" when they are shared by collectives. Societies vary in the number of stereotypes beliefs they hold concerning males and females and the degree of consensus among societal members concerning them. Again, the specifics undoubtedly vary across time and space, but the same themes operative for gender norms underlie gender stereotypes in gender-stratified societies.

In some times and places, a substantial number of the members of a disadvantaged group come to question and subsequently reject dominant social definitions pertaining to them and the socially dominant group. They develop usually in the process of social movement formation—a set of counter definitions. This counter set rejects the ideology and stereotypes as false and encourages people to violate norms that are redefined as vehicles for their oppression. In short, the legitimacy of the social definitional system is questioned and then withdrawn. It is typically replaced by a set of counter definitions that includes different norms, ideology, and possibly stereotypes. When women do this, it is called "gender consciousness". No less than gender social definitions, gender consciousness is a phenomenon. Both the rejection and the reconstitution are accomplished and shared by collectivities of women (along with some male allies). Variation exists in the number of people who share a gender consciousness and in the radicalness of the rejection and reconstitution.

Three types of gender social definitions were presented–gender ideology, norms, and stereotypes. Each can vary along two dimensions–the level of societal consensus and the extent to which gender differences are presumed. Gender ideologies serve to justify or legitimate differential and unequal rights, responsibilities, restrictions, and rewards for men and women by "explaining" how and why they differ. How many such distinctions are legitimated varies. But in gender stratified societies there will be at least some. There will also be substantial, although rarely total, societal consensus about them. Gender norms specify particular behaviours, as well as the degree of societal consensus about, both vary. Nonetheless, in gender-stratified societies there will be atleast some behaviours so designated by a substantial proportion of societal members. Likewise, gender stereotypes, or beliefs concerning gender differentiation, will vary in the number of traits and level of agreement among societal members. Nonetheless, the levels of neither dimension will approach zero.

Gender ideology constitutes the basis for the other two types of social definitions. Gender ideologies are more stable and resistant to change, because they are typically embedded in yet broader belief systems, especially religions, along with overarching sociopolitical cultural views of the world. A given gender ideology is likely to be sufficiently flexible to survive minor to moderate changes in the specific content of gender norms and stereotypes. For instance, suppose a deity is believed to have mandated that men's primary obligation is to the world outside the home and family, and women's to family members.

Given gender stratification, gender ideologies typically legitimate male authority over women. Especially the major world religions, which all arose in highly gender stratified societies, explicitly grant men dominion over their wives and other family members. Gender ideologies often enumerate rights specific to women, which are required for their protection precisely because men have substantially more power and authority. They typically define the outer boundaries of men's use of their power / authority, by prescribing or restricting certain male behaviours. Men may be restricted in their ability to divorce or at least be required to continue supporting the family financially; they may be restricted in their ability to physically chastise their wives or to deprive them too much of basic resources needed for survival. It is possible that the more disadvantaged their status, the more the gender ideology of a society will specify concrete, protective rights for women.

Given ideologies are also likely to include certain rewards for women, courtesies offered as recompense for their otherwise devalued and disadvantaged status. Substantial deference to mother or to virgins constitutes an example of this. Women are likely to be ideologically placed upon a pedestal, but only if they are "good women" who subscribe fully to gender social definitions. The pedestal is, in fact, a "gilded cage". Women's rewards are thus primarily symbolic in nature.

Gender ideologies are likely to specify responsibilities for men (e.g., service in the defense of nation or religion) that are more onerous than those prescribed for women. However, these are recompensed with more concrete and meaningful rights and rewards than those offered to women, and include dominion over women.

Women are likely to face far more ideologically rooted restrictions on their behaviour and demeanor than are men, especially concerning sexuality. Virtually all gender ideologies in substantially gender-stratified societies insist on female chastity, probably to ensure that men are secure in the knowledge of paternity of their own offspring (heirs). An implicit (if not explicit) sexual double standard is widespread. To ensure chastity, all manner of other restrictions are often imposed specifically on women (e.g. *purdah*, chaperoning, veiling, "modest" clothing and behaviour). Gender ideology, alongwith gender norms, usually also prescribe sharply gender differentiated. Moreover, especially parents, but also other relatives, neighbours, teachers, clearly, and so on, are likely to react in a consistent manner by defining and responding to behaviour on the basis of children's gender. Room décor, clothing, hair styles, gifts, books, forms of play, and so on are likely to convey a constant and consistent gender content. Explicit rewards and punishments in response to children's behaviours and utterances will do likewise. Reactions to others that can be observed by children will further reinforce this process. Analytically separate from, but obviously related to the extent to which the adult generation is gender differentiated is the extent of the gender division of labour. When men and women perform sharply different work roles, they provide models that suggest to children the kinds of work they can and cannot do as adults, given their gender.

Recommendations

There are certain recommendations to emphasize equal opportunity. They are :

1. Representation of women in top management positions in universities and other higher educational institutions.
2. Presence of women in the decision making positions, in all fields whether family or society.
3. An appropriate time should be set to dwell on issue on women's effort and ability to take leadership positions.
4. Seminars should be conducted on the following aspects :
   - Barrier faced by women manager
   - To discuss different strategies for empowering women
   - Women and Law.
5. Increase in the age of marriage and adoption of family welfare measures.
6. Faculty at each school/department/institute must decide the mission and establish a strategic plan to achieve this mission.
7. Immediate action programmes to universalize early education should be taken up as the first and the most challenging assignments in the interest of girls.
8. Immediate steps to be taken to prepare guidelines for scrutiny of textbooks and teaching material.

9. Materials have to be produced to be incorporated in textbooks and teaching materials should enhance the status of women.
10. Vocational education needs heavy strengthening material and support by strong studies in the interest of women at all levels.
11. Block-wise national information of female situation must be developed and compiled and be made available for educational planning and administration.
12. Research on what can be the different incentives that would help integrating girls in education and also reducing the drop-out rates.
13. A locale specific programmes for girls must be developed so that the model is used by different segments.
14. More of use links between women studies at the university department and women education unit at the NCERT must be developed so that "what research tells about the studies on Women Education" are compiled, classified and analyzed for priorities.
15. To teach in non-formal and formal education programmes and especially in the news media around the world, sensitizing the people about gender issues.
16. To establish compulsory education for both males and females with special concern for keeping children in school and providing career counselling for students and parents.
17. To increase motivation and empowerment of youth by providing resources and instructions for both females and males to gain skill for household production, such as food preparation and preservation, home improvements, childcare and education.
18. To empower females by giving information on basic human rights. They can then take more readily, responsibility for seeking improvement of laws and practices, such as those pertaining to freedom of speech, equal protection, inheritance, and property right.
19. To have better facilities for women in their work place as well in schools.
20. Need to have more residential schools wherein parents can send their daughters with confidence.

Conclusion

A measurement of the 'gender gap' in mortality, morbidity, literacy and work participation provides only a partial explanation of why earnings and productivity differ by gender, that is, by identifying differential endowments. This is an approach policy makers are receptive to. Investments in girl's schooling, hostels for working women are relatively uncontroversial ways of increasing opportunities for women.

In India, state interventions to promote access to schooling work and health facilities take some note of constraints specific to women. But such interventions do not address to the broader structural constraints on women.

An important development in the last few decades in the developed and in many developing countries has been the occupied increase in female education and labour force participation. Over a period of time, women's earnings have risen relative to men's in almost all countries. A careful analysis of male-female wage difference and an estimation of the extent of this wage discrimination is important for the development of appropriate anti-discrimination.

The Indian Constitution guarantees equality between men and women and number of laws have been enacted from time to time to implement this guarantee. The dowry prohibition act is in the process of being amended to plug loopholes in it and make it more effective. However, legal rights can never ensure social practice. Despite constitutional and other legislative provisions aimed at generating equality for women under law, a gap still remains between the de-facto and de-jure status of women. The main obstacle to the realization of this equality is the pervasiveness of social attitudes deep rooted in tradition.

References

Andrews, A.C. (1982). Towards a Status of Women Index, Professional Geographers 34 (1) 24-31.

Bezbaruah Supriti, Janeja K.M. Situational analysis of adolescents in India: A Profile UNFPA for UN system in India, Sept 2000, pp. 19-25.

Bhadra Mita, *Girl Child in Indian Society*, Edition I, Rawat Publication, Jaipur, 1999.

Chandhoke, Neera (1995). State and Civil Society : Exploration in Political Theory Sage Publication. New Delhi.

Chapter II–EFA in the Indian context Education for all, the Indian Science, Department of Human Resource Development, Government of India, Dec. 1993, pp. 18-27.

Cunha D. Jean, Women and Education in India, *Femina*, Pradeep Guha, August 8, 1995, pp. 15-21.

Datta Amindita & Sinha Sachidanand, *Indian Journal of Gender Studies*, Gender Disparities in Social well-being : An overview, Vol. 4(1), Jan–June 1996.

Haiman, F.S. (1950). Group Leadership and Democratic Action. Houghton Miffin Company, New York.

Hess B. Beth & Marya M.F. *Analysing Gender : A Handbook of Social Science Research, Gender Inequality in Paid Employment*, Sage Publications, New Delhi. 1987.

Jain, R. (1990). Year of the Girl Child. Let's Stop Discrimination Against the Girl. Social Welfare. Jan.-Feb. 1990. pp. 21-25.

Joshi, S.C. (1996). Indira Mahila Yojna Empowerment of Women. Kurukshetra, XLIV(6), 24 & 50.

Kannan Kavita, Gender Benders, *Femina*, Pradeep Guha, April 1, 2002, p. 123.

Krishnaraj Maithreji, Sudarshao M. Rathwa, Shariff Abusalen, *Gender, Population and Development*, Oxford University Press, Calcutta, Chennai, Mumbai, 1998.

Madumita Majmudar. The Female Child in Family Setting in *Indian Journal of Social Work* Vol. 529. No. 1 Jan. 1991.

Memoria, C.B. (1981). Social Problems and Social Disorganisation in India, Allahabad, Kitab Mahal.

Nair, B.S. Is Status of Women Crucial to Quality of Life ? Social Welfare, October, 1988, pp. 2-13.

Narayan, V.N. and Sabharmal, Jyoti. (1997). India at 50, Bliss of Hope and Burden of Reality Sterling Publishers, New Delhi.

Rao, N.J.U : Women in a Developing Society Ashish Publishing House, New Delhi, 1985.

Sandaarbini, Library and Documentation Center, AIACHE, Documentation on Women's Concerns New Delhi July-Sept. 1996.

Saxena Sadhna, That's Mr. Einstein for you, Femina, Pradeep Guha, April 2002, pp. 108-109.

Thomas, P. (1964). Indian Women Through the Ages. Asia Publishing House, Bombay.

Upadhyay, H.C. (1991). Status of Women in India, New Delhi, Anmol Publication.

Venkatesaram Samdaya, *Environment, Development and the Gender Gap*, Sage Publications, New Delhi 1995.

Vohra, R. and Sen, A.R. (1985). Status, Education and Problems of Indian Women, Akshar Publications, Delhi.

8

Women and Environment

Anuradha Mathu, Rameshwari Pandya

Abstract

The relationship between women and environment attains a significance because women are perceived as victims of environmental degradation.

It is important to understand that everything in nature is connected and one can never do just one thing as everything we do has numerous effects on nature, which are often unpredictable. Women from low SES/ poor families are closely dependent on environmental resources like fuel wood and water. Deforestation adversely effects income generating activities of women in several ways. There is a strong interconnectivity among Human activities, Social and Natural environment.

As is evident all development activities have impact on environment. It is high time that environmental issues are tackled systematically by bringing newer innovations in techniques, training the change agents and increasing people's initiatives or by organized people's movement through NGO's.

Redefining the objectives, activities and methods of implemention, both of education and of contemporary communication technologies for imparting environment education through non-formal adult education as well as through well structured classified stage-wise course content in formal education. These are several strategies like organizing excursions, field trips, co-curricular activities, organizing debates, drama, role play and campaign to impart messages for environmental conservation and sensitize people for conservation and sustainable development. Empower women as environment manager and reduce their drudgery.

Introduction

The relationship between women and environment attains significance because women are perceived as victims of environmental degradation, but though they have been traditionally playing the role of efficiently managing natural resources and possess a valuable knowledge base, they have been completely marginalized from processes that seek to formulate strategies for use and management of these resources. In this process of marginalization they have further lost status and power, by losing access to resources and control over their manpower.

The daily contact with water of poor quality due to pollution, stagnation, etc. exposes women to the risk of water borne diseases. Shortage of water leads to poor sanitation especially among women in reproductive age groups. Lack of toilet facilities increases the chances of infections. Type of housing also affects women's health–small houses with lack of ventilation and privacy to manage personal sanitation can also lead to morbidity.

U.N. Conference on Environment and Development (UNCED) linked environment and development internationally, to facilitate national mechanisms to meet global challenges due to degradation of the planet. As mentioned earlier, the preparatory committee of UNCED (1991) linked the topics namely–that the gender dimension is important in implementing the resolution on "Women in Environment and Development", and secondly, "the national and international emphasis on eco-system management and the control of environmental degradation" should be strengthened and that women should be recognized as active and equal participants in this process.

In this context, two pertinent questions emerge. First, what are the mechanisms by which women would be a part of the eco-system management at the national and international levels? Second, through which mechanisms should women participate in the control of environmental degradation? Partial answers appeared at the 1991 Global Assembly on Women and Environment and various recommendations were made by the NGO's and Regional Assemblies on increasing women's participation in decision making and enhancing their status.

The Global Assembly basing itself on women's experiences at national levels arrived at some important conclusions, which brought together environmental concerns and development needs. There were three priority themes of UNCED : Energy, water and waste.

- Conservation of energy starts in the household and is often related to tasks women predominantly perform.

- Designers of all water supply and sanitation systems should be required to consult women who are the primary users in the home.
- Women have often found ways to deal with waste economically and safely, whether by recycling or by responsible consumer behaviour.

As Meining (1971:23) demands :

"A much larger body of citizens whose eyes have been opened to see their surroundings with a fare great appreciation and who thereby are not only enriched by what is good, but appalled by that which is bad and refuse to countenance the continued despoliation of their surroundings".

And the media certainly has an important role to play in environmental education, conservation and sustainable development thus making environment better place for women to live.

Women should be mentioned as specific target groups for all agricultural development programmes. Efforts should be made to involve them in decision making at all levels. Continuous monitoring should be done of women's programmes so as to improve the programme designing and implementation.

In the allied sectors of sericulture and animal husbandry, dairying, fisheries, forests, handloom and handicrafts, the Commission recommends greater inputs of training and credit and as in the case of agriculture, women's co-operatives should be encouraged, and they should have greater access to extension workers.

Fuel, Fodder and Water

Large sections of women in the unorganized sector, living in rural areas, are involved in collection of fuel and fodder. With the process of deforestation, this task has become more strenuous as women have to walk long distances to collect fuel. Non-availability of grazing land has increased their problems. Social forestry was visualised both for satisfying the basic needs of rural households and for reducing pressures on the forests by generating resources for community needs outside the forest land. However, the programme, as implemented has developed a slant in favour of the larger farmers urban markets and industries, while the fuel fooder crisis continues to grow. Government policies in the last few decades have hastened degradation and privatization of the common property resources through land allotment policy. Illegal encroachments by large farmers and operation of market forces have led to further deterioration of the state of the common land, affecting women adversely, specially with large tracks of agricultural land being diverted from food crops to cash crops and tree farming for commercial gains. The social forestry programme has not resulted in increased employment opportunities for women.

The National Commission agrees with the recommendations of the Workshop on Women, Social Forestry and Wasteland Development, held by Centre for Women's Development Studies as reported in their document:

1. If Social Forestry or Wasteland Development is to provide economic independence for women, it is essential to build in adequate wage and other technical/managerial support through the period of rearing, maintenance and protection of the plants.
2. The basic aim of social forestry should be to create village woodlots on a sustained yield basis which will yield resources according to village needs.
3. Any social forestry programme which allows for clear felling of village woodlots must be avoided and only rotational harvesting should be permitted and need-based cutting cycle should be worked out.
4. All social forestry programmes should be simultaneously agro-forestry programmes of which multi-layering and multi-cropping should be essential features, as per the local situation, to provide for both short and long-term returns since poor cannot wait for long. Species should be selected which compliment each other rather than compete for nutrients.
5. The planning for social forestry programme should be based on a long-term perspective rather than short-term perspective.
6. Women's access to productive resources under social forestry programmes should be backed by State marketing supports. The market structure for their products, under social forestry programmes, are controlled by distant monopolistic agencies and intermediaries which deprive them of their just returns. To ensure their participation as equal partners in this nationally vital activity, it is essential to guarantee strong and effective State support in the marketing of their products.
7. Direct benefits to women are in the form of wages. In consideration of the short-term nature of the employment, and in view of the high financial output of the projects, the wages must be upwardly revised.
8. In all kinds of social forestry/wasteland development programmes, budget lines must include provisions for the development of women's organisations.

9. Review of forest regulations is needed to make possible the achievement of social forestry goals.
10. Creation of tanks for water grown plants, and multi-layered useful plants below and above the soil, should be the basic strategy in community controlled and community managed social forestry system for involvement of women.

Modernizing water supply systems should aim not only at releasing women from traditional tasks, for this might determine what is the social status that they enjoy in the rural communities. The aim instead should be to modernise women's role in rural water supply, preserving the importance of their contribution, but reducing hardships. Such a course of action is also supported by evidence showing that village involvement in the construction and maintenance of rural water systems is crucial for their success.

Water is one of the basic necessities of human kind. Water sources are getting either depleted or the water table is becoming difficult to reach in places like Rajasthan, some parts of Gujarat and places where rain-fall is scanty or scarce.

Thus, our basic role is to sensitize common masses to reduce wastage, recycle and conserve water, wherever and whenever possible and re-use it to its optimum level.

Women in particular and generally children need to be made aware all the more because they are at the heart of the problem. Let us save each drop of water last we have no water at all !

The necessary industrial support in the manufacturing of various small equipments should be created, e.g., manufacture of small water storage systems, forage harvesting systems, etc. Women and small entrepreneurs should be involved in such ventures with suitable subsidies.

The decision makers both at the bureaucratic and political levels should be sensitized to the importance of programmes specifically targeted for women in the context of national development.

The socio-cultural and traditional practices must be suitably modified for conservation of various resources and more efficient utilization of time, energy and capital. For example, cooking recipes which require more fuel and time in cooking have to be pointed out and corrected. Where possible, community kitchens should be encouraged. Especially in the periphery of towns, the food prepared in neighbouring areas can be brought in packages. This would reduce the load on fuel, provide employment to women in the surrounding areas while benefiting many working women.

Many of the local hardware and software problems especially with respect to fuel and drinking water are not easily solved at the household level. The right level of scaling has to be planned, keeping in view both the economic viability and the consumer's convenience. For instance, in a biogas system, a 80 m^3 community biogas plant is more economical than a 2 m^3 household plant but the former calls for a more elaborate management system. Perhaps a sub-community biogas plant of 15-20 m^3 for 15-10 families could be a solution. Thus for each problem, a suitable community or sub-community system has to be worked out.

Some of the above recommendations have been noted both in the 'Country Report of 1985' presented at Nairobi and "Forward Looking Strategies for the Year 2000". However, at the level of implementation, the programmes of various governmental departments tend to get superimposed. Hence it is important to identify one of the Ministries as the 'Nodal Ministry' for coordination and keeping abreast of all programmes related to women. The Ministry of Human Resource Development could perhaps take this up so that a Master Table could be prepared of all action/ projects having a bearing on women, noting the time schedules for implementation, and the agencies involved in planning and action at the central, state, regional local levels. This "Nodal Ministry" for women may constitute sub-committee with members drawn not only from government but also from other participating agencies to discuss the various issues and evolve strategies.

Rapid growth of population, urbanisation and industrialisation has resulted in over-exploitation of resources and overcrowding. At such overcrowded places women face a lot of problems regarding the procurement of the food, fuel, water and other essential needs of life. Water, which is a main source of life also becomes a major killer of life. Majority of death among children are due to water-borne diseases. In Rajasthan 70 per cent of children deaths take place on account of water-borne diseases. Therefore, women can control this situation. If they are well-educated and aware regarding water disease and causes of infant and child mortality. Further, they can improve the nutritional and health status of their children.

Women have a crucial role in the improvement of environment. However, in many developing countries including India their lower social and economic status has made them suffer from poverty and environmental degradation. Although, many environmental movements throughout the world have been led by women they are poorly represented in decision making activities.

According to Gupta (2000), A natural calamity, sudden or progressive invariably impacts with sudden severity that the affected communities especially the vulnerable populations despite all their coping mechanisms and exceptional measures need external assistance and input for their survival. Women happen to be more than half of these vulnerable population, the other vulnerable groups being older people, children especially abled and it's invariably seen that whenever relief measures are taken by the government and other agencies more than 80 per cent of the people working on these relief measures are women. The drought which is been taking place in Rajasthan in varying proportions has an instant impact on the availability of fuel wood, drinking water and agricultural operations which has a direct correlation with women who are the predominant players in the rural environment in these activities. Any reduction or decrease in the availability of water, fodder and firewood increases the immediate hardship of not only the women who normally manages but also of their families which resultantly affect the children and some of the older people who might be dependant on them. In effect natural calamity effect women and their families to a much larger extent than men.

It's the women who first reduces her intake of food and nutrition at the onset of drought when she starts of only one meal a day in order to provide sufficient nutrition to other members of the family.

The expectant and lactating mothers suffer the most due to lower haemoglobin levels and vitamin deficiencies which are in consequence of the reduced availability and intake of nutrition. The long-term effects on newly born children and infants can only be visualised. Empirical data collected in various parts of the states very clearly suggest the direct cause and effect relationship between the onset of drought and the reduction of the health and nutritional status of the women and consequently of that of her children which can have a very long lasting impact on the quality of the future human resources.

Management of droughts which could best be possible with effective management of natural resources, water harvesting and drought proofing would have women as the key player as they are intimately associated with all these activities and it is not only them but their entire family which could benefit from the above stated endeavours in the short-term and also for the long-term management and mitigation of drought in Rajasthan and elsewhere.

Hossain (2000) explored the inter-linkages between homestead forests, rural women and economic development in Bangladesh. The contribution of rural women to economic development by showing their historical role in forestry activities and economic development. The women's involvement and economic role in the planting and management of trees. There is a relative contributions of women and children (female) as compared to other household members in the planting and management of homestead trees in rural Bangladesh. The rural women of Bangladesh contribute their labour in collecting fuel items from forest resources and spend a higher proportion of their working time in forestry related household activities.

Madan (2001) explains philosophy of Dr. Homi Bhabha who believed in the continuum of development of human society. He coined the expression "no energy is more expensive than no energy," meaning that nothing is grimmer than living without any other energy except that of your body. Thus, development in any society is inevitable. However, for the human society to exist and continually evolve, it is imperative that the development model should promote and/or guarantee sustainability. The issue is whether or not women's empowerment and gender equity is sufficient to promote sustainability.

Women's empowerment is an important issue and has been addressed favourably by many organizations, governments, and non-government organizations (NGO's). Women's empowerment is a justifiable objective and there is full consensus about this.

The dominant literature supports that if only women and environment were considered for development, the environment crisis would be solved. This argument is correct but is largely valid for the poor and the traditional context. In rural context women are preservers and managers of bio-diversity and help in sustainability. Women in such societies hold the key to the future of the agricultural systems and to food and livelihood security through their role in seed selection, the management of livestock, and conservation and sustainable use of plant and animal diversity. The poor farming communities in heterogeneous environment have not benefited from the modern methods. The women's empowerment and gender equity and equality in such societies is sufficient to promote sustainability.

However, advanced societies are facing sustainability problem from the current development model. The societies have achieved greatest progress in terms of gender equity and are responsible for the most critical environment problems. Thus, simply enhancing women's empowerment, gender equity and equality would not eliminate the problem of sustainability. Women do not have any genetic advantage in promoting environment. However, it is important to take women into account, include men in the analyses, as well as relations between men and women to address the problem of sustainability. Hence, it is imperative to include empowerment as well as cultural traits to enhance sustainability.

Nasreen Mahbuba (1999) from Bangladesh points out that floods are a common phenomenon in Bangladesh and one of the main concerns of most rural households. Floods affect both women and men but it has a gender dimension. The flood-related problems affect rural women more severely than men because of the wider responsibilities they have for their households and the fact that those responsibilities keep them tied to their households more strictly and more effectively than those of their male members. Those responsibilities, including food processing and cooking, cleaning, collecting water and fuel, bearing and rearing children, looking after livestock and income generation, become much more difficult to perform under flood conditions. Despite the heavy burden, which women bear in extremely difficult circumstances, they demonstrate considerable fortitude and ingenuity in their attempts to maintain the livelihoods of their households. Explanation of these phenomena should be sought in the economic, cultural and political structure of the country. Factors should be stressed in the patriarchal structures of a Muslim society; the dominance of pardhan in the sub-culture of women and the position of women within the socio-economic context of their households: gendered culture and gendered economics. It is here that we need to make an attempt to highlight some of these issues and the survival methods adopted by women in rural areas. Extensive research in one of the remote villages in Faridpur district proves that it is women who adopt many of these strategies, which are crucial for their household survival.

Singh (2002), says, Orissa, has been the seat of large-scale initiatives by local communities to protect and manage state forest-lands. Several thousand villages in Orissa are involved in active protection and management of forest patches in their vicinity. Most started protecting degraded forests on their own initiative as a spontaneous response to the problem and process of forest degradation.

The State has been struggling with the process of formalizing these initiatives and bringing them to the Joint Forest Management's fold. The forest protecting villages find the standard JFM deal offered by the state unacceptable, as they feel that this does not put management powers and locus of decision-making in the hands of local communities. There exists considerable mismatch between formal JFM system and locally evolved Community Forest Management (CFM) arrangements.

(Singh, 2000), Community leaders and NGOs have been advocating for community rights over forests and forest products, and there has been considerable discussion in the State on the need to move beyond JFM to CFM.

CFM in Orissa and women's involvement and presence in CFM. A discussion on alliances amongst forest protection groups follows, with special focus on women in federations of forest protection groups. Discussion and debate around community rights issues in Orissa, highlight some of the equity concerns within CFM, and introduce the concept of trusteeship rights as opposed to ownership rights to safeguard the interests of forest dependent sections.

Acharjee (2000) brought forth that Arunachal Pradesh, with a geographical area of 83,743 sq. kms. is blessed with rich cultural and ecological heritage but suffers from colossal problems like flood, earthquake and landslides. About 82 per cent of the total area is covered by forest displaying rich biodiversity. The total population amounts for 8.6 lakhs of which female population is 3.9 lakhs (1991 census). Since North-Eastern region is considered as a hotspot in terms of global biodiversity, it is felt that women's role to maintain its sustainability is paramount. Many researchers believe that the critical work of maintaining the ecological cycle is done by women whom they consider as the "invisible workers". In recent times, the state is witnessing wider conscious-rising among the different tribal groups because of NGO's and other activists to prioritize and initiate conservation of environment, but a proper implementation of any environmental awareness programme accounts for better understanding of the socio-economic compulsion of women whose dependency on forest resource is more or less 100 per cent.

Fig. 1. Adjustment to Environmental Control.

The above figure explains the various components involved in and their interplay in the society with human beings.

Singhal (1997) highlights that poor women in developing countries are closely dependent on environmental resources for their productive responsibilities. Hence, they suffer heavily from the negative consequences of environmental degradation, especially deforestation that affects not only their own health but also the health of their family and economic status. Two central activities women perform to ensure the health and nutrition of their families are–maintaining a clean and hygienic environment, and preparing meals. It has become increasingly difficult to provide a clean and hygienic household and community environment due to increased environmental contamination. A direct link between fuel wood scarcity leading to fewer cooked meals per day has been reported in some studies. Thus, deforestation and the resulting fuel wood scarcity has negatively affected the preparation of cooked foods, besides increasing the already high health risks to women from indoor pollution.

Molnar (1993) argues that the fuel wood crisis is as much an issue of quality as of quantity. Further, deforestation increased the time spent by women in collecting fuel wood, thereby decreasing the time they can devote to agricultural production and childcare. Substitution of cow dung and crop residues, which fertilize soils, for fuel wood in domestic cooking and heating, is another facet of the impact of deforestation, as this leads to high use of pesticides and increased risk of pesticide poisoning. Fuel wood scarcity caused by deforestation adversely affects income generating activities of women in several ways, thereby having a direct impact on women's economic well-being and their ability to contribute to the support of their households. The dependence of women's domestic and economic roles on the environment and the importance of their economic contribution in poor households has been explored.

The Mc Graw Hill *Encyclopaedia of Environmental Science* defines environment as, "A sum total of all the conditions and influence that affects the life and development of organisms".

The Tibilsi Conference (1972), defines "Environment as a sum total of natural, artificial and social components of the material world which are or may be in direct interaction with man. Here man means mankind as a whole. Environment thus has two basic components, which includes all living organisms like plants, animals, bacterial, viruses, etc. and the biosphere comprising lithosphere, hydrosphere and atmosphere. It also includes climatic factors like light, temperature, precipitation and physiographic factors like attitude, steepness, weathering and erosive agents like sea, wind, rain, ice and soil. The interaction between these biological and physical factors decides the type of habitat and organisms in an area. The socio-cultural factors consists of man's economic, social, political and their products such as mode of production, industry, education, technology, means of transport and commerce, culture, housing, bridges and highways, etc. Darwin's Descent of Man, describes man's biological evolution to the present stage through continuous interaction with environment.

Environmental problems have attracted the attention of a wide cross-section of people all over the world during the last two decades. People are becoming increasingly conscious of a variety of problems like global warming, ozone layer depletion, acid rain, famines, flood, droughts, scarcity of fuel, firewood and fodder, pollution of air and water and problems from hazardous chemicals and radiation, which have adverse effect on the environment.

It was in the early seventies that along with the rest of the countries in the world, India realized another disheartening trend. The same efforts which helped bring people above the poverty line, also put greater pressure on the natural resources of the country. Irrigation facilities provided also produced salinity in the land. Industrial development provided products but it also polluted water and air. Medical facilities improved the health of the people, but increased the population thereby increasing the usage of nature, which is another reason for creating environmental pollution.

A new era has entered the age of environmental awareness or "The Age of Ecology". Human survival is at stake. We are facing several environmental problems. If man has to survive, it is imperative that all the problems can be dealt with simultaneously. This dimension can be achieved only when we enlighten the younger generation and make people aware in order to develop the right attitude and enlarge the area of commitment towards checking environmental deterioration. In recent years there has been a growing demand for higher environmental quality.

Environmental management must regulate the demands and activities of man in such a way that the ability of the environment to sustain future development remains unimpaired. Efficient environmental management is a pre-requisite for sustaining economic development. Environment management can be defined as–'Environment management consists of the set of activities aimed at choosing appropriate institutional arrangements, technologies and incentive for achieving whatever goals are specified as environmental quality targets'.

Environment management as an operational concept might best the defined as describing the actions of those involved in decision making who make a deliberate and systematic attempt to understand how their interaction activities affect the environment and how their concern about the environment will affect their activities.

Thus, environmental management is a positive concept, not a negative "whole progress" or "back to nature" concept. Some of the key aspects involved are–

1. Identification of the 'needs' and 'wants' of man in his individual and social development.
2. Identification of the resources that are needed for such development.
3. Identification of how meetings of the needs and wants will inhibit or increase the ability to meet others as a result of destruction, degradation or enhancement of resources.
4. Identification of the factors who gave a stake in the conflicts that may arise between meeting needs and protecting resources.
5. Resolution of the conflicts.

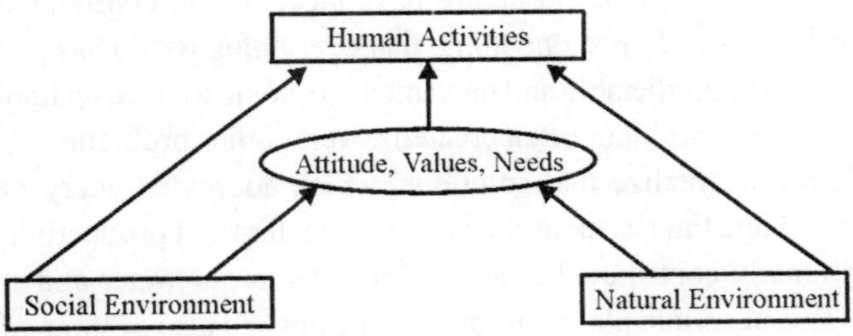

Fig. 2. Figure Explains How Environment is Interrelated.

No matter how the concept of environmental management is defined, the attainment of its objective will necessarily require significant change in the values, attitudes and behaviour of those concerned with the maintenance of the society. Institutionally, sound management needs to be developed and these need to be based on concerns other than the traditional monetary values.

In India, concern for environmental management have emerged and are reflected in the successive five year plans. The Sixth Five Year Plan (1980-1985) for the first time had a specific environmental objectives. This was expressed in the following words, "Bringing about harmony between the short-term and the long-term goals of development by promoting the protection and improvement of ecological and environmental effects".

The approach of the Seventh Five Year Plan (1985-1990) also recognized the ecological and environmental conservation as one of its principal objectives. In terms of integrating environmental consideration with national economic planning, the Seventh Five Year Plan emphasized that, "The environment must not be considered as just another section of national development. It should form a crucial guiding dimension for plans and programmes in each sector. Although we have come a long way since the invention of the steam engine. We can now travel a lot faster. We can produce much more food. Our lives have become more comfortable with modern conveniences. But much of this technological progress has also created many problems, which we today perceive as environmental problems. Why this has happened? Perhaps because the highly educated specialists who created many of the modern technologies, and society, which used them, did not understand two fundamental environmental principles–

(1) That everything in nature is connected, and consequently, (2) That we can never do just one thing, that everything we do has numerous effects, often unpredictable and unwanted. So, sophisticated technological solutions to one problem often created several other problems.

Today we realize that solutions, which addressed every pressing problems at one time, such as the need for greater food productivity, have unintentionally contributed to adding poisons to our water and soil and causing loss of certain plants and animal species and also of some essential microbes and soil nutrients. Environmental problems have reached a level where almost everyone is conscious of them.

This rising consciousness has also given rise to a widespread responsiveness to the idea for the need to do something about it.

Environmental education is a comparatively new area of the discipline of education. It is a new source of concern for educators, teachers and students. With the rapid development in each area of environment there are both internal and external problems to be confronted and resolved.

Meaning and Definition of Environmental Education

1. *UNESCO Working Committee (1970)*. "Environmental education is the process of recognizing values and clarifying concepts in order to develop skills and attitude, necessary to understand and appreciate the interrelatedness among man, his culture and his bio-physical surroundings. It also entails practice in decision-making and self-formulation of a code of behaviour about problems and issues concerning environmental quality".
2. *UNESCO Seminar at Jammi (1976)*. "Environmental education is a way of implementing the goals of environmental protection. It is not a separate branch of science or field of study. It should

be carried on according to the principles of life-long integral education".

3. *Mishra (1993)*. "Environmental education appears to be a process that equips human beings with awareness, knowledge, skills, attitudes and commitment to improve environment".
4. *Sharma (1996)*. "Environmental education refers to the awareness of physical and cultural environment and perceive its relevance for real life situation. The problems and issues are to be identified. The imbalances of environment are to be improved in view of sustainable development".

Environment and Education

Education is the process of development. Environment is the aggregate of all the external conditions and influences affecting the life and development of man and other living organisms. Every organism has its own environment. Man's environment consists of natural as well as socio-cultural environment. Education may change and improve the quality of man's environment to achieve desirable modification of his behaviour.

Illustrating the relationship of environment and education Bernard points out that the educational process of development is organized formally in the educational institutions' class-room, where an interaction takes place between teacher and taught.

While most people recognize an urgent need for environmental education, only some have clear ideas about what should be done. Very few have the actual experience or knowledge about the courses that the individual and social groups should acquire awareness and knowledge, develop attitudes, skills and abilities and participate in solving real life environmental problems. This perspective should be integrated, interdisciplinary and holistic in character. The public in rural, tribal, slum and urban areas; students and teachers in schools, colleges and universities as well as planners and policy makers, programme implementators and workers all need to be educated about the environment.

To generate conducive social and emotional climate to provide the new experiences to the students for desirable changes and modifications in their behaviour a teacher performs certain activities verbally and non-verbally. Thus, the process of development is carried on in schools. The organization, climate and health of the institutions provide new experiences to their students. Educational process of development occurs in physical, social, cultural and psychological environment. This may be understood from the following figure :

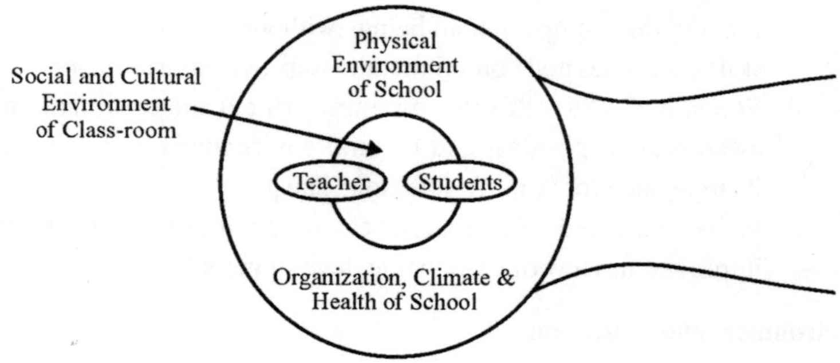

Fig 3. Environment Education.

Education and Environment

Education deals with the various problems and principles governing the relationships between students and their environment. Formally and

Table 1 : Impact of Development Activities on Environment

Development activities	*Impact on Environment*
Forest clearing and land settlement	Extinction of rare species of flora and fauna, create breeding grounds for mosquito.
Shifting cultivation in upland agriculture	Soil erosion in upland areas. Soil fertility decline. If shorter cultivation cycle, flooding of low land areas.
Agro-industries, e.g., Sugar and tapioca	Air pollution due to burning of bagasse as fuel in mills, large amount of highly polluting organic with surface water pollution.
Use of pesticides	Organisms develop resistance and new control methods needed. Leads to complex and widespread environment problems. Biological magnification, poisoning.
Timber Extraction	Degrades land, destroys surface soil, reduces production potential of future forest.
Urbanization and industrialization	Concentration of population, making huge dent on rural environment, air and water pollution.
Water resources projects	Human settlement and resettlement, spread of, e.g. extensive irrigation, waterborne irrigation disease schist to somiasasis as in Egypt after Aswan construction, reduction of fisheries, salutation, physical changes, e.g., temperature, humidity.

Source : Lohani, Bindu, N. 1984. Environment Quality Management, Delhi.

informally this is related by the school and the teacher. Ecology is a new science, which deals with the various principles governing the relationship between organisms and their environment. Education is Human Ecology dealing with the relationship of man and material in the context of growth and development.

Environmental education has now been included as a part of the formal curriculum in colleges and universities. Realization and educating the people about their environment is indispensable to the conservation process has led to a sharpies in the incidence of various national and international seminars/workshops on environmental education. (See table 2).

Table 2 : Important Events in Environmental Education Movement

International working meeting on 'Environmental Education in School Curriculum'. Carson City, Nevada, USA, 1970.

Workshop on 'Environmental Education at University Level'. Tours, France, 1971. European working conference on 'Environmental Conservation Education', Rushikon, Switzerland, 1971.

International Seminar on 'Environmental Conservation Education in the School Curriculum' in East European Countries, Kioscenko, Poland, 1972.

United Nations Conference on "The Human Environment" Stockholm, 1972.

International Workshop on 'Environmental Studies in Higher Education and Teacher Training', London, Ontario, Canada, 1972.

'Eastern Africa Youth Meeting on Environmental Conservation' Nairobi, Kenya, 1974.

International working meeting on 'Environment Education Programmes Egypt, 1974.

Pilot Seminar on 'Environment Education Methodology in East Manbasa, Kenya, 1974.

Seminar on 'Educational for the Conservation of Renewable Natural Reserve in High School Curricula, Cordoba, Argentina, 1971.

'International Environment Education' workshop at Belgrade, 1978.

First Inter-Government Conference on 'Environment Education', Tiblisi, 1977.

Workshop on 'Environmental Education' held at Indian National Science Academy, New Delhi, 1979.

International Conference on 'Environment Education', New Delhi, 1985.

Second International Seminar on 'Environmental Education', New Delhi, 1985.

Inter-governmental conference on 'Environmental Education', Moscow, 1987.

Source : P.R. Trivedi and Gurdeer Raj (1992) Management of Environmental Education and Research. Akashdeep Publication House.

Communication Strategies for Environmental Conservation

Harol D. Lawell identified environmental surveillance as one of the most important functions served by communication (Laswell, 1948). It is only through a better and wider communication network that we can reach people quickly, creating awareness of the environment and triggering a positive action towards conserving it. Communications must assist citizens and policy makers to make sound and well informed decisions on environmental conservation. A substantial and effective communications component must be employed and carefully integrated with the message. The people must first be made aware of the problem, the problem must be relevant to their personal aspirations and concerns and they must pursue the course of action that is practical and worthwhile, and should be motivated to act.

The necessary steps are :

DEVELOP AWARENESS → CREATE INTEREST → BUILD SUPPORT → GET ACTION

It is not just enough to communicate reasonable solutions. People must be educated on what is rationally possible in the universal desire to cope with the problem of environmental degradation. In this regard, the media, one of the crucial modern day communicator has an important role to play. The communes concept of school as adopted today remains a closed concentration of human beings for learning in a systemized manner, often within the boundaries of rigid syllabus and limited to the confines of the instructor's experience. The media message in contrast are available to anyone, anywhere, encompassing a wide range of topics and enriched by the participation of a number of resource persons. Hence the task now remains to build a coherent relationship between education and the media, evolve a rational plan of action and balance instruction through the two means.

"Thought should be give more systematically than in the past to ways and means of combining organically and harmoniously, the objectives, activities and methods of implementation, both of education and of contemporary communication technologies. In the years to come, all those who are concerned with the problems of education and communication and are aware of the inter-dependence will be seeking to build bridges between the two and institute a practical operational symbiosis between the two cultures, that of school and that of the media, each with its own individuality and without order of preference (Moray, 1984).

Environmental Education Through Media : A Shifting Focus

Initially environmental coverage by media received only common place treatment becoming newsworthy relative to other development of the day. As also, there was no separate environments report department, with experts in this field to chalk out the programmes, it would require major catastrophes to environment to receive adequate coverage, such as the Union Carbide pesticide factory accident in Bhopal, the Chernobyl nuclear reactor explosion or the Swiss Chemical Warehouse fire. The coverage even then was more on lost lives, damaged property and the economic setbacks than the environmental fallouts. The Stockholm conferences received sufficient coverage by the Indian media due to the participation of Indira Gandhi who earmarked poverty as a threatening crisis. Gradually new environmental problems mushroomed and the media responded to the need for education and awareness among people regarding them. Previously ignored areas such as wildlife conservation, forestry, alternative energy sources, threat to bio-diversity and habitat destruction received wider coverage. The psychological and emotional impact of such programmes has been on the rise with the media going one step further and supporting localized people's movements against exploitation of the environment and winning wider support for the cause from people all over the globe.

People's Initiatives

India has witnessed growing concern and agitation among people to the destruction of their habitat. Most of these protest movements have stemmed up due to the efforts of a single person on community. During recent times, awareness of the environmental issues and the related social and economic degradation is motivating the aware citizens towards proving against inimical development projects, reckless exploitation of natural resources and indiscriminate pollution of our habitat. It is important to note that people's participation is vital and integral component of development. Participatory communication development recognizes the fact that people with their own inherent potential and cultural identity can generate their own source of power to achieve the objectives they set for themselves and their community. If his power is supplemented with systematic functional knowledge, then liberation from powerlessness and ignorance will set the pace for a self-reliant development.

The numerous cases for environmental conservation projects becoming successful through people's initiative and participation is a testimony to the fact that participation of the people is an important decisive factor in the conservation process. Issues have ranged from opposition to tree felling, to fighting exploitative and cost ineffective development projects. One famous instance of people's enterprise is the Chipko movement in the Chamoli district of Uttar Pradesh. The felling of some 2500 trees was stopped due to protest by the villagers. Another instance came in 1978-79 when a campaign was undertaken against a World bank sponsored "Social Forestry Project" in which the adivasis cut down teak trees planted at the expense of the Sal tree, the centre of their social and economic life. The campaign resulted in for the first time, a World Bank project being called to halt.

There have been movements opposing big dams and development at the cost of environmental harmony. The Narmada Bachao Andolan, The Tehri Garhwal resistance movements, are two classic examples of mass people's movements against destruction of the environment in relation to development, often they have been the organized efforts of a small group. In all the above efforts of the people which have resulted in mass movements, the media has played a tremendous role in creating an awareness of the issues and bringing the protest to the notice of the policy makers and to people all over the country. The media has united the people of the sub-continent to one common cause and has accelerated the process of observation. Often they have provided the motivation required in the people of other areas faced with similar problems. Communication media offer a tremendous potential for bringing the environmental issues closer to people all other and forging networks for action. The media has helped place environmental conservation and improvement among the top national, even international companies and thus media are the most effective means of reaching the people out of the news line.

Non-Government Organisations (NGOs)–Organised People's Movement

The World Bank's Operational Directive defines them as, 'Groups and institutes that are entirely or largely independent of government and characterized primarily by humanitarian or cooperative, rather than commercial objectives'. In the Bank's operational directive, the term NGO is used to refer principally to those private organizations that pressure activities to relieve suffering, promote the interest of the poor, protect the environment or undertake community development.

NGOs have certain advantages and disadvantages. Some of them are small, flexible, close to people with good local roots and contracts. They work at grassroots levels in underdeveloped areas. Their sense of purpose and voluntarism along with high values for the development of people enable them to work with the people with their support and participation. Innovation and creativity along with humanness help the

NGOs to achieve their social purpose. Many NGOs work to develops people by helping them to become self-reliant using the available resources and developing their own competencies. Team work, high quality leadership and committed people work in rural areas are some of the strengths of NGOs.

In the changing scenario a good number of responsibilities have been handed over to the government organisations by the government and by the people to protect the society from the adverse effects that follow the changes to ensure welfare needs and to enable to grow and to develop. Earlier the NGOs were established with the purpose of solving the problems of health, economy, literacy, etc., and to develop the society for national development.

Many voluntary agencies have taken up the issue of environment protection. Among these agencies are the Dasholi Gram Swarajya Mandal that has started the Chipko Movement in which women play a very important role. The Chipko Movement has received international acclaim and was initiated by hill women. Women embraced (Chipko) the tree to prevent them being felled and some women were killed while thus protecting trees with their own bodies. Trees to these women and others are the source of life. The impact of environmental degradation and of soil erosion is first felt by women. Many grassroots level women's organisations have begun to take up environmental issues in institution to their continuing concern for rural poverty due to the intrinsic link between environment, poverty and gender.

The responsibility for creating awareness, mobilizing public opinion and building a strong people's movement lies mainly with the voluntary agencies. The awareness generated by individual women pioneers/leaders and all types of women's organizations on environmental issues has focussed on the fact that women and men have the capacity to manage their environment, and their access to productive resources should be sustained and enhanced. It is also recognized that the requisite knowledge and information can be disseminated by voluntary organizations to reinforce the self-help potential of women in conserving and improving the environment.

Demystification of Technology

A number of voluntary agencies are involved in commendable work in the demystification of appropriate technology for the advancement of rural women. The programmes implemented by voluntary agencies in this area include, providing opportunities for gainful employment and self-employment for women, reducing the drudgery in their lives, ensuring adequate medical and nutritional facilities, improving sanitation and environmental conditions and protecting women from occupational hazards. However, there is a need for further voluntary action in this direction that can develop and disseminate appropriate technology for women. Since the technological marginalization of female work is endemic in both the agricultural and the non-agricultural informal sector, voluntary agencies should be involved in over-coming gender differentials in the application and generation of technology. There is a need to actively deploy technology to reduce the drudgery of the poorest working women in back breaking tasks such as gathering of fuel, fodder and water.

Training constitutes another important input, particularly for upgradation of skill and augmentation of earning capacities of women. There is a strong need for a diversification of training undertaking by voluntary organizations. Their role should be particularly geared to the sensitization of administrators functionaries and catalysts on the issues and needs of women in development and in the delivery of comprehensive training programmes that have a component of knowledge, attitudes and skills for women's development.

It is well recognized that the management of the environment requires the participation of people as they are closest to it and have a stake in its preservation. Active involvement of women and their organizations in environment protection is of paramount significance since women are most affected by the issue. There is a serious threat to the environment due to its degradation and pollution arising from various factors such as policies of government as well as the private sector, unplanned discharge of residual and waste, handling of toxic chemicals, indiscriminate construction of dams, large scale deforestation, expansion of settlements and unplanned mining and quarrying work. Such conditions have pushed great numbers of women into marginal environment where floods, droughts, shortage of fuel, and excessive utilizating of grazing land have deprived women of their livelihood.

NGO's in India concerned with various aspects of environmental education and conservation have been making their presence felt by working slowly towards improvement of environmental conditions in their areas of concerned India and has 900 NGO's working for environmental conservation.

NGO's constitute a valuable information source and can be a source of education and information on environmental issues. They have also acted in groups in various instances when the administrative system has been ineffective and NGO's can also act as a bridge between the government and people bringing crucial information to policy makers regarding environmental issues and NGO's played a major role in educating the people about their environment and providing a range of educational and motivational aids as well as by providing directly in public education. The Agha Khan Rural Support Programme is one such NGO working with village communities in Gujarat to provide and catalyze community participation in natural resource management and with relentless dedication has seen the increase in agricultural productivity upto 100 per cent over a two year period. Soil loss has been reduced. Foundation of Organizational Research and Education (FORE) promoted self-management of slums by women at Janata Jeevan Camp and promoted 1000 slum dwellers in Tigri, a village of Delhi, VICAS, a women's organization of FORE is crusading towards improving the environmental and other issues of the camp. The movement arose out of disillusionment with the facilities provided by the government.

However, governmental interference must be kept to a minimal level to ensure effective functioning of the NGO's. Ghosh (1991) points out how voluntary action was previously organized at the local level to solve local problems identified by the people themselves, today, the majority of NGOs are mere emissaries or carriers of governmental policies and programmes. However, the task they are performing towards conservation of the environment is highly commendable.

What is needed is active coordination between different NGOs working for the cause of conservation, the schools and Universities, media, NGOs, government and the activities to effect a better level of awareness and motivation among the people.

"To effectively perform management of the environment, there must be integration of single purpose groups, their outlooks must be topographic on jurisdictional lines, permitting inter-related activities to perform jointly and cooperatively, in parallel, or in correct sequence, rather than in competition, out of phase, or in a communication vacuum". (Bouner and Co. 1995).

In the long-term this crusade for the establishment of nation wide environmental classroom through media may lead to growth of an environmental religion which will involve the recognition of environmental issues or factors in the development and nature of human insight. In fact, from the ancient times, environment has been linked with religion and people in India worship nature as a part of their spiritual beliefs. For example the Black Buck is worshipped by the Bishnoi community in Rajasthan,

Palm trees and Grey Pelicans in Kokrebellur in Karnataka, Langur and Ficus species all over India. It is this deep religious bond that people share with nature and has led to the conservation of some of the priceless species of flora and fauna.

Today, what is needed is a whole lot of dedicated "environmental communication" who can help shape the attitude of people towards the conservation of the environment. A well informed public is essential to form the process of conservation because abuse of the environment can only be slowly bringing about behavioural changes among the people and help them make significant informed decisions about their own behaviour. A deeper understanding of the functioning of the ecological processes and an empathetic view is required to bring about this change in behaviour. There must be therefore, a very comprehensive and effective communication system to inform and educate the public of the risks of biological damage. For an effective dissemination of information to a wide network of people, heavy reliance upon television, community groups, information aids such as letters, posters, educational pamphlets is a must.

Non-Formal Environmental Education

The environment education has been designed both formally and non-formally. The environmental education is lifelong process for the welfare of mankind and the development of the society. It is designed for every age group, participating in social, economic, cultural development of the community. Groups or clubs arrange exhibitions, public lectures, meetings and environmental campaigns. The following constitute main content of non-formal environmental education.

1. *Adult Education :* It may influence adult members for better ways of life, through local language, information packs, posters, slides, audio, audiovisuals, etc.
2. *Rural Youth and Non-student Youth :* Organizing these into group the programmes of education may be taken up by involving their community leaders, women and youth in an important content of our forest wealth for tribals and forest dwellers.
3. *Children Activities :* These may include essay competitions of different age groups. With the help of United School Organization of India, the Department of Environment organizes such activities. On the spot painting, modelling and poster design contests are conducted for children by the National Museum of Natural History (NMNH). Short-term courses are also given by NMNH every year.

4. *Eco-development Camps :* These help in sound rural development involving youth. A set of guidelines has been prepared by Department of Environment in 1984. Its main objectives are to create awareness in student and non-student youth about basic ecological principles; to identify root cause of ecological/ environmental problems; and to develop a spirit of national integration and emotional integration.

Problem of Water Scarcity : Women

Water is a vital resource which is a basic need for any human being. But it is of limited source as most of it is not consumable. Water is a luxury for many living in semi-arid, arid deserts, hills, coastal and rocky regions of the world, particularly the less developed parts of the world.

The consumable water is less than one-third of the water source available. The sources of consumable water are rains, atmospheric humidity which is mostly frozen in terms of ice. Safe drinking water supply and basic sanitation are vital human needs for health and efficiency. Disease and death particularly of children every year and drudgery of women are directly attributable to lack of these essentials.

In a developing country like ours, there are many villages and cities either with scarce water supply or without any source of water. In many rural areas women still have to walk a distance of about 2.5 kms. to reach upto the source of water. She reaches home carrying heavy pots not to rest but to do other household chores of cooking, washing, cleaning, caring of children, other family members, and caring for livestock. Water may get used up by all family members by the end of the day since it is used for all these purposes. This creates the need for fetching water again by evening. Thus, a rural woman's life is sheer drudgery. Hence, modern or alternate water sources and storage methods need to be planned and promoted in the villages to solve the problems related to women and water.

Fast approaching desert or desertification in many areas of India creates a disastrous effect on the habitants in these areas who are required to be helped through various ways and means to meet the challenges in desert for survival as well as development. Constant changes in the eco-system brings about basic changes in the composition of its environment and converts fertile land into deserts. The main reasons for desertification are high pressure on grazing lands, specially in view of its low carrying capacity results in over use of these lands and in depletion of natural vegetation, often necessitating migration of people and livestock in search of pastures.

Cultivation on sand dunes and marginal lands is also a menace, causing soil erosion. The increased population has led to increasing demand for wood for fuel and over exploitation of vegetations. Cultivation on the rain-fed, steeply sloping lands and other erosion-prone areas, clearance of forests and jungle for resettlement and cultivation, resulting into water erosion.

The desertification processes in the Indian sub-continent are extremely varied. Efforts to combat should be location specific with the broad objective of increasing productivity and restoring the biological potential of the land. In India, the arid zone covers about 12 per bent of the country's geographical area and occupies over 3,20,000 sq. km. of hot desert. The percentage-wise spread over of desert area in various states of India indicate the following, situation–

About 62 per bent in Rajasthan, 18 per cent in Gujarat, 10 per cent in Andhra Pradesh and 9 per cent in Punjab and Himachal Pradesh. Gujarat has the second largest spread over of desert and the people living in the north-west of Gujarat are affected by desertification year in and year out. A huge area in this zone is lying barren and uncultivated which can be used through massive afforestation programmes which can be initiated involving women in the programme which will be of great help because women are engaged mostly in the job of procuring water, storing water and utilizing the water for various purposes like drinking, washing, cleaning themselves and cattle. A household is a main institution of which the woman is the manager. All the drudgery involved in fetching storing, purifying and managing water are faced by women so, it becomes all the more necessary to make them aware about water management. As aim the above activities are physically and psychologically tiring it is hard on the part of the household manager to manage other household activities alongwith managing of water which is very time and energy consuming.

Rural Water Supply Programmes in India

This programme is essentially an investment in human resource development. The provision of free or subsidized services through public agencies is expected to improve the consumption levels of those living below the poverty line and thereby improve the productive efficiency of both the rural and urban workers.

A new policy direction for solving the drinking water problem, coverage of problem villages both under, Accelerated Rural Water Supply Programme (ARWSP) and Minimum Need Programmes (MNP) had the following priorities :

1. To cover sixth plan spill over problem villages 1980 list.
2. To cover all villages with no water source according to 1985 list.
3. To cover all the 'no source' problem villages and certified subsequently but not yet covered.
4. To cover all villages with contaminated drinking water (chemical and bacteriological).
5. To cover all villages with per capita water supply less than 10 litres per capita per day.
6. To cover all villages with per capita water supply less than 40 litres social consumption obtain not only between income groups but also between areas. The level of development of the various social services and infrastructure varies widely from state to state.

National Technology Mission

The technology missions on drinking water and related water management was set up in 1986 under the department of rural development as one of the five technological missions, to solve the problem of drinking water in the country. The technology mission's main objective was to mobilise resources of water supply authorities and various experts and government departments on the priority basis to study the problems at a grassroots level, to ensure supply of adequate and acceptable quality of drinking water on a long-term basis.

Main Theme of Water Mission

(a) Scientific source finding and development.

(b) New dimension and application of sciences and technology inputs in an integrated manner for generating cost-effective long-term solution to predominant problem associated with rural water supply.

(c) Thrust to computerise Management Information Centre (MIS) for collection of data base analysis, monitoring and evaluation.

Water Management and Role of Women

In the gender division of household task, fetching water, apart from other chores like cooking, washing, child-care, etc. are considered as women's task. Women are first acceptors of water, hence, every water related project should focus on reduction of their drudgery. By virtue of their domestic roles, women are regularly in touch with water which is often polluted in rural areas. Women are thus vulnerable to water related diseases which, according to estimates of the 'World Health Organization' account for 80 per cent of all sickness and diseases in the developing world. The women's roles are usually ignored when community involvement is called for. Women should be viewed more than mere target groups. Since women in rural areas are involved in water collection, maintenance and usage, they can play an active role in developmental efforts related to water management as well.

The impact of the lack of concern has been two fold on women. It has affected their quality of life including the health of the entire family and kept morality rates high, particularly, infant morality with high incidence of gastroenteritis, cholera and various other water-borne diseases. Second, it has confined women and female children to the drudgery of spending long hours and walking long distances for fetching water. This has deprived them many a times of education, skill development and better employment opportunities.

In terms of water supply and management women must be viewed as:

1. The acceptors of the plan and project of water supply.
2. The users of new water facilities.
3. The managers for better utilization and for training the members of the household in water conservation practices.
4. The change agents promoting acceptance of new sources of water, thus removing the cultural inhibitions to sources of water and its utilization.

Strategies for Water Management

To cope with water management following strategies are required:

1. Water has to be managed as a commodity in exactly the same way as any other resources.
2. Supply of water to consumers should normally be based on the principle of effective demand which should broadly correspond to the standard of service, that the users are willing to maintain, operate and finance.
3. In rural areas, water tariff may not be feasible in all places. However, wherever house service connections are given, it is suggested that appropriate water tariff is levied, and realised whereby operation and maintenance become self-sustaining to the extent possible.
4. Private sector efforts for construction and maintenance of drinking water projects should be encouraged and mobilized to the maximum extent feasible.
5. Local bodies whether in rural or urban areas should be made responsible for the operation and maintenance of the system installed with technical guidance from government agencies.

6. Appropriate lengths should be forged between water supply and environmental sanitation (solid and liquid waste management) in the planning of new programmes.
7. The concept of primary health care, water availability, women's welfare, immunization and provision of sanitation facilities all linked to cleanliness as a basic human need should be emphasized. Every effort would be made to adopt a low cost approach, employing technical and scientific know how and the experience already gained by several non-governmental organizations in this regard.
8. Emphasis on efficient exploration of available water for various uses, should be made necessary in order to take timely steps for recharging and rejuvenating the water sources. At the same time appropriate linkage between all conservation and land / water management and drinking water supply schemes should be made available to sustain water supply.
9. An effective mechanism for ensuring proper operation and maintenance of existing assets is necessary. "Village Water Committees" should be actively involved in the maintenance of drinking water supply schemes and a system of beneficiary participation should be introduced.
10. Studies should be undertaken on the preventive maintenance of water distribution system with reference to leakages and carrying capacities of the mains, leak detection measures, hydraulic analysis and optimum design of the water distribution systems, extension of rapid bacteriological techniques, development of springs for water supplies, development of natural and inorganic coagulants etc. Use of solar energy in the rural water supply, hydraulic rams for the rural water in the hilly areas, development of package water treatment plants, etc. should be given a major thrust. Focus should also be given to research and development on the conversion of brackish water and sea water to drinking water.
11. Women should be made focus of users, education accompanying water management programme.
12. Women should be selected as health promoters and designers of education programmes. Addressing groups of women in markets, clinics, bus stops and so can be taken up.
13. Women should be developers of education materials for illiterates and neo-literates using women in illustrations and

projecting women's preference for acquisition and disposal of water.

14. The educational programmes should be directed to change the practices relating to water handling, its disposal, storage as well as use in food preparation.
15. Water users and education for women should also take advantage of social system compared to friends and reinforcing behavioural change.
16. Where actually women should be trained in technically and managerial aspects of water supply.
17. Some can be trained as trainees of other women jobs and specific skills as supervisors.

Empowering Women as Water Managers

To reduce drudgery on the part of women in carrying water and in order to make the women aware regarding various methods of water recycling, multiple use of water and scientific ways of purifying water and also to enable women to become decision makers in water management. She needs to be empowered :

1. Consciousness needs to be developed in women by discussing her problems and by attacking common problems they face in water management.
2. Women need to be empowered in building up a sense of solidarity among themselves.
3. Greater control needs to be given to women while implementing water management programme. This can be done by providing technical skill.
4. Some organizations should decide to train women in water management.
5. Help them provide valuable expertise regarding water management.
6. They can also be helped by empowering them within their household and in their community as a whole as there is a great discrimination between men and women due to her illiteracy and ignorance. Women like men require opportunities for developing their intellectual potential to the maximum. National policies and programmes should provide them with full and equal access to education and training at all levels of water management. While ensuring that such programmes and policies consciously orient them towards new occupations and new roles consistent with

their need for self-fulfilment and the needs of national development.

Role of Home Scientists in Water Management

The process of involving the university system to participate in extension programmes was initiated by the University Grants Commission with the specific objective of securing equal importance to 'Extension' as the third dimension with teaching and research.

The infrastructure of higher education provides a large reservoir of human energy and resources. It is, therefore, imperative to mobilise the resources for nation building activities and utilise the infrastructure for national development to achieve the desired objective.

Home scientists can play a very important role in water management as:

1. Academician
2. Communicator
3. Non-formal Educator
4. Researcher

1. Academician

As an academician she can play a vital role by–

1. Continuing to develop and refine the objectives, scope and content of 'environment education' at various levels with special emphasis on "water management".
2. Helping in stimulation and orientation of various concerned agencies is another major task that Home Scientists can undertake.
3. Teaching the students about water source, water management practices, pollution of water, drudgery of women, techniques of purifying water, use and reuse of water and water-borne diseases. In this way she can educate the students as part of the curriculum.
4. Guiding students to take up action projects related to water management.
5. Home scientists can take up studies and researches and provide invaluable help by carrying out attitudinal, cultural and other studies to evolve the content and methodology essential for a new and unprecedented programme dealing with "water management".

2. Communicator

1. As a communicator the Home Scientists can also impart environment education. In the rural areas as well as in the urban

communities the Home Scientists can arrange talks, discussions on importance of good nutrition, energy conservation, labour saving devices, health and nutrition, and benefits of drinking clean water.

2. The education can be effectively given by using teaching aids like charts, posters, flashcards and flannel boards.
3. Home Scientists can write scripts, guide students, arrange role plays, street plays, bhavai and puppet shows for giving information related to "water management".
4. Set of slides, manual, audio cassettes and video films can be developed for imparting knowledge to the people, related to water, purification, recycling and conservation.
5. Developing, using and harnessing both traditional and mass media at the field level. As the modern mass media like radio, T.V., cinema and powerful instruments for creating a suitable climate in favour of sensitizing people about need for proper water management.

3. Non-formal Educator

1. Department of Home Science Extension and Communication can undertake different activities like organizing seminars, symposia and debates on environmental issues, related to water.
2. Organising field trips for students to make them study the eco-system, plantation of trees and water management in rural areas.
3. A comprehensive training programme can be developed so that women become more effective by acquiring skills and knowledge essential in contributing to the solution of water problem.
4. Home science students can conduct house to house survey to meet women, develop rapport with them and make them aware of the importance of water management.
5. Meet village leaders and key persons and seek their cooperation in organising training programmes, on the related issues and problems.
6. Organising exhibitions and awareness campaigns to publicize the importance of recycling of water, use of filters, importance of forestation, danger of water pollution and water-borne diseases.
7. Arranging demonstrations on use of renewable source of energy like solar, biogas as it has greater potential for providing the energy for lighting, water pumping, generating electricity.
8. Organising training programmes on maintenance of water sources, water quality assessment at the village level and creating

awareness about water pollution, its sources and preventive measures.

9. Increasing knowledge of water and health relationships.

This can be done by organising campaigns, talks by experts and film shows regarding the health hazards caused by unhygienic drinking water, symposia and exhibitions regarding the various techniques used for the filtration of water or for problems involved in storing, bringing and managing of water. This can be done by materials like photographs, flash cards, flip charts, booklets, leaflets, folders, posters and charts etc. This may help in increasing the knowledge of our women regarding water and its relation with health.

10. Promoting positive attitudes and practices related to hygienic use of water supply and storage facilities.

This can be done by creating awareness with the help of discussions, from reports on topics like drudgery of women in water management, so that everyone becomes aware of work which she does either in her extra time or during her ongoing household activities, group discussions, symposia can be held, demonstrations regarding the hygienic storage of water, street plays, bhavai and puppet plays regarding the health hazards caused by its consumption and video films.

11. Promoting practices related to water handling that contribute to better health.

This can be done by telling them about the importance of clean storage vessels, covering of water for drinking purposes, and purifying water before use. This can also be done by creating an awareness in the masses through audio visual-aids and individual discussions, on topics related to drinking water.

12. Promoting appropriate use of waste water :

This can be done by recycling water by watering plants in kitchen gardens or by cleaning courtyards or verandahs.

4. Researcher

The area of research in the field of water management has so far remained neglected. The different research thrust areas where Home Scientists can play an active role are–

Studies can be carried on the–

1. Time spent by women on water collection.
2. Problems faced while collecting water.
3. Awareness regarding water-borne diseases.
4. Promotion of different indigenous water filters.
5. Knowledge and practices of recycling and conservation of water.

6. Action projects on setting up / developing adoption of water filters.
7. Survey to find out water management practices.
8. Effectiveness of different media in imparting environment education.
9. Identification of sources of contamination and new potential water resources.
10. Experiment on effectiveness of media, demonstration and workshops in promotion of better water management practices.

Suggestions to Reduce Water Problems

1. Water tap connection to each rural household through pipe line connections plan can be made for extending pipe line to long distance to provide tap water in no source villages also.
2. Collection and processing of rain water in the village itself for daily use.
3. Involvement of other members male and children in fetching water, since all the time it is the women who brings the water, but all the family members are the users.
4. Users education should include suggestions for reuse of water for cleaning livestock, for watering kitchen gardens.
5. The NGOs must participate very actively in advocacy campaigns and in action research programmes related to water management.
6. Sanitation and cleaning programme.
7. Afforestation and tree plantation.
8. Construction of tanks.
9. Digging up of new wells.

Role of the Home Scientist in Tackling Environment Problems

1. She can correlate the topics of environmental issues while teaching different subject matter.
2. She can help individuals in providing awareness and sensitizing the students about the total environment and its allied problems.
3. She can create awareness regarding renewable and non-renewable resources or environment.
4. She can help her students to acquire basic understanding of the total environment, its associated problems and humanity's critically responsible presence and role in it.
5. She can use play-way techniques to make them understand the significance of food chains and food web and ecological balance.

6. She can help her students to acquire social values, strong feelings of concern for the environment and the motivation for active participation in its protection and improvement.
7. She can conduct activities like drama on environmental conservation.
8. She can help individuals to acquire the skills for solving environmental problems.
9. She can organize field trips to zoos, national parks, polluted cities, polluted rivers, birds sanctuary, etc.
10. She can help her students to evaluate environmental measures and education programmes in terms of ecological, social and aesthetic factors.
11. She can organize seminars and workshops on environmental issues like soil erosion or population explosion, etc.
12. She can help students to develop a sense of responsibility and urgency regarding environmental problems to ensure appropriate action to solve these problems.
13. She can arrange lectures from experts on topics of environmental concerns.
14. She can teach the interdependence of living things as the relationship between the needs of society and the interaction with the environment.
15. She can discuss environmental issues alongwith simple teaching activities through which people understand the significance of environmental resources.
16. She can motivate and train the students to acquire and spread knowledge and skills that will help society solve interrelated environmental problems and prevent their occurrence.

Conclusion

It is important to understand that everything in nature is connected and cause quaintly one can never do just one thing, as everything we do has numerous effects, which are often unpredictable Environmental Education has become a concern for educators, teachers and students. As is evident all development activities have impact on environment. It is high time that environmental issues are tackled systematically by bringing newer Innovations in Techniques, training the change agents.

The recent government policy measure of making environmental education a part of the school curriculum in India will go a long way in sensitizing young minds and responding to the challenge of environmental preservation. The media can effectively supplement this effort, apart from involving the whole community in sustaining the delicate balance in the environment. The media can yield better results due to the fascinating blend of education and entertainment : a stimulating information dissemination.

The need of the hour is citizens who are more aware, educated and active towards solving the existing environmental problems and conserving the natural resources which are in a limited proportion to the human population. It is only an aware citizenry who can enhance the longevity of our planet and ensure the survival of other inhabitants sharing this planet with us, fostering an emotional and empathetic bond resulting from millions of years of co-existence.

References

Annual Report, Ministry of Rural Development published by Government of India, 1993-94.

B.N. Neelima, Communication for Environmental Education, JRF, Deptt. of Journalism, Sri Padmavathi Mahila University, Tirupathi.

B.R. Kukreti, Environmental Education–A Blue Print, University News, August, 16, 1993.

Behera, S.N., Rainfed Agriculture in Dryland Areas of Orissa. XXXVI (10) July 1998, pp. 47-50.

Bharat B. Dhar, Environmental Education in India, University News, 38(6), February 2000.

Contingency Action Plan for Natural Calamities, Ministry of Agriculture, Government of India, 1990.

Datta, M.N., Rural Drinking Water Supply in India. Kurukshetra XXXVI (10). July 1988, pp. 16-21.

Datta, S.K. and Kapoor S., Collective Action, Leadership and Success in Agricultural Co-operatives. A Study of Gujarat and West Bengal, 1997.

G.R. Chhatwal, Encyclopaedia of Environmental Education, Anmol Publications Pvt. Ltd. New Delhi, 1998.

Gopalan, S. Integrated approach to resolve the problem of water, Kurukshetra XXXVI (10), July 1998, pp. 4-7.

Horan, N. Wastewater collection, Treatment, Disposal and Reuse in the book "The Global Environment, Science, Technology and Management" Vol. 2 Ed. by Brune. D : Chapman. D.V. A Wiley Company 1997.

K.B. Powar, Environmental issues and University, University News, November 22, 1993.

Kottern, D.C. and Felipe, B.A. "Bureaucracy and the Poor : Closing the Gap" Asian Institute of Management, Manila, 1981.

Menon. N.V.C. Role of NGOs in Disaster Management, Indian Journal of Adult Education, Vol. 59. No. 3. July-Sept. 1998, pp. 33-39.

Natural Disaster Reduction–South Asian Regional Report, Ministry of Agriculture, Government of India, 1994.

Onkar, N. Srivastava. Environment and Sustainable Development, University News, January 13, 1992.

Rs. 60 crore for environmental studies. University News, November 12, 1990.

S. Lakshmi, Challenges in Indian Education 1991.

Sen, S.R. Development of Drought Prone Area, Kurukshetra 12(8) 73-80. 1969.

Sreenivas Chary P. 'DPAP Outlay and Expenditure' Kurukshetra Vol. XXVII. No. 21, 1979.

Subramanium, C. The new strategy in Indian Agriculture, Vikas Publishing House, New Delhi, 1970.

Upadhyay, J.N. Role of Education and Training in Disaster Mitigation, Indian Journal of Adult Education. Vol. 59. No. 3 July-Sept. 1998. pp. 27-32.

Workshop Report on Women and Development in India - Issues and Challenges, BITS, Pillani 19-20 Jan. 2001.

Yogendra, K. Sharma, History of Problems of Education, Vol. 2, Kanishka Publication, 2001.

9

Women Studies Cells and Centres

Anuradha Mathu

Abstract

Women's Studies has now emerged as a full fledged academic discipline which calls for a thorough investigation into the subject. We have many cells and centres now working in many colleges and universities. These cells and centres do three things in particular viz.–research, extension and training. It is now over one and a half decades that the term 'Women Studies is being used in India. Initially, women studies would focus mainly on women's problems and issues. S.N.D.T. Women's University was the first university to establish a centre in the year 1974.

Further, in the year 1975, Indian Council of Social Science Research (ICSSR), launched a programme of research on women which is designated women's studies. In Delhi, ICSSR also supported an autonomous institute, 'Centre for Women's Development Studies'.

It is here that the Extension Communicators need to motivate and mobilize women for participation in various programmes and activities, conducted by centres and cells. Also help women from low socio-economic status families in building skills.

Introduction

Women's studies has now emerged as a full fledged academic discipline which calls for a thorough investigation into the subject. Within the University structure, centres and cells are now functioning in several universities and colleges. They take up research, extension and training activities.

There have been several studies analysing the existing status of females in terms of their rights, and their socio-economic, social, political, legal and educational are well-known. Compartmentalisation of problems of Dalit women, of working women, of housewives, of tribal women, of Muslim women or of unlettered rural women are all related to gender issues. conjugal relationships among educated couples, violence against women is there as well. Domestic violence in one form or the other is not confined to one's culture or one place. It is everywhere globally. Even in advanced countries single, divorcee or separated women are seen inferior to 'wives' and this leads to tolerance towards violence more so in Indian culture where one believes in fate and hopes that things may improve one day. Even in Hindu texts, where loud mouthed masculinist propaganda about so called glorification of femininity create figure devices in the form of Durga, Lakshmi and Saraswati, the patriarchal metaphysics see women only as females, a weaker sex.

The mainstream struggle between the 'haves' and 'havenots' encompasses undifferentiated domain of women's liberation. Inter-socio linkages in our social milieu can narrate long standing discrimination between the two sexes. Dowry, divorce, child bearing, harder struggle for food, fuel, water and fodder, sexual abuse, political participation and career are only some of the problems. Through micro level investigations and macro level assessments the present and the prospects for the future can be narrated constructively for the optimum utilisation of Stri Shakti. More and more participation of formal education sector is needed.

It is now more than two and a half decades that the term "Women Studies" began to be used in India. Women's studies in India began with research and were associated with a few individuals and institutions committed to women's cause. A few universities established small units or centres of women's studies with their own resources. S.N.D.T. women's university was the first university to do so when in the year 1974, it established an independent research unit on women's studies.

The Indian Council of Social Science Research (I.C.S.S.R.) after 1975, launched a programme of research on women which it designated as "women's studies" and many individual scholars did research. In Delhi the I.C.S.S.R. also supported an autonomous institute, "Centre for Women's Development Studies". After that a number of other universities opened women's studies cell / units in particular disciplines or as inter-disciplinary cell / centres.

From the early 1980's several exercises have been conducted, on why we need women's studies. In 1981, the First National Conference on women's studies hosted by S.N.D.T. Women's University propagated the message of the need for women's studies. As a result of the Conference, the Indian Association for Women's Studies was born. Since then, the term "Women's Studies" have spread more widely and rapidly. The University Grants Commission for the first time in their sixth plan, granted special assistance to women's studies centres / units in three universities. The S.N.D.T. women's university research unit on women's studies received the title "Centre for Advanced Studies and Research in Women's Studies" in the year 1984. The other two institutions were Tata Institute of Social Sciences, Bombay and School of Social Science, University of Hyderabad. By 1987-99, there was more support to lead centres at Kerala, Punjab, Pune and Benaras Hindu University. By 1988-89, a year later, many other universities / colleges were extended support.

Concept of Women Studies Centres or Cells and Status of Women

Status means position, so status of women means position of women in society. Malani has said that status of women refers to position of women as an individual in the social structure defined by her designated rights and obligations. The sociological viewpoint of the concept of status implies a hierarchical arrangement of social positions, each involving a set of rights and obligations which the occupant is expected to fulfill.

To this sociological view, two important aspects have been added, which are the degree of access to and control over material resources, including food, income and other forms of income and to social resources including knowledge, power and prestige, within the family, community and society at large.

Women Studies Centres / Cells : The term women's studies is a borrowed term from the west. Women's studies was pioneered in the United States of America in the late sixties. In India, the term was used more frequently after the International Women's Year, i.e. in 1975. Women's studies can change women's lives and mobilize other women to change their position. Women studies change the society and its values. For these goals of women studies. "Women studies Centres and Cells were established, where Women Studies Centres–works on national level and Women Studies Cells–works at local level.

Women's Studies Centres and Cells within the University System

The main objective of women's studies centre and cells within the university system is promotion of women's studies through reading and research, curriculum development, extension services, documentation and dissemination. The women studies centre and cells works for the common cause of women's development.

Role of Women Studies Centres and Cells for Enhancing the Status of Women

Women studies centres and cells promote research into the conditions and status of women, to recover women's history, literature and art, to initiate programmes to disseminate ideas and information related to the women's questions both at the scholarly and the popular levels.

Women studies centres and cells undertake various research projects, e.g., working of Mahila Mandals, etc. They conduct research on women's issues and organize seminars at national level and also have panel discussions on themes like 'women and social action' and drug abuse. They organize lectures on 'Women in development', 'Women in Politics' and 'Women in Religion'. Women studies centres organize workshops for leaders of women' voluntary organizations and activists from rural areas with the objective of creating awareness among them. Women studies centres perform extension activities which includes promotion of self-employed projects, creation of media equipped community halls for creating awareness and providing entertainment, rehabilitation projects, adult education, first-aid training, day care services for working women, information bureau for young girls to provide guidance about courses, employment opportunities, etc. They also identify the problems of women and try to provide alternatives.

They build contacts with women's organizations to initiate income generating activities like tailoring, etc. Women's studies cells organize adult education centres for illiterate women. They initiate work in slum areas for women's training, education and organization. They strengthen the Mahila Mandals to enhance the socio-economic status of the women.

Role of Women Studies Research Centre the M.S. University, Baroda, Gujarat

The centres main objectives are that it inculcates and promotes values that are necessary to achieve women's equality in a patriarchal society. It aims at effecting a change in the present attitudes and values regarding women's roles and rights. The outreach and training programmes are designed to empower both the privileged and underprivileged women. The centres activities and programmes are channeled through teaching, research, training, outreach, documentation and publications. The centre organizes seminars and workshops regularly relating to women's issues.

Role of Research Centre for Women's Studies (RCWS), SNDT, Juhu Road, Bombay

It is the first women's university in the country. In 1974, Research Centre for women's studies was established in the university with the main objective of identifying issues and problems of women and to undertake studies pertaining to women's role and status in society. The centre aims at collecting information and building documentation and reference material on women, and assists in the preparation and teaching of women's studies, liaison with individuals and institutions in India and abroad and encourages and supports action programmes for the improvement of women.

This centre regularly organizes seminars and workshops to provide an important forum for exchange of ideas and sharing new research findings. It publishes research reports and brings out a newsletter regularly. The centre also promotes networking through support to campaigns and struggles by women's action groups.

The Role of Extension Communicator in Strengthening the Role of Centres and Cells

- To motivate and mobilize the women for participation in various programmes and activities, conducted by centres and cells.
- To help in building skills amongst women, especially those belonging to low socio-economic status.
- Supply information and follow up support to women through extension work, in other words to become a liaison and bridge the gap between the centres and cells and the communities.
- To reflect the aspirations of women. It can be achieved by involving women in identifying issues, defining priorities, formulating and implementing need-based action programmes.

A three-day workshop on 'Women's Studies–Research and Curriculum' was organized by The Indian Institute of Advanced Studies, Himachal Pradesh University, Shimla.

There are 33 women studies and development centres and six women cells supported by University Grants Commission. The workshop was conducted to share the significant researches conducted by these centres as well as by the renowned scholars, professors, college principals, policy planners and action research experts. The main objective was to explore the ways of inducting gender sensitization in the classroom through suggested curriculum.

There were wide ranging deliberations on various aspects of women's studies with ten major recommendations. Setting up of a forum for women's studies in India as an effective network for exchange of ideas was one of the important recommendations. Some of the other recommendations include:

Establishment of a national level women's studies resource centre with adequate grant and organizational support for high quality sustainable programmes for materials collection, research and activities.

Curriculum design should be supported by a publication programme for Indian contexts of women's studies so that appropriate teaching material was available.

The teaching material should be translated in regional languages. A website for the women's studies centres and other institutes and individuals contributing to the development of women's and research should be setup.

IIAS should encourage women's studies through fellowships and by holding regular workshops and conferences, promote gender sensitization through modules in the IUC programme and disseminate information about its extensive library holdings in gender studies.

UGC Standing Committee for Women's Studies should convene regular meetings of directors of centres and cells and enhance the grant support in the Tenth plan.

Conclusion

It can be concluded that women studies centres and cells are playing an important role in enhancing the status of women. These centres are working for the common cause of women's development. They initiate programmes to disseminate information related to women's problems, create awareness among women, organize adult education centres, etc.

But in order to make the proposed women's study centres more action based and meaningful, we should try to involve agencies who are working with women in both the urban and rural areas. We must realize that development is constantly dynamic, enriching and an evaluative process. Therefore, the proposed centres must endeavour to work at research, training and also implementation. Only then, can we hope to walk a step towards real equality.

Total Number of UGC Supported Centres and Cells

Centres	*Cells*	*Total*
20	8	28

Statewise Distribution of UGC Supported Women's Studies Centres/ Cells in India

	State	*Number*
1.	Andhra Pradesh	4
2.	Assam	1
3.	Delhi	1
4.	Goa	1
5.	Gujarat	1
6.	Haryana	1
7.	Karnataka	1
8.	Kerala	2
9.	Madhya Pradesh	2
10.	Maharashtra	3
11.	Orissa	1
12.	Punjab	1
13.	Rajasthan	2
14.	Tamil Nadu	1
15.	Uttar Pradesh	4
16.	West Bengal	2
	Total	**28**

Distribution of UGC Supported Centres / Cells as per Year of Establishment

Year	*Number*
1984	3
1985	-
1986	-
1987	7
1988	13
1989	5
Total	**28**

UGC Women's Studies Centres / Cells as per discipline

Discipline	*No*	*Name of the Institution*
• Continuing and Adult Education	1	Kurukshetra University
• Education	2	Gauhati University, University of Kerala
• English	1	Gulbarga University
• Home Science	1	M.S. University, Baroda
• Humanities and Social Sciences	1	University of Hyderabad
• Interdisciplinary	1	Jadavpur University
• Sociology	5	(i) Goa University
		(ii) Barkatullah University
		(iii) Rani Durgawati Vishwa Vidyalaya
		(iv) University of Poona
		(v) University of Jodhpur
• Telugu	1	Nagarjuna University
Total	**13**	

Independent Centres

(i) Alagappa University
(ii) Banaras Hindu University
(iii) Berhampur University
(iv) Calcutta University
(v) University of Delhi
(vi) Punjab University
(vii) University of Rajasthan
(viii) SNDT Women's University
(ix) Tata Institute of Social Sciences

Type of Activities Undertaken by UGC Supported Centres/Cells

1. Research	7
2. Documentation	1
3. Research and Academic	5
4. Research, academic and action	1
5. Research, academic, action and training	11
6. Research, action, academic, training and documentation	1
7. Research, academic and training	2
Total	**28**

Colleges

(i) College of Arts and Commerce and Law–Andhra University
(ii) B.N.K.B. postgraduate college–Faizabad.
(iii) PG College of Social Work, Hyderabad.
(iv) Acharya Narendra Dev–Mahapalika Mahavidyalaya, Kanpur.
(v) S.D. College, Muzaffarnagar.
(vi) College for Women, Trivandrum.

List of Women's Studies Centres and Cells

Women's Studies Centres

1. Research Centre for Women's Studies–Osmania University of Hyderabad, Registered in 1985.
2. Centre for Women's Development and Extension Programme, Mawabagh Women's College, Jabalpur. Registered in 1988.
3. Women's Studies College of Arts, Commerce and Law, Andhra University, Vishakapatnam, Registered in 1988.
4. Centre for Women's Studies, Department of Adult and Continuing Education, University of Rajasthan, Jaipur.
5. Centre for Women's Studies, Department of Political Science, Punjab University, Chandigarh.
6. Centre for Women's Studies, Goa University, Bamboim, P.O. Santacruz, Goa.
7. Centre for Women's Studies, Gulbarga University, Jnanaganga, Gulbarga.
8. Centre for Women's Studies, Nagarjuna University, Nagarjuna Nagar.
9. Centre for Women's Studies, University of Kerala, Karyanattom, Trivandrum.
10. Centre for Women's Studies, University of Rajasthan, Jabalpur.
11. Centre for Women's Studies and Development, Banaras Hindu University, Faculty of Social Sciences, B.H.U. Varanasi.
12. Department of Human Development and Family Studies, Faculty of Home Science, M.S. University, Baroda.
13. Centre for Women's Studies, Alagappa University, Karaikudi.
14. Prakriti Centre for Women's Development, College of Home Science, Nirmala Niketan, Bombay.
15. Priyadarshini–Women Studies and Development Centre–Acharya Narendra Dev Mahapalika Mahila Mahavidyalaya, Harsh Nagar, Kanpur.

16. Research Centre for Women's Studies (RCWS) Shrimati Nathibhai Damodar Thackersay Women's University (SNDT), Juhu Road, Bombay.
17. Women's Department Studies and Research Centre, Rani Durgavati Vishwa Vidyalaya, Jabalpur.
18. Women's Studies and Development Centre, Chatra Marg, University of Delhi.
19. Women's Studies Centre, Department of Sociology, University of Pune.
20. Women's Studies Centre, Karnataka University, Dharwad.
21. Women's Studies Research Centre, Berhampur University, Berhampur.
22. Women's Studies Centre, Ranchi University.
23. Women's Studies Centre, St. Christopher's College of Education, Madras.
24. Women's Studies Research Centre, Centre for Adult, Continuing Education and Extension, Kurukshetra University, Kurukshetra.
25. Women's Studies Research Centre, Darbanga Building, Calcutta University.
26. Women's Studies Research Centre, Education Department, Guwahati University.

Women's Studies Cell

1. Women's Cell, Fathima College, Madurai.
2. Women's Cell, H.C. Home Science College, Ambikapur.
3. Women's Studies Cell, BNKB (PG) College, Akbarpur, Faizabad.
4. Women's Studies Cell, College for Women, Trivandrum.
5. Women's Studies Cell, Department of Sociology, University of Jodhpur.
6. Women's Studies Cell, Kanaria Mahila Vidyalaya, Jaipur.

List of Women's Studies Centres and Cells

Women's Studies Centres

1. Research Centre for Women's Studies–Osmania University of Hyderabad, Registered in 1985.
2. Centre for Women's Development and extension programme, Mawabagh Women's College, Jabalpur. Registered in 1988.
3. Women's Studies College of Arts, Commerce and Law, Andhra University, Vishakapatnam, Registered in 1988.

4. Centre for Women's Studies, Department of Adult and Continuing Education, University of Rajasthan, Jaipur.
5. Centre for Women's Studies, Department of Political Science, Punjab University, Chandigarh.
6. Centre for Women's Studies, Goa University, Bambolim, P.O. Santacruz, Goa.
7. Centre for Women's Studies, Gulbarga University, Jnanaganga, Gulbarga.
8. Centre for Women's Studies, Nagarjuna University, Nagarjuna Nagar.
9. Centre for Women's Studies, University of Kerala, Karyanattom, Trivandrum.
10. Centre for Women's Studies, University of Rajasthan, Jabalpur.
11. Centre for Women's Studies and Development, Banaras Hindu University, Faculty of Social Sciences, B.H.U. Varanasi.
12. Department of Human Development and Family Studies, Faculty of Home Science, M.S. University, Baroda.
13. Centre for Women's Studies, Alagappa University, Karaikudi.
14. Prakriti Centre for Women's Development, College of Home Science, Nirmala Niketan, Bombay.
15. Women's Studies Cell, P.G. College of Social Work, Hyderabad.
16. Women's Studies Cell, S.D. College, Muzaffarnagar. Women's Studies Cell, School of Social Sciences, University of Hyderabad. Women's Studies Cell, Sociology Departments, Barkatullah University.

Also, gives immediate protection to distressed women, family counselling, gives free legal services to women. Training is given to women for income-generating activities.

References

Asthana Pratima, (1974). Women's Movement in India, Vikas Publication. New Delhi.

Chakrabarti, V. Women's Education in the New Millennium *Social Welfare* 47(6), Sept. 2000, 3-5

Chatterji, S.A. (1988), Indian Women's Search for Identify, Vikas Pub., New Delhi.

Desai, Neera, (1977). Women in Modern India Vora and Company, Bombay.

Ganguly, G. Critical issues on the Status of Women, 1990.

Hakshar, Nandita and Singh Anju (1986), Demystification of Law for Women Lancers Press, New Delhi.

India Government of India, Towards Equality, Report of the Committee on the Status of Women in India. Dec. 1974:20-22.

National Educational Policy - 1986 and Programme of Action. AIFUCTO Publication, 1990.

National Perspective Plan for Women - 1988-2000 A.D. Department of Women and Child Development, Ministry of Human Resource Development, Government of India, 1988.

Patel, Vibhuti Women's Participation in Policy and Decision Making Process: Need for a network.

Patni, S. (1994). Political elite-search for identity, Maknagar Publishing Ltd. Jaipur.

Pillai, J.K. Empowering women in India. University News, 28(47), Nov. 1990 : 1-5.

Shams, S. (1991) Women Law and Social Change, Ashish Publishing House. New Delhi.

Sharma, U. (1995) Women's Education in Modern India, New Delhi Commonwealth Publishers, pp. 64-69.

Sunita, K. and Sunanda, G. Review of Researches in Women's Studies Conducted in the M.S. University of Baroda (1962-1985).

Suryakumari, A. (1989). Strategies for Political Empowerment of Women. *University News*, June 5, p. 17.

Talesra, H. (1989). Higher Education among Women, National Publishing House, New Delhi.

Women Studies - In Search of Alternatives, *Social Welfare*, Vol. 43(7) October, 1996.

Women's Studies, A Current Awareness Bulletin, Dec. 1990.

Workshop on Gender Analysis in Project Planning for Policy Makers and Project Managers (9-12 Aug., 98) Puri.

Workshop on Women's Studies, *University News*, Vol. 34(45), Nov. 5-11, 2001.

10

Women and Widowhood

Rameshwari Pandya, Priti Shah

Abstract

With the death of her husband, women have to face deprivation which are severe and widespread. Widows are deprived of their universally acknowledged human rights to food, shelter, clothing and discrimination in relation to work, dignity and participation in the community life. Study was conducted in 2002 to study their problems, coping up strategies and their suggestions. 123 Hindu widows of Baroda were contacted by purposive and snowball sampling method, statistical measures like percentages, Intensity Indices, F-test (ANOVA) and t-test were used. Majority of them were above 40 years from middle SES having 2 children. They were extrovert living with their children.

Majority of the respondents had low awareness regarding government widow pension scheme. Overall coping up strategies were found to be moderate. Major suggestions given by widows were be optimistic, do not trust any one, be extrovert. Government should increase the amount of widow pension. Above all widows must save money for accidental and medical expenditures.

Introduction

In India, a married Hindu woman is most commonly blessed with the words, "Sada Suhagin Raho" meaning may you never be snatched off your wifehood. These words reflect the general attitude of society towards the widow versus the married woman, whose husband is still living. The problems of Indian Hindu Widows is not confined to Vrindavan, Mathura,

Tirupati and the other holy towns where widows have traditionally congregated. In every fourth household in India there is a widow. Only a very small minority of widows could claim to be comfortable, secure and well looked after (Sachdev, 2000). The dictionary meaning of the term widow is, "A woman whose husband is dead and she has not married again".

In India, Hindu widows have to cope up with profound changes and tackle the stormy inner debates. Conflicting pressures are put from all sides and actions are demanded in all kinds of ways. A widow has to bear much pain and humiliation as long as she lives. On the death of her husband, a widow is first shocked by the reality that she may have to face the world on her own, perhaps for the first time in her life. This is particularly the case with Indian women who have spent most of their married lives depending on their husbands for support, decisions and protection. They are therefore unprepared to face the situation on their own.

Hindu society is a patriarchal society and has patriarchal attitude to women's role and values in society. The status of women shows that Hindu society is a male dominated society and bias, discriminatory attitude and inhuman practices prevails towards women. An andocentric society followed Manu's codes and did not allow women to develop a sense of autonomy or personal freedom. In India, women are rarely educated, married early, not encouraged to take up employment and their public participation is limited. Moreover, they were neither expected nor encouraged to develop a sense of autonomy or have control over their lives. The status of Hindu women cannot be studied in isolation but has to be seen in the light of social, economic and political development of the nation.

In the Indian context, widowhood also means a loss of self-esteem, dignity, social position and rights. Widows are the unfortunate victims of nature and for centuries they have been ill-treated. India has the highest prevalence of widowhood in the world (Sachdev, 2000). With the death of her husband, women have to face deprivation which are severe and widespread. It is a tradition with Indian culture to accept them as dependent because of poor economic status, lack of social support, poor health and low education. Widows are deprived of their universally acknowledged human rights to food, shelter, clothing and discrimination in relation to work, dignity and participation in the community life. From all over the developing world there are evidences that millions of Hindu widows and their children live in conditions of acute insecurity, deprivation and even violence. This is a matter of great regret and disappointment.

Those left behind by the dead die a thousand deaths. Nothing could be closer to this truth for the widows and their families. Widowhood is a critical and a very hard period in a woman's life. Widowhood brings sudden and unhappy change in the life of a woman. What ruins the enjoyment of widow life? Is not the use of capacity still retained, but the hankering after a capacity already lost. (Srivastava, 1989). Death of a husband means not merely a loss of financial and emotional support but creates a big void in a woman's life. The problems of widowhood are manifold.

Psychological Problems

Each decade of human life span has its own emotional problems and the moments of uncertainty. Widowhood brings in its fold, a number of problems for the widow, and she lives a life of isolation, dependency, anxiety, depression and mental morbidity which are some of the pscycho-social problems associated with widowhood. Emotionally she suffers the most and she has to make many compromises with her life. A large number of widows feel anxious about their future.

The Hindu widows are pitied or shoved aside because of the structure of society which makes them feel more useless and insecure. It is a trap of a piece of bad luck for which they are unprepared, feel uncertain, sensitive and self-conscious.

Widowhood implies a shift in position from that of secured to an unsecured woman. Widowhood compels the woman to reassess her own worth and ability in the light of changed position. The self-evaluation of new position and roles depend not only on her own characteristics like age, educational level, economic status, nature of obligations, family support, but also on the evaluation of others including her in-laws, neighbours, peers and others. As a widow she feels insecure, isolated, depressed and has an unwanted feeling. She also faces difficulty in dealing with day to day activities. In such a situation, widows expect help from the group of people around her, which may be her parents, in-laws, children, friends and relatives with whom she can share her views and feelings, who will listen to her patiently and try to understand her.

For the widow the death of husband means the loss of love and security, increase in household work especially in the handling of children and redistribution of household work especially home-related responsibilities. It takes a long time and lot of courage for a widow to pick up the threads of her life, to get over the loneliness, emptiness and to start living a normal life.

Social Problems

India is a land of diverse geography and culture–its natural that social problems will also be diverse. A sensitive person can experience the different anomalies that beset ones local environment. Women suffer a lot due to this heterogeneous nature of the Indian society with its structure based on social and economic inequalities. These inequalities are inherent in the traditional Indian social structure.

In the traditional Hindu culture, a woman's life had meaning only in relation to other men such as husband or son. In childhood, a female must be subjected to her father, in youth to her husband, when her lord is dead to her sons : a woman must never be independent.

In a traditional society like ours, a woman derives her social status from her husband. Thus, there is a drastic change in a woman's life after the death of her husband. Widowhood not only disrupts her social environment but also brings change in her life style and it affects her dress, food, makeup, participation in various social and religious functions. She feels out of place in her in-law's as well as parent's house. Added to this she is not trained or accustomed from the beginning to lead an independent life. In fact widowhood pervades almost all the spheres of widow's life. She has to shun all ostentation in life. They remain subjugated and their self-esteem gets injured. Widowhood brings in its fold number of socio-economic problems not only for the widows but also for the young children and other dependents in the family. Rasundari Debi (2001), correctly expressed her feelings for a widow by saying–

"Why was I born a member of the female sex? Would I had been a boy, I would not have to be married by other's choice, I would have flown like a bird, What am I to do now! I am a widow, a caged bird."

Widowhood may be perceived as a new position involving major changes in a woman's role, both in the family and society. They are expected to confirm to an enormous burden of restrictive customs like:

- Wearing white sarees
- Foregoing all decorations and cosmetics
- Foregoing pickle, spices and eating only bland food
- Never singing and dancing
- Remaining in seclusion and avoiding social gathering such as weddings, puja, etc.
- Never looking at any man outside the immediate family.

And if a Hindu widow is caught not following any of these customs, she is criticised. Punishment ranges from psychological abuse, fines, social boycotts, disinheritance, ex-communication and even death. Widows have deleterious effects not only because of the sudden loss of the spouse but also because the community feels obliged to feel sorry for them which arouses an unconscious hostility. Socio-economic conditions aggravate this social problem.

Financial Problems

In India husbands are the main bread winner, therefore, their death brings in fold a number of socio-economic problems, not only for the widow but for the young children and other dependents in the family also. The sudden demise of husband reduces the family income drastically and puts the whole family into financial bankruptcy.

The problem of financial stringency gets more aggravated where the late husband leaves no savings or assets. In such circumstances, the family looks forward to financial help from parents, in-laws, relatives, friends, etc. The widows generally gets such help for the mourning period which varies normally from 6 months to 1 year. The widow has no alternative but to become self dependent but this becomes difficult for those who have little or no education or vocational training before widowhood.

A widow is called apathetic if she stays at home and does not earn for supporting her family. On the other hand she is also blamed if she goes to work. A widow in either case is suspected of infidelity and cursed for indulging in immoral acts. But still a widow has to continue with her job until her children mature or she gets regular support from somewhere else. The death of a husband becomes catastrophic for widows in economic terms, living arrangements and access to property.

Giri (1999), former chairperson of the "National Commission for Women" reported.

"Majority of rehabilitation measures are working out unsuccessfully for war widows. Economic needs have increased, moral attitudes have changed and future is even more difficult".

Widows have few options for their source of income :

1. *Business* : Widows normally cannot take part in it, as in majority of the cases, husbands do not discuss the business with wives. So after the husband's death they feel lost.
2. *Property* : In-laws do not like to give the property rights to the widows if she is issueless, as they fear that if she remarries the property will unnecessarily go to the other family.

3. *Handling of finance* : Like going to banks and dealing with financial matters becomes difficult for widows as in majority of Indian homes, money is handled only by the males who are the sole bread earners and after his death, widows find it difficult to take control of the financial matters and faces multiple problems.

Singh (1986), conducted a study on widows their age varying between 25-70 years. In all 140 respondents were selected from Ludhiana city. The findings revealed that 85 per cent of the widows faced a variety of financial problems. They were unable to fulfill their children's basic needs like clothing, food and school fees. Other financial strains were– pay back loans taken by husband, purchase of luxurious items, provision of dowry for daughters and children's marriages. Above all the major problem experienced was to fulfill their routine requirements. Main areas from where the respondents tried to cut down were social and recreational activities, clothing and food.

Singh, Singh, and Sharma (1987), interviewed 100 widowed women of Kidhall Pahladpur of Sonepat district in Haryana State in the year 1984-85. Purposive Sampling technique was used for selecting sample. The study revealed lack of involvement in family decisions and functions. This was due to unrespectable behaviour of married son(s) and daughter(s)-in-law and increasing dominance of daughter(s)-in-law in household affairs. These were the major social problems experienced by the respondents.

Joni (1988), conducted a study in suburban area of Calicut District in Kerala. The respondents were below 30 years (youth) and above 60 years (old). The main aim of the study was to find correlation between age and adjustments. And it was found that respondents who lost his/her spouse were the worst sufferers of loneliness and agony. They had nobody who could understand their misery. Further, it was revealed that those living in joint families did not have a feeling of being neglected. Also those who had more number of friends and visited them were better in adjustment than those who had no friends. Better adjusted men had positive self-concept in comparison to a widow.

Shah (1989), conducted a study with 150 respondents where 50 widows, 50 widowers and from couple group–25 women and 25 men were selected from Bhavnagar District of Gujarat State. It was found that in less than 1/4th families, respondents were taking decisions and in more than half of the families, sons were taking decisions. Majority of the widowers were consulted in all types of decision and marriage, whereas majority of the widows were consulted in their own matters. On the whole, respondents were consulted in decision related to marriage, religion and other such social association. They were not much consulted in economic decisions. Further findings regarding, "Time use pattern" revealed that respondents on an average spent seven hours in sleep and one-half to two hours in rest. Grossing and praying were the activities done by majority of the respondents. Also playing cards was their favourite time pass. Very few read books during leisure time and time spent on personal care was 4 hours.

Lemonas (1990), examined the relationship between old age; security and child bearing patterns among 30 widows in a rural Indian village between 1975-1987. It was expected that women, because they were less likely to remarry, have an inheritance, or earn sufficient wages, would value offsprings as means of support in old age. Analysis of Indian inheritance law and data from case studies showed that sons were important regardless of their economic support value. Sons provided certain nurturing function, assume religious obligation on the mother's death and carry on the family name widows who lived with daughters or other relatives were less happy than those who lived with sons, widows who lived with sons and received visits from daughters were the happiest.

Chen and Dreze (1992), conducted a study on 262 widows in 8 different villages of North India found that :

- There is low mortality risk among widows staying in families headed by adult sons (40 per cent) and when staying with adult sons in family headed by others (10 per cent).
- There is high mortality risk among women living in households that are headed by others (13 per cent) and among women living alone (12 per cent).

Further, it revealed that position of widows is strongly influenced by practices that govern gender relation as a whole in North Indian society. It is important not to discriminate widows from women in general because of their specific situation. Instead a pervasive link must be generated between widows and women in general. Women in North India are alienated from her parental home after marriage. It leads to vulnerable situation for widows as she does not get social support even from husband's family. This is all because of patrilineal norms particularly pronounced in the case of widows. As a result widow is deprived of living a comfortable and happy life.

Mohit (1994), conducted a socio-psycho active study of widows in Ambala Division of Haryana State. Survival was their biggest problem without any adequate means of income. Their first priority was to feed the family and then look after the other needs and requirements.

Accommodation was another problem mentioned by nine per cent and ten per cent of urban and industrial respondents respectively. Too much of work beyond their management capacity was also one of the problems faced by (8 per cent) rural and (17.65 per cent) industrial widows. The major findings of the study was :

- Rural young widows faced change in the dressing pattern.
- Rural widows usually live with son(s) instead of living with in-laws.
- Young widows experienced more lowering in their status compared to old widows.
- Life seemed to be burden for widows because of social customs.
- Encouragement for widow remarriage was reported in very few cases.

Sarah (2000), conducted a research on widowhood in India. A total of 69 widows were selected from Magaldihi village, West Bengal. Debate was on widow remarriage, the perceived dangers of widow sexuality, a young widows anomalous childlessness which largely concerned the social and economic issues surrounding young widows. For the many women widowed in late life, the social expectations and dilemmas faced were significantly different. The differences were considered on the basis of gender, sexuality and age of Hindu widows, who have not remarried.

After the extensive perusal on related literatures, it was found that the research, which was undertaken, proved to be of immense value in the execution of the present investigation. It was revealed that studies were conducted in different parts of India as well as abroad. Most of the studies used Interview schedule and Questionnaire as the methods of data collection.

It was found that, very few indepth studies were conducted to find the problems and difficulties which widows faced. Thus, from the various studies, it could be conducted that, widowhood is inevitable, because in majority of the countries, widows outnumber widowers not only because women tend to outlive men even in the poorest countries, but because women usually marry men who are older than themselves. The status of widows are very stigmatized and they have had enough of bureaucracy. When widowhood occurs, there is a complete withdrawal from productive activities and means of carrying social role disappears. Moreover, she is treated as an isolated person and is unable to perform her former role. Widows begin to find a different evaluation of herself in the minds of others. She no longer finds respect in the eyes of people around her. The looking glass composed of her former group, throws back a changed image. Her old image which was part and parcel of her, is no longer dependent upon her current reflections that she sees of herself, in the words and gestures of others. Her self image is in conflict with the reflection. She finds change in the attitude and actions of others.

Some of the studies have found that, the widows who lost their spouse were the worst sufferers of loneliness and agony. Their present situation was distasteful and unrewarding for widows. They had nobody who could understand their misery and they were unable to anticipate the partner's death which led to higher level of emotional loneliness. They also experienced mental stress, which affected their relationships with children and family members. Concomitant role exit of widows exacerbates the feelings of alienation and isolation among many of them.

Studies have all suggested that, society views widows to be inauspicious and stigmatized as a woman who has failed to safeguard her husband's life. She is expected to manifest inconsolable grief for the rest of her life. Social problems included social customs and change in dressing pattern. Factors that affected coping with husband's death included widow's personality, religious belief, marital relationship and cause of husband's death has been highlighted by many researchers and found that, widows interacted more with widow friends than married ones.

It could also be concluded that widows faced variety of financial problems like fulfilling basic needs of children, dues left back by husband and children's marriage. Widows have tried to find new perspectives that would incorporate loss and provide them with a new meaningful direction in life. Recommendations have been provided for the future development in social services, social work practices, social welfare, civic education and research related to life of widows.

A Study was Conducted in Baroda City in 2002 with the following Justification

Few problems in contemporary society are receiving lot of attention and care, like many people are concerned about issues of child labour, problems of adolescent and old age. But not many people have expressed their concern about the status of Hindu widows in India. The basic aim of the society should be to work with people in order to find out their needs and interest and plan programmes according to them. It helps the people in becoming self-reliant and thereby, raising their standard of living and preparing them for a better life.

A. Women Empowerment

Majority of the Indian women are illiterate, poverty stricken to such an extent that they cannot even satisfy their basic needs of food, clothing and shelter. Thus Empowerment of Women is receiving due attention. The year 2001 was declared as "The Womens' Empowerment Year" to achieve all tangible results.

B. Unexplored Research Area

The present study has been undertaken as this important research area has not been explored much in the past. Intensive library search indicates that, literature are available on different women related issues, books on crime against women, reproductive health, problems related to marriage and violence against women, but there is a dearth of literature on widowhood. Hence, it is essential to study the problems of widows and how the lives of widows can be uplifted.

C. Challenge for Policy Makers, Social Workers and Administrators

This issues has posed a challenge to policy makers, social workers and administrators, particularly because so far in India, no comprehensive schemes have been developed for Hindu widows. So more and more such studies are required to formulate measures for the welfare of widows by suggesting remedies to widow's problems.

D. Home Science Extension and Communication

This department focuses on the projects and activities thus contributing in raising the status of women in society. Department of Extension and Communication has introduced courses related to women's issues in its curriculum like :

1. At B.Sc. level course on "Women in Changing India" and at M.Sc. level course on "Women and Development".
2. Various projects are taken up for improving the condition of women in society like income generation projects which includes candle making, literacy programme through adult education and legal awareness projects for womens' rights. Researches have been conducted on issues like dual role of women, decision regarding family planning, role of media in improving the life style of women and many more.

Therefore, the investigator was interested in studying the problems of Hindu widows and to obtain suggestions for improving their lives.

Major Objectives of the Study, was

1. To study the problems of Hindu widows.

Specific Objectives of the Study, were

1. To study the overall differences in the problems reported by widows according to the following aspects :

(a) Psychological
(b) Social
(c) Financial

2. To study the coping up strategies followed by widows according to the following aspects :
   (a) Psychological problems
   (b) Social problems
   (c) Financial problems

Methodology

Selection of the Sample

The sample for the study comprised of 125 Hindu widows residing in Vadodara during the year 2001–2002.

Construction of the Tool

An interview-cum-structured questionnaire schedule was constructed to collect the data from the respondents. The final questionnaire was divided into 3 sections as follows :

	Sections	*Aspects*	*Response System*
I	Background Information	• Age • *Socio-economic status	Checklist
		• Employment Status	2 point scale
		• *Personality Dimension	2 point scale
		• Number of children	Open ended
II	• Problems	• Psychological • Social • Financial	3 point scale
III	• Coping up strategies	• Psychological problems • Social problems • Financial problems	2 point scale

*For socio-economic status, K.G. Desai's standardized scale (Adapted).

*For Personality Dimension, V.S. Shantamani and A. Hafeez's standardized scale.

Collection of the Data

The investigator started data collection in the months of December–January, 2001–2002. The investigator, personally interviewed all the Hindu widows and before starting the interview, rapport was established with them. The total time taken to fill a questionnaire with each widow was approximately 60 to 90 minutes.

Scoring Plan and Categorization

Scoring of the Data

Each item of the study was given scores as follows:

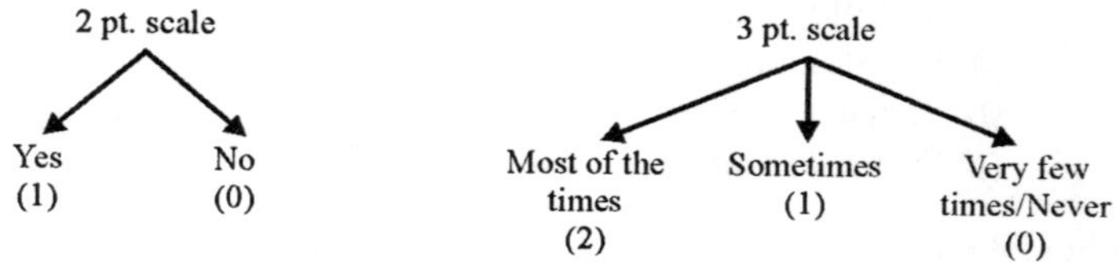

Scoring of the Data for Statistical Analysis

Section	*Response System*		*Weightage*
Section II			
• Problems	3 point scale	Most of the times	2
		Sometimes	1
		Very few times/ Never	0
• Coping up strategies	2 point scale	Yes	1
		No	0

Intensity indices were calculated to find out the overall and itemwise problems reported by widows and coping up strategies.

Response System	*Range of Score*
Most of the times	1.60 to 2.00
Some times	0.60 to 1.59
Very few times never	0.00 to 0.59

Categorization of the Variables

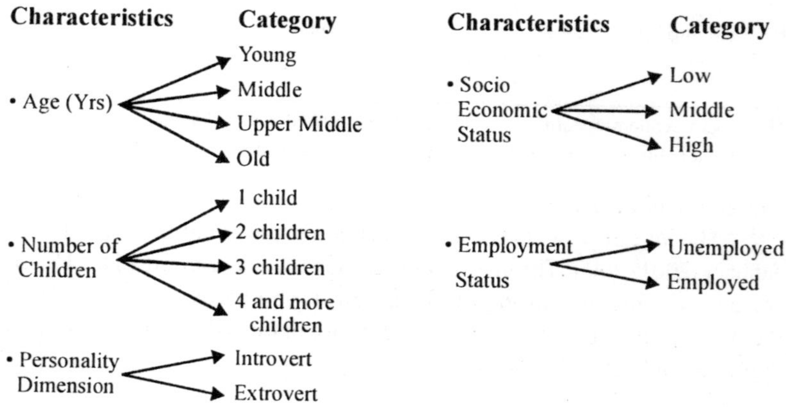

PLAN FOR STATISTICAL ANALYSIS OF THE DATA

Different Statistical Measures Used for the Analysis of the Data

Purpose	*Statistical Measures*
• Background information of the respondents	Percentages
• Overall differences in the problems reported by widows	Percentages Intensity Indices
• Overall coping up strategies followed by the widows	Intensity Indices

Background Information of the Widows

Table 1 : Percentage Distribution of the Respondents Showing their Background Information

N = 125

Sr. No.	*Variables*	*Frequency*	*Percentage*
A.	Age group :		
	(i) < 34 years	13	10.4
	(ii) 35–44 years	32	25.6
	(iii) 45–54 years	38	30.4
	(iv) ≥ 55 years	42	33.6
B.	Socio-economic Status		
	(i) Low	50	40.0
	(ii) Middle	50	40.0
	(iii) High	25	20.0
C.	Number of children		
	(i) 1 child	18	14.4
	(ii) 2 children	48	38.4
	(iii) 3 children	29	23.2
	(iv) 4 and above	30	24.0
D.	Employment Status		
	(v) Employed	72	57.6
	(vi) Unemployed	53	42.4
E.	Personality Dimension		
	(vii) Introvert	18	14.4
	(viii) Extrovert	107	85.6

Table reveals, that 33.6 per cent of the respondents belonged to the age group of 55 years and above, 30.4 per cent of the respondents belonged to the age group of 45-54 years, whereas very few (10.4 per cent) of the respondents were in the age group of below 35 years. Further, it was seen that equal number (40 per cent) of the respondents belonged to both low and middle socio-economic status, whereas only 20 per cent of the respondents belonged to the high socio-economic status.

The table also indicates that 38.4 per cent of the respondents had 2 children, whereas 24 per cent of the respondents had 4 and more children. Further, it was found that 23.2 per cent of the respondents had 3 children and in comparison 14.4 per cent of the respondents had only 1 child. It is further seen that little more than half (57.6 per cent) of the respondents belonged to the employed group, whereas 42.4 per cent of the respondents were not gainfully employed. Table also indicates that majority (85.6 per cent) of the respondents were found to be extrovert in comparison to only 14.4 per cent who were introverts.

Problems

Table 2 : Percentage Distribution of the Respondents According to the Overall Differences in Problems Reported by Widows

	Percentage (%)			
Problems	*Low*	*Moderate*	*High*	*I.I.*
Psychological	23.2	49.6	27.2	1.56
Social	54.4	34.4	11.2	1.02
Financial	57.6	35.2	7.2	0.62

The Table 2 reveals differences in problems according to intensity indices that majority of the respondents reported psychological problems as their major problem, followed by social problems and least was the financial problems.

It is worse in India, because of the sex segregated character of society, the conditions of poverty and the traditional value system. Widows are the most vulnerable section of the society and their position become more precarious because of the set boundaries.

Thus, it can be seen that widows lives are always surrounded with problems and some or the other worries. All the problems and botherations in a way are interrelated to each other. But still the trend and the data indicates that widows have more psychological problems, than social problems and followed by financial problems.

Problems Reported by Widows, which Shows Significant Differences According to Variables :

A. Psychological Problems

Table reveals that ANOVA test showed significant differences with socio-economic status. So to get more of indepth differences, t-test was applied to find out which categories–low, middle or high socio-economic status showed significant differences with psychological problems. The detailed data is shown in Table 3.

Summary of ANOVA Showing Differences in Psychological Problems Reported by Widows According to Socio-economic Status

N=125

Source	*Df*	*Sum of squares*	*Mean squares*	*F-Cal.*	*F-Prob.*	
Between group	3	852.91	426.45	3.23	0.04	S*
Within group	122	16081.46	131.81			
Total	124	16934.37				

*Significant at 0.05 level with df = 3, F-tab = 3.07

Table 3 : t-values Showing Differences in Psychological Problems Reported by Widows according to Socio Economic Status

N=125

SES	*X*	*SD*	*Low*	*Middle*	*High*
Low	48.78	13.21		2.19*	1.87 NS
Middle	43.56	10.46			0.13 NS
High	43.24	9.48			

*Significant at 0.05 level with df = 98, F-tab = 1.98.

When data were analyzed to test null hypothesis that there will be no significant difference in psychological problems faced by widows according to he socio-economic status, the data reveals as per the Table 5, that the t-Cal. value of 2.19 when compared to t-tab value was found to be significant at 0.05 level of confidence with df=98. This indicates that a significant difference existed in psychological problems faced by widows according to socio-economic status. Table revealed that low socio-economic status respondents faced more psychological problems in comparison to middle socio-economic status respondents. Hence the null hypothesis was not accepted.

Socio-economic status of the respondent plays an important role in increasing or decreasing their psychological problems. Most of the time, low socio-economic status respondent were occupied with activities, which included interaction with many people and satisfying the basic needs of her family members and in this routine had no time for herself. This held true with the Middle class respondents also as they faced psychological stress. But in contrast, the respondents with higher socio-economic status, lived a luxurious life and spent their time in parties, clubs involving in recreational activities. They did not have to worry about financial adjustments and thus comparatively needed to make less compromises. They had sufficient time and money to spend in the activities of their interests.

Thus, in the light of the above findings it was found that psychological problems faced by widows varied according to socio-economic status.

Summary of ANOVA Showing Differences in Psychological Problems Reported by Widows According to Personality Dimension

N = 125

Source	*Df*	*Sum of squares*	*Mean squares*	*F-Cal.*	*F-Prob.*	
Between group	1	1354.93	1354.93	10.69	0.00	S*
Within group	123	15579.44	126.66			
Total	124	16934.37				

*Significant at 0.05 level with df = 1, F-tab = 3.92.

Table, indicates that personality dimension showed significant differences with respect to the psychological problems. Thus, to study in greater depth, t-test was applied to know which category extrovert or introvert showed significant difference with psychological problems. The detailed data is shown in table that follows.

Table 4 : t-value Showing Differences in Psychological Problems Reported by Widows According to Personality Dimension

N= 125

Personality Dimension	*X*	*SD*	*Introvert*	*Extrovert*
Introvert	53.61	11.97		3.27*
Extrovert	44.23	11.13		

*Significant at 0.05 level with df = 123, F-tab = 1.98.

When data were analyzed to test null hypothesis that there will be no significant difference in psychological problems faced by widows according to personality dimension, the data reveals as per the table, that the t-Cal. value of 3.27 when compared to t-tab value was found to be significant at 0.05 level of confidence with df=123. This indicates that a significant difference existed in the psychological problems faced by widows according to personality dimension. Table 4 revealed that introverts faced more psychological problems than extroverts. Hence the null hypothesis was not accepted.

When extrovert and introvert personalities are compared, there is more chance of an extrovert widow readjusting and resettling in her life quickly. This is because an extrovert knows how to let out her emotions and feelings through words and actions. Her motto in life is to remain happy in all circumstances and she can adjust easily with people from all age groups and tries to forget her sorrows. On the contrary, an introvert widow never expresses her feelings and emotions and therefore, others are not aware of her likes and dislikes. She lives in her own world and never participates in any social activities be it discussion, debate or social functions.

Therefore, personality of an individual respondent motivates them to behave and adjust accordingly.

B. Social Problems

Summary of ANOVA Showing Differences in Social Problems Reported by Widows According to Age

N = 125

Source	*Df*	*Sum of squares*	*Mean squares*	*F-Cal.*	*F-Prob.*	
Between group	3	3534.63	1178.21	19.92	0.00	S*
Within group	121	7157.49	59.15			
Total	124	10692.13				

*Significant at 0.05 level with df = 3, F-tab = 2.68.

From table, it is seen that age showed significant differences with social problems. To study in greater detail, the t-test was applied to analyze which category of young, middle, upper middle or old showed significant differences with social problems. The detailed data is shown in table that follows.

Table 5 : t-values Showing Differences in Social Problems Reported by Widows According to Age

N= 125

Age	*X*	*SD*	*Young*	*Middle*	*Upper Middle*	*Old*
Young	29.53	10.10		2.32*	5.91*	7.03*
Middle	22.15	9.48			3.58*	4.89*
Upper Middle	15.31	6.41				1.51^{NS}
Old	1316	6.29				

*Significant at 0.05 level with df=43, t-tab=2.02, with df=49, t-tab=2.01, with df=53, t-tab=2.01, with df=68, t-tab=2.00, with df=72, t-tab=2.00

When data were analyzed to test the null hypothesis that there will be no significant difference in the social problems according to age, the data reveals as per the table, that the t–Cal.values when compared to the t-tab value were found to be significant at 0.05 level of confidence. This indicates that significant difference existed in the social problems faced by widows according to age. The Table 5 revealed that young and middle age group respondents faced more social problems than upper middle and old age group respondents. Hence the null hypothesis was not accepted.

There seems to be a metamorphosis in widows life from their previous way of life. The death of the partner, the movement and mobility of families, reduced income and growing social distance in relationship with other generations appear to confirm widowhood as a period of loss and abandonment. Many of the social problems which widows face are mostly due to the restricted opportunities which widows get. Widows turn to self-contemplation, retrospection and concern over the meaning of life. Thus, a widow who has lost her spouse and friends develop new ways for providing for such basic needs as self-expression, recognition and emotional security but it varies according to different age group.

Table 6 : Summary of ANOVA Showing Differences in Social Problems Reported by Widows According to Employment Status

N= 125

Source	*Df*	*Sum of squares*	*Mean squares*	*F-Cal.*	*F-Prob.*	
Between group	1	1129.26	1129.26	14.53	0.00	S*
Within group	123	9562.87	77.75			
Total	124	10692.13				

*Significant at 0.05 level with df = 2, F-tab = 3.92.

If a respondent is young, she faces more of criticism, humiliation, and misbehaviour in comparison to respondents who are of older age, as they get more respect, care and are well adjusted to situations with time. Thus, the social problems of widows vary according to their age.

Table 6, reveals that employment status shows significant differences with social problems. Data was further analyzed through t-test, to find out which category–employed or unemployed showed significant differences with the social problems faced by widows. The detailed data is shown in table that follows.

Table 7 : t-value Showing Differences in Social Problems Reported by Widows According to Employment Status

N= 125

Employment Status	*X*	*SD*	*Employed*	*Unemployed*
Employed	20.40	9.32		3.81*
Unemployed	14.32	8.08		

*Significant at 0.05 level with df=123, t-tab=1.98.

When data were further analyzed to test null hypothesis that there will be no significant difference in social problems faced by widows according to the Employment Status, the data reveals as per the Table 7 that the t-Cal. value of 3.81 when compared to t-tab value was found to be significant at 0.05 level of confidence with df=123. This indicates that a significant difference existed in the social problems faced by widows according to employment status of the respondent. Table revealed that respondents who were employed faced more social problems than respondents who were unemployed. Hence the null hypothesis was not accepted.

Employment status to some extent changes a woman from her submissive behaviour to assertive behaviour with a broader perspective in life. If a respondent is employed then family income increases which raises the standard of living in areas of food, clothing, education, entertainment and facilities of modern amenities at home. But at the same time, employment of women increases her physical labour as she has to manage two fronts, the home and her job. On the other hand not gainfully employed lady has less sources of income as she is dependent on others for her survival. Compared to employed respondent, she lives more of isolated life and period of forced mourning is quite prolonged for them. She as such contributes in different household activities, but it remains unaccounted in economic terms.

Thus, it was found that employment status made difference in the social problems faced by widows.

C. Financial Problems

Table 8: Summary of ANOVA Showing Differences in Financial Problems Reported by Widows According to Age

N = 125

Source	*Df*	*Sum of squares*	*Mean squares*	*F-Cal.*	*F-Prob.*	
Between group	3	2582.07	860.69	16.35	0.00	S*
Within group	121	6370.19	52.65			
Total	124	8952.27				

*Significant at 0.05 level with df = 3, F-tab = 2.68.

Table 8 reveals that age shows significant differences with financial problems. Data was further analyzed through t-test to find out which category–young, middle, upper middle or old showed significant differences with the financial problems faced by widows. The detailed data is shown in table as follows.

Table 9 : t-values Showing Differences in Financial Problems Reported by Widows According to Age

N = 125

Age	*X*	*SD*	*Young*	*Middle*	*Upper Middle*	*Old*
Young	21.38	11.96		1.59 NS	4.31*	5.82*
Middle	16.43	8.33			3.51*	5.42*
Upper Middle	10.36	6.12				1.96NS
Old	7.88	5.20				

*Significant at 0.05 level with df =49, t-tab=2.01, with df=53, t-tab=2.01 with df=68, t-tab=2.00, with df=72, t-tab=2.00.

When data were analyzed to test null hypothesis that there will be no significant difference in financial problems faced by widows according to age, data reveals as per the Table 11, that the t-Cal.values when compared to t-tab values were found to be significant at 0.05 level of confidence. This indicates that a significant difference existed in financial problems faced by widows according to age. The table revealed that young and middle age group respondents faced more financial problems than upper middle and old age group respondents. Hence the null hypothesis was not accepted.

At all stages of life, widows have to face financial problems in some or the other form. The financial situation of widows irrespective of their age group is far from satisfactory. Most of them do not have much of savings. On the other hand, they continue to have financial liabilities such as completing education of their children, arranging marriages of their daughters and so on. Inflation has made their financial condition even more miserable. The financial problem of widows belonging to upper middle and old age is comparatively less, as they have already accomplished their goals and finished all their major responsibilities. But at times, they too face financial problems as grown up children prefer to stay away from them. Many widows seem to squander the provident fund amount and experience serious difficulties in their later life. Some of them invest their money in dubious schemes and lose everything. A few do not know where to invest and get regular income out of it. So overall according to the data, we see that widows of all age groups experience financial problems, but the frequency of problems varies according to the age group.

Thus, according to the age group of the respondents, the financial problems varies.

Table 10 : Summary of ANOVA Showing Differences in Financial Problems Reported by Widows According to Employment Status

N=125

Source	*df*	*Sum of squares*	*Mean squares*	*F-Cal.*	*F-Prob.*	
Between group	1	450.68	450.68	6.52	0.01	S*
Within group	123	8501.59	69.12			
Total	124	8952.27				

*Significant at 0.05 level with df = 3, F-tab = 3.92.

Table 10, reveals that employment status showed significant differences with financial problems. It was further analyzed through t-test, that widows being employed or unemployed showed significant differences with the financial problems faced by widows. The detailed data is shown in table that follows.

Table 11 : t-values Showing Differences in Financial Problems Reported by Widows According to Employment Status

N=125

Employment Status	*X*	*SD*	*Employed*	*Unemployed*
Employed	13.86	8.01		2:55*
Unemployed	10.01	8.70		

*Significant at 0.05 level with df = 123, t-tab = 1.98.

When data were analyzed to test null hypothesis that there will be no significant difference in financial problems faced by widows according to employment status, the data reveals as per the table, that the t-Cal. value of 2.55 when compared to t-tab value was found to be significant at 0.05 level of confidence with df=123. This indicates that a significant difference existed in financial problems faced by widows according to employment status. Table revealed that respondents who were employed faced more financial problems than respondents who were unemployed. Hence the null hypothesis was not accepted.

This could be due to the fact that an employed widows can well plan for the future and can even have savings as they had a definite source of income. The main sources of income for the respondent whether employed or not gainfully employed could be family pension, financial support from children or other family members.

Thus, if a respondent is employed, then she is more aware of her rights when compared to the respondent who is not gainfully employed. Most of the time, widows preferred to be engaged in some or the other economic work so that they were not dependent on others. Widows opted for hardship and pain and even took up small jobs with less salary. It is a known fact, that the more you are financially dependent, the more you are suppressed by the society which includes the family members. Earning even a small income increases the status of widows not only in family but also in society and they were consulted in decision making and were given the right to participate and share their views in family matters. If a widow is not gainfully employed, not only herself, but even her children has to face humiliation, ill-treatment and abuse. Thus, employment status solved many problems. Hence, according to employment status the financial problems of respondent varies.

Coping Up Strategies followed by Widows

Table 12 : Itemwise Distribution of the Respondents According to the Coping up Strategies Related to Psychological Problems Followed by Widows

N = 125

Sr. No.	*Items*	*I.I*
1.	Close contacts with following	
	(a) Children	1.84
	(b) Parents	1.00
	(c) In-laws	0.78
	(d) Brother	0.53
	(e) Relatives (other than in-laws)	0.52
	(f) Sister	0.49
2.	Confide in the following persons	
	(a) Children	1.66
	(b) Friends	0.70
	(c) Parents	0.65
	(d) In-laws	0.42
	(e) Colleagues	0.36
	(f) Relatives (other than in-laws)	0.30
	(g) Ex-colleagues	0.08
3.	Persons in whom you confide and they help you when you have a problem	1.62

It is seen from the Table 12, that most of the time, respondents had close contacts with children and respondents confided in them only if they had a problem. Further, it was observed that sometimes respondents had contacts with parents, in-laws and they confided in her parents and friends for sharing their feelings. Table also reveals that widows had close contacts with their brothers, relatives, sisters and they confided in their in-laws, colleagues, relatives, ex-colleagues, but this happened very few times only.

Effect of widowhood differs from individual to individual due to different socio-economic background, education and living pattern. Those living with their near and dear ones are better adjusted and happier than those living alone. The self-determination of the widows gave them an extra courage to fight against obstacles. They began with doing their choice of work and started living life as they wanted to as it would provide them with satisfaction at all fronts. By doing this, they could become ideal role models for other widows too.

Table 13 indicates that the respondents coping up strategies were related to social problems. Sometimes respondents watched television, participated in religious activities during leisure time. Some of the respondents visited friends and relatives daily or once a month, it was mainly for change of mood, attending ceremonies, during illness or religious functions and ceremonies.

Table 13 : Itemwise Distribution according to the Coping up Strategies Related to Social Problems Followed by Widows

N = 125

Sr. No.	*Items*	*I.I.*
1.	Leisure time activities–	
	(a) Watching television	1.34
	(b) Religious activities	1.19
	(c) Shopping	0.48
	(d) Reading	0.40
	(e) Morning walks	0.39
	(f) Evening walks	0.28
	(g) Listening to radio	2.23
	(h) Playing games	0.14
	(i) Watching movies	0.11
2.	Visit friends and relatives–	
	(a) Daily	1.07
	(b) Once a month	0.67
	(c) Once a week	0.07
	(d) Twice a week	0.07
3.	Reasons for visit to friends and relatives	
	(a) Change of mood	1.38
	(b) Attending ceremonies	0.90
	(c) During illness	0.85
	(d) Religious functions	0.71
	(e) Whenever you need help	0.26
	(f) Birthdays	0.09
4.	Encouraged to participate in following–	
	(a) Discussion on current news	0.50
	(b) Various activities and competitions organised at community level	0.41
	(c) Organise functions	0.34
	(d) To take up leadership roles	0.28
5.	Associated with any welfare organizations	0.06

Respondents spent leisure time in shopping, reading, morning walks, playing games, listening to radio, watching movies and visiting friends and relatives once a month or twice a week. Very few times respondents were associated with welfare organizations or were encouraged to participate in activities, competitions, organizing functions, discuss on current news and take up leadership roles.

Widows should be encouraged to remain active, engage in social activities, get more and more involved in the society. A few hours of useful social activity will help them in getting companionship outside their homes. They will be in a better frame of mind to accommodate to their new form of life. Members of the family will also be eased of considerable stress of trying to find ways of keeping the widows occupied fruitfully and thus give them the necessary change. So, widows now have both the alternatives, whether to involve in active life or withdraw into her own shell of loneliness. They must choose from these alternatives depending on one's own inclinations.

Thus, the respondents were encouraged to regularly participate in social gatherings, functions and activities which kept them busy as well as active all the time. It acted as coping up strategy to overcome their social problems.

Table 14 : Itemwise Distribution of the Coping up Strategies Related to Financial Problems Followed by Widows

N= 125

Sr. No.	*Items*	*Intensity Indices*
1.	Take financial help at the time of money crisis from	
	(a) Family members	0.55
	(b) Sons	0.30
	(c) Friends	0.30
	(d) Savings	0.26
	(e) Relatives	0.25
	(f) Asking for credit	0.18
	(g) Daughters	0.06
2.	Assets other than liquid assets	
	(a) House	1.12
	(b) Ornaments	0.45
	(c) Land	0.30
	(d) Vehicle	0.30
	(e) Any other	0.06

Table 4, indicates that sometimes respondents asked for help from family members during financial crisis and as assets they mainly possessed house. Very few of them asked for help during financial crisis from sons, friends, relatives or used their savings or asked for credit. In the form of assets they possessed ornaments, land, vehicle or had own business.

In our patriarchal society, women right from birth are over protected. When they suddenly find themselves widowed they are completely directionless due to lack of education, proper knowledge and are unaware about the realities of life. Many of them are such, that they had never thought of becoming independent, or doing a job. Once they are widowed, financial crisis was a major problem as the bread winner was no longer with them. They are bound to take up jobs to take care of people dependent on them. At times inspite of earning, widows face financial crisis and thus they seek help from family members, sons, friends, and relatives. Thus, according to priorities widows have to plan, whether they should give importance to their children's education, their marriage or buy assets for a secure future. Thus, with lot of hardships, widows resets to the sudden new changes in their life. Thus, respondents are encouraged to plan their expenditure priority-wise, keeping in mind the amount of money an individual has. This careful and priority-wise planning strategies will lead to overcome the financial problems.

Awareness among widows regarding Government Widow Pension Scheme

Table 15 : Percentage Distribution of the Respondents According to the Awareness among Widows Regarding Government Widow Pension Scheme

Awareness of Pension scheme	*Frequency (f)*	*Percentage (%)*
Low	105	84.0
Moderate	19	15.2
High	1	0.8

Table 15, reveals that majority (84 per cent) of the respondents had low awareness regarding government widow pension schemes, whereas 15.2 per cent of the respondents had moderate awareness and respondents with high awareness were almost negligible (0.8 per cent).

Reason for low awareness regarding government widow pension scheme, could be the fact that widowhood increases with an increase in age–50 per cent in the age group of 50 years, 64 per cent in the age group of 60 years and 80 per cent in the age group of 70 years and above (Sachdev, 2000). With an increase in age, their responsibilities were less as their children got settled, and therefore they did not require financial help for their primary needs. These could be the reasons for low awareness about any scheme. This holds true for government widow pension schemes, also.

This could be mainly due to lack of publicity as schemes are not much publicized through mass media, and widows are also not much exposed to media, and therefore, are not aware of things around them for their betterment. If a widow is working, she is very busy with her dual responsibilities of home and job and thus does not have time to concentrate on other activities. Contrary to this, widowed women who are at home are less educated and therefore, ignorant about the different schemes or policies meant for them. They are totally dependent on others for emotional, social and financial support.

Widows on the whole faced psychological, social and financial problems. Widows trying to adjust with their psychological problems are unable to come out of it throughout their life, as worries always persist in their minds.

Due to various social problems that widows face, majority of them prefer not to expose themselves to the outside world and therefore, they are not able to get information about the benefits available to them. Government has set up the government widow pension scheme from several years for financial help to widows, but widows are ignorant about this scheme as government does not take the initiative of publicizing this scheme, so the beneficiaries are unaware of these scheme.

The Table 16 reveals that respondents gathered information about the government widow pension scheme from friends, government officials, family members and shared it with other friends during social gatherings.

Moreover, widows had few sources of income like salary, support from family, few assets other than liquid assets which declined the need for government widow pension scheme. Therefore, widows never tried to gather more and more awareness regarding the government widow pension scheme.

After data collection, it was found that out of total respondents, very few of them were availing of the government widow pension scheme. This was due to the rules are regulations of the State government and Social Welfare Department for financial resettlement of widows.

Table 16 : Itemwise Distribution of the Respondents According to the Awareness among Widows Regarding Government Widow Pension Scheme

N=125

Sr. No.	*Items*	*Intensity Indices*
1.	Source of information about the government widow pension scheme	
	(a) Friends	0.38
	(b) Government officials	0.36
	(c) Family members	0.05
	(d) Television	0.02
	(e) Social workers	0.02
	(f) Radio	0.01
	(g) Newspaper	0.01
2.	Discussed government widow pension scheme with friends	0.34
3.	By which means government widow pension scheme was discussed	
	(a) Interacting during social gatherings	0.33
	(b) Through letters	0.02

Such as :

- Son's age should not be more than 21 years
- Age of widow should be between 18–60 years
- Annual income of family should not be more than Rs. 3600/-
- Personal annual income should not be more than Rs. 1200/-
- Resident of Gujarat State.

Majority of the widows did not qualify in all the criteria's mentioned above and thus were unable to avail of the widow pension scheme.

Suggestions Obtained from Widows

Table 17 indicates that the respondents suggested awareness regarding government widow pension scheme by viewing television. Further, it was suggested to increase the amount of pension money by the respondents, so that widows could get better benefits.

Table further reveals that respondents felt that society should support and help them and suggested that regular interaction with friends is one of the way of improving one's life. It was also observed that Government and NGO's can also extend help to widows by associating with social groups and organizations.

The table also depicts that more of the respondents felt the need for counselling and guidance services for improving their life, whereas, majority

Table 17: Itemwise Distribution of the Respondents According to the Suggestions Obtained from Widows for Improving their General Condition

N = 125

Sr. No.	*Items*	*Intensity Indices*
1.	Ways to develop awareness :	
	(a) Television	0.88
	(b) Posters, leaflets, pamphlets, newspaper	0.54
	(c) Radio	0.08
2.	Ways of improving government widow pension scheme	
	(a) Increase the amount of money	0.87
	(b) Short procedures	0.54
	(c) Efficient administration	0.40
	(d) Regular distribution of pension amount	0.10
3.	Social participation that could change widow's life	
	(a) Regularly interacting with friends	0.79
	(b) Passing leisure time in doing hobby work	0.77
	(c) Participating in social gatherings	0.53
	(d) Accompanying family members for picnics, movies	0.27
	(e) Participating in major decision making	0.13
4.	Institutions recommended for widows	
	(a) Guidance and counselling services	0.74
	(b) Employment placement services	0.56
	(c) Recreational institutions	0.32
	(d) Special institutions	0.14
5.	Vocational training to increase their income	0.91
6.	Society's attitude should change towards widows	
	(a) Support and help them	0.82
	(b) Give equal importance to them	0.77
7.	NGO's and Government organizations can help in improving life of widows	
	(a) Associating widows with social groups, organizations	0.71
	(b) Starting widow clubs	0.61
	(c) Encouraging widow remarriages	0.49
	(d) Organising conferences and seminars	0.22
	(e) Opposing wearing of white saree	0.18
	(f) Opposing practice of shaving head	0.10
8.	Support from organizations	
	(a) Helping widows to get husband's job	0.94
	(b) Getting husband's financial assets	0.93
	(c) Understanding legal and property rights	0.30
9.	Financial actions to help widows	
	(a) Opening joint accounts	0.86
	(b) Having joint property	0.26
	(c) Proper knowledge about shares	0.22
	(d) Having joint business	0.05

of the respondents wanted to increase their income by taking vocational training. Above all, majority of the respondents wanted organizations to provide them with their husband's job, so that the total amount of monthly income and facilities provided to widows do not vary and the situation remains the same as before widowhood.

Very few widows suggested that awareness regarding the government widow pension scheme can be developed through posters, leaflets, pamphlets, newspapers, radio and suggested improvement in administrative procedures so that they do not face too many problems in attaining the benefits due to them. Moreover, they recommended regular distribution of pension amount. They wanted more recreational institutions and wanted encouragement towards remarriages and seminars organized so that they could understand their legal rights and have better knowledge about financial aspects. They also suggested social gatherings, accompanying family for picnics, movies and participating in major decisions to change and improve their life.

With time, widows wanted to improve their life. On the basis of the responses given to the open ended question, the following suggestions were given:

Psychological : Do not trust anyone. Make yourself strong and confident so that society's comments, abuse do not bother you. Self-respect is the biggest thing, so do not involve in matters, where people do not respect you. Above all, be optimistic, then everything will be easy to achieve.

Social : If by wearing coloured sarees, ornaments, sticking bindis and wearing black thread you believe that you are saved from mis-happenings and comments, then you should go ahead and do it as feelings for your husband will not decline by doing so. Widow remarriages should be encouraged and one should find one's own way of living.

Financial : Government should give facilities like jobs, free girls' education, opening training centres, low cost raw materials and other facilities to start with small business. Widows should be given husband's job or other jobs, so that she can take care of her children, and in-laws who are dependent on her. Above all, widows must save money for accidental and medical expenditures.

Conclusion and Implications

It can be concluded that widowhood is faced by millions of women in India. It was found that widows mainly faced psychological problems followed by social and financial problems. Widows mainly wanted their self-respect, where they wanted society to be more sympathetic towards them. They wanted more financial aid in helping them to become independent. As psychological problems were the most, which widows faced, special help and training should be given to widows to make them mentally strong and confident so that society's attitude do not disturb them. Also, different legal aid centres should be started to help them. More awareness among widows could be spread through the electronic and print media regarding the different schemes, policies and programmes beneficial to them. Society must support and help widows and should not discriminate them. Widows must also regularly interact with friends and participate in decision making.

The result of the present study draws the attention of social workers towards this section of society. It also creates awareness among society of their responsibilities towards this vulnerable group. The academicians can train the people to foresee and understand the reasons for the problems that widows face, and therefore solutions to the problem could be sought through better management of resources. Another purpose of the study was to highlight the awareness regarding government widow pension scheme and coping up strategies followed by widows to overcome their problems. For this, government and voluntary organizations could be approached and results got from this study could be used in preparing their future plan. All this will help collectively in improving the lives of widows.

Implications

1. Sensitization must be made among people regarding problems of Hindu widows.
2. With decline in joint family system, there should be change in traditional belief that sons have the sole responsibility in looking after their mothers. Thus, daughters must also be encouraged to look after their mothers.
3. Facility like free education for children must be encouraged for widows, to reduce their financial problems.
4. A positive attitude must be inculcated among people towards widows regarding their social and recreational needs, so that widows can actively participate in the social stream.

References

Bordavekar, K.S. Retirement and its Social Implications. Dissertation (M.Sc.), The M.S. University, Baroda, 1973.

Bothra Payal (2000). Widow : Socio Economic Aspects. Dissertation (M.Sc.) M.S. University, Baroda.

Byles Julie, E., Feldman, Susan and Mishra G. For Richer for Poorer in Sickness and in Health : Older Widowed Women's Health, Relationship and Financial Security. *Sociological Abstract*, April 2000, p. 1025.

Chen, M.A. (1998). Widows in India. Sage Publications, New Delhi. p. 450.

Chen, M.A., and Dreze, J. Widows and Health in Rural North India, *Economic and Political Weekly*, Vol. 27, October 1992, pp. 24-31.

Cherubini, C. Widows in Post Tridenate Rome. *Dissertation Abstract International* Vol. 59(10) April 1999, p. 3930A.

Dave, Tejal, Life style of Single Women. Dissertation (M.Sc.). The M.S. University, Baroda, 1998.

Jain, Ashima. Frail Elderlies and their Associated Problem. Dissertation (M.Sc.). The M.S. University, Baroda, 1997.

Joni J.C. Interaction between the old and the youth. *Journal of Social Welfare* Vol. 35(6) 1988, pp. 17-23.

Kohli, A.S. (1996), Social Situation of the Aged in India, Anmol Publications Pvt. Ltd., New Delhi.

Mishra Arti. (1989). Problems of Retirement Dissertation (M.Sc.) M.S. University, Baroda.

Mohit Sandhya (1994). Widowhood - A Socio-psychiatric Study, Mohit Publications, New Delhi.

Pollock, L. Private Women, Public Needs : Middle Class Widows in 19th Century England, Dissertation Abstract International. Vol. 56(6) Dec. 1995.

Sachdev, R. Women in white. *Human Scope*. May 2000, pp. 6-7.

Shah Dipa Problem faced by aged and their attitude towards old age. Dissertation (M.Sc.) M.S. University Baroda, 1989.

Singh, K. Problems of Widowhood, *Indian Journal of Social Work*, Vol. 7(1), 1986, p. 67.

Stronger, L.A. Lifting the Veil off Widowhood : Portraits of Transformation, Dissertation Abstract International Vol. 60(2) Aug. 1999. p. 562.

Susan, R, Single, Older Children Women : Differences between Never Married and Widowed Women in Life Satisfaction and Social Support. Journal of Gerontological Social Work Vol. 13 (3) 1989. pp. 35-47.

Tripathi, Smita. (1984). Problems of Single Elderly Parents Residing with Married Children. Dissertation (M.Sc.) M.S. University Baroda.

Wisnewski Wendy, M. The Coping Resources of Elderly Widows and their Relationship to Depression and Self Transcendence. Dissertation Abstract International Vol. 61(4) Oct. 2000.

11

Women Development and Efforts of NGO's

Anuradha Mathu, Rameshwari Pandya

Abstract

Voluntary organisations in India has always been an integral part of the cultural and social tradition. The role of NGOs in national development has been considered vital due to their direct and first hand experience and knowledge of local needs, problems and resources at the grassroots. The rationale for involvement of voluntary agencies in women's development is quite clear. Women in India suffer from multifarious constraints such as a low level of literacy, lack of access to resources and obstacles caused by the cultural and social customs and traditions that are discriminatory of women. In a situation such as this, the role of voluntary agencies in creating awareness among women of their rights, capacity to earn. Since voluntary organisations have the advantage of community involvement and help to promote voluntary action the National Commission recommends that they should be actively assisted by providing finances training and managerial inputs.

The NGOs should be encouraged to enlarge their activities to create awareness, carry out training programmes. The government should provide legislative support and removal of restrictive legislation, need to be done.

Introduction

NGOs are generally small, flexible and cost-effective organisations and they work with and very often on behalf of others. Most of them aim at building self-reliant development. They recognise that when people set their own goals, develop their own approaches and take their own decisions, human creativity and local problem solving skills are released and the resulting development is likely to be self-sustaining.

NGOs cover a wide spectrum from small loose knit local organisation to nation wide federations and international networks. Issues they tackle might be from human rights of one group to the entire mosaic of development concerns, they might focus on women's issues. Many NGOs place more emphasis on empowerment of disadvantaged or marginalized groups in society. The main purpose of a programme may be improvement in health, literacy or legal aid, but NGOs are also concerned with how much each project enhances peoples power. NGOs are collection of organizations, which are different in their origin, structure, size, programmes and ideology. To begin voluntary organization were a conglomeration of volunteer joined together with shared values of concern for a specific goal. NGOs are expected to play a critical role in all conceivable aspects of development. NGOs are expected to play a very vital role in aspects of development. Some of the important roles ascribed to NGO's are to act as:

1. Planner and implementor of developmental programmes.
2. Catalyst enabler and innovator.
3. Builder of self-reliant sustainable society.
4. Mediator of people and government.

The greatest potential of NGOs lies in their capacity to generate self-help initiative. It is this vein that NGOs are viewed as vehicles for development and more specifically as vehicles for democratic development. NGOs have the potential to be significant vehicles of empowerment because of their ability to reach the grass-roots. Empowerment can be measured by the ability of the collective action to alter conditions that it finds intolerable.

Voluntary action in India has always been an integral part of the cultural and social tradition. A variety of social services were provided by voluntary agencies prior to independence and in the first few decades of planned development in India. Traditionally, voluntary agencies undertook a wide variety of activities in the areas of social reform in the pre-independence period. Independence resulted in government policy and commitment to support and strengthen voluntary agencies. Voluntary agencies have currently opted for several alternative roles depending on their objectives, location (rural/urban and resources available).

The role of voluntary agencies in national development has been considered vital due to their direct and first hand experience and knowledge of local needs, problems and resources at the grassroots. Further the commitment and zeal of the voluntary action movement is considered effective as it is not bound by rigid bureaucratic systems and is more responsive to people. The voluntary sector is observed to operate with greater flexibility and base its activities on felt needs. There is a process of continually learning from past experiences in programme planning and implementation, etc.

The essential strength of voluntary agencies derives from the fact that they are closer to the community and people. They represent in many cases the needs and aspirations of the people. Voluntary agencies often function more effectively than the government managed agencies in areas such as motivation, problem identification and analysis, project formulation, innovative methods of service delivery and involvement of the community, due to their spirit.

The organization of women by voluntary organizations has acquired importance as the need has emerged for organizational structures to ensure women's participation in the development process. Many old established voluntary agencies have undertaken the task of setting up welfare development services for women in the country.

The increasing interest of the government in enhancing the role of voluntary agencies in the development of women is quite evident. Considering the magnitude of problems faced by women, the government has rightly felt that it cannot assume the entire responsibility of service provision and development. It has sought to associate voluntary agencies in the various programmes aimed at women. The thrust of the current programmes is more towards development of women's potential and their productive participation in development rather than merely providing welfare services to them. A meaningful partnership with the voluntary sector has thus been an avowed goal and an essential variable in government's attempts to integrate women in development.

Women and the Voluntary Sector

Voluntary agencies have contributed immensely to the new directions and impetus provided to women's programmes during the decade for women. A number of innovative features in several government formulated schemes/programmes are based on the experience of the projects run successfully by voluntary agencies.

The rationale for involvement of voluntary agencies in women's development is quite clear. Women in India suffer from multifarious constraints such as a low level of literacy, lack of access to resources and obstacles caused by the cultural and social customs and traditions that are discriminatory of women. In a situation such as this, the role of voluntary agencies in creating awareness among women of their rights and mobilizing women as well as developing in them appropriate motivation and leadership to realize those rights cannot be minimized.

Beginning in 1958 with Delhi Pilot Project financed by Ford Foundation, there has been a series of Urban Community Development Projects in India. Community Development in India could be seen as an effort to mobilize manpower and participation of village or city people for economic, political and social reconstruction activities. The ultimate of these programmes is composite national development leading to an overall process of modernization. These are the projects of local significance initiated and carried out by local people. Development is achieved by moving in stages towards modernization through mobilizing sizeable people's participation and their efforts towards improving conditions of community life and the capacity for community integration and self-direction.

Voluntary associations and community councils are structured groups in which numerous individuals work towards some common objectives. What do people actually do in their non-working hours? Dr. Saxton Graham has made such a study in Butler Country and in his findings more leisured persons are found in the upper than lower classes, but only 25% of Butlers population belong to one or more organization. Most persons are "bench sitters" spending a large portion of their leisure time watching video, television and motion pictures which are passive, non-creative and non-commercially organized activities. More urban than rural folk engage in recreational and religious activities, which are most likely to produce warm and personal relationships and enriching experiences.

The literature suggests that the rapid growth of urban areas in developing nations is accompanied by social disorganization and that individuals living in these urban centres experience great stress as a result of their being caught between two worlds—the modern and the traditional.

From the mid 1970s onwards there was an emergence of many newly established organizations and activist groups. A large part of the activities of these groups has centred around combating atrocities and violence committed on women, dowry murder, brutal forms of maltreatment and exploitation. In many cases, women in distress have approached such groups for assistance in registering and follow up of cases, providing shelter, etc. These activist groups have identified themselves with oppressed, victimized, and harassed women and awakened new hopes, aspirations and consciousness among women on these issues. Recently many formal and informal groups have emerged throughout the country which have successfully mobilized women's awareness and have preferred to work directly with the women, relying less on material imputes from the outside and more on increasing the internal capabilities and resources–economic, social, cultural and political. These activist groups have also elicited the intervention of the State, especially of the judiciary and of the fourth estate, to project the rights of women and ameliorate their situations. At the same time, they have organized the women themselves for struggle.

Inhabitants of urban centres may leave traditional patterns and learn to adopt new patterns. There are certain organizations which have developed in urban areas. They take the form of voluntary association which are either rooted in traditional patterns or which are Western in form they are said to provide meaningful substitutes of traditional identities and patterns of living and to act as socializing agents for the adoption of new roles more in harmony with the urban environment and a modern society.

Voluntary organizations play an important role in the lives of modern means of living and working in an urban environment. In the industrialised cities these associations have flourished without precedents. One of the outstanding characteristics of urban living is said to be the great number of variety of clubs, organization, societies, leagues and similar associations into which people group themselves and through which they pursue their interests.

Philosophy of NGO's

Self help has been the philosophy of these projects since the beginning. The projects proceed with the assumption that any neighbourhood, no matter how poor, can do something to improve itself by its own efforts and that any approach from outside help should be resorted to only after it has exhausted its own resources. This is not always an easy message to get across to poor people, who sometimes felt that the government should meet all their needs because they are poor. The success of the projects depends almost entirely upon the work of each individual community organiser who had to stimulate, guide and sustain the whole process by working with individuals and groups, and bring in outside help when needed. The task requires a great deal of patience, sensitivity and commitment to the aims of the projects.

Rise of NGO's

Urban groups and associations arise and exist to help the urban people to adjust to their social and cultural environment. The rise of special interests are fewer in rural areas, a small number of such interest groups are found there, people who are socially and culturally conscious tend to form into groupings of their own kind, cities foster many such special interest groups. City life and conditions also give rise to many welfare associations.

It has been theorized that voluntary organisations flourish in a social setting in which the community loses its cohesive and organised character and ceases to function as an all inclusive social group. The growth of big urban centres have created conditions fertile for the extensive development of associations.

Social differentiations, heterogeneity and large urban aggregates are some of the major factors responsible for this development. The loss of economic, educational, protective and recreational functions of family, neighbourhood community largely contribute to the growth of voluntary associations. Consequently, voluntary associations have been increasingly relied upon to make up for these losses. These voluntary associations are also considered to be integrative both for society and for the individual as well as providing a direct way for the individual.

Social Organisations and Segmentation

One chief reason for segmentation of the social world of many urbanites lies in the number and importance of the voluntary association in which they participate. Many men with similar interests tend to associate with others of like interests and of the same economic class–lawyers with lawyers, executives with executives, regardless of local area of residence. City life proves to be a particularly fertile breeding place for voluntary associations not only because of similarity of specialized interests and problems as the part of many person but because most of these people do not normally come to know one another personally through family or neighbourhood.

Thus, a whole series of association parallels the various branches and activities of government and extends into many areas where government is relatively inactive. The people involved often meet face to face but do not have such intimate contacts. They see each other as persons in certain categories.

Functions of Voluntary Associations

It is difficult to categorize the associations and their functions as such because they tend to overlap each other. However, one can always identify the main functions from the subsidiary ones which can help in placing them in almost exclusive categories for analysis purpose.

N.K. Bose in his social survey of Calcutta sponsored by the Anthropological Society of India, points out a similar preponderance of voluntary organizations. Members of different linguistic groups have built up, in course of time, a little less than two thousand voluntary institutions to cater to residents, educational, recreational, welfare, religious and cultural needs.

It is always found that professional, recreational and welfare organization have the largest membership. Studies reveals that formal organizational membership with other variables, suggest that this significantly associated with respondents urban exposure and experiences, socio-economic status and education.

An obvious explanation of this correlation pattern can be the fact that people with good education, high income and status occupation usually have an easy access to voluntary organisations especially those organisation which function on a relatively more secular and specialized interest based pattern. These organisations such as Rotary and the Lions have a restricted and selective membership based on the factors discussed above. Although NGOs are plentiful, they do not reach all elements of the population equally. It is generally the people in the higher income brackets, the better educated those having high SES and greater urban exposure and experience that are more active in formal organisations.

The voluntary organisations are one of the basic community structures found in modern urban society. A voluntary agency is a non-political, non-commercial and non-government organisation engaged in various human care services to the people. These are the projects of local significance initiated and carried out by local people.

A detailed analysis of activities, services and projects of the voluntary organizations reveal striking similarities which indicates that they share a common cultural pattern. These similarities appear in recreational interest, income generating activities, religious, educational and social pattern of Baroda.

Voluntary organisations are structures in which numerous individuals work towards some common objectives. Voluntary organisations play an important role in the lives of modern women living and working in an urban environment.

Voluntary organisations and agencies have contributed immensely to the new directions and impetus provided to women's programmes during the decade for women. Although, the government made lot of efforts through various programme like IRDP, TRYSEM, DWCRA, ICDS and Adult Literacy Programmes. Still, involvement of Voluntary Action in the organisation of Women to Empower them needed to be taken seriously. It is with this background that a micro-research study was undertaken to find out what are the women doing in these-voluntary organisations.

Objectives of the Survey

To analyse the performance of women's voluntary organisations in terms of their structure, functions and overall activities.

Methodology

A questionnaire was made and eighteen voluntary organisations of Baroda city which worked exclusively for women were studied.

Results and Discussion

A range of human care services is being provided in the fields of education, health, economic and women's upliftment etc. It is difficult to categories the associations and their functions as such because they tend to overlap each other. However, one can always identify the main functions from subsidiary ones which can help placing them in almost exclusive categories for analysis purpose. The various voluntary organisations have undertaken several programmes to attain their objectives. They may be divided into these categories :

1. Cultural and religious programmes.
2. Economic programmes.
3. Welfare and relief programmes.

These categories are not mutually exclusive. The investigators have differentiated them for the purpose of convenience.

Table 1. Percentage Distribution of Voluntary Organisations According to the Type of Activities Undertaken

N=18

Type of Activity	*N*	%
Economic activities	15	83.5
Social activities	14	77.9
Religious activities	13	72.3
Cultural activities	12	66.7
Health and Nutrition Education	10	55.6
Counselling services	6	33.3

As indicated in Table 1, more than 80 per cent of the agencies are involved in economic activities. These include assistance in the form of providing raw materials for preparing masalas, snacks, uniform, providing equipments like sewing machine, typewriter, and so on. Activities related to health and nutrition education are undertaken by little more than 50 per cent. The health education is imparted through meetings and discussions.

Nearly one-third of the various agencies have provision of counselling services for family, social and marital problems.

Table 2. Percentage Distribution of Voluntary Organisations according to the Courses Offered by Them

N = 18

Course Offered	*N*	%
Sewing	15	83.5
Embroidery	13	72.3
Knitting	10	55.6
Typing	10	55.6
Book Binding	10	55.6
Adult Education	10	55.6
S.S.C. Tuition	05	27.7
Hand painting	05	27.7
Aya training centre	03	16.8

Different organisations have schemes of self-supporting economic activities. Sewing classes seem to be most widely offered course. Embroidery classes are held in about more than seventy per cent voluntary organisations. This is followed by courses in knitting, adult education, typing and book binding. Least offered course is of Aya training as seen in Table 2, only 17 per cent organisations were offering this course.

Table 3. Percentage Distribution according to the Extent of Service Provided by the Various Voluntary Organisations

N = 18

Extent of Service	*N*	%
Provide training only	18	83.33
Placement after training	03	16.66
Retraining and Refresher course	00	00.00

The most striking finding of Table 3 is none of the agencies have facilities of retraining or for refresher course for the women. More than 80 per cent of the agencies have facilities only for training for their trainees.

Table 4. Percentage Distribution of the Beneficiaries According to their Characteristics

N=18

Characteristics		*N*	%
Age	Below 20 years	03	16.8
	21–30 years	05	27.7
	31–40 years	06	33.3
	41 and above		
	Age is no bar	16	66.7
SES	Belong to LIG (Low Income Group)	17	94.4
	Belong to MIG (Middle Income Group)	17	94.4
	Belong to HIG (High Income Group)	04	22.4
Education	Illiterate	17	94.4
	Primary	15	85.5
	High School	13	72.3
	College	03	16.8
Caste	Brahmin	03	16.8
	Baniya	06	33.3
	Patel	07	38.9
	Scheduled Cast Scheduled Tribes	03	16.8
	Caste no barrier	11	61.11

As far as the age of a woman is considered to become a member of organisation, it is no bar in more than sixty-six per cent organisations. So women from all age groups are present. Majority of women who came to take advantage of the different organisation are either illiterate or educated till primary level and from lower or middle income groups. The women from Patel and Baniya caste are in majority and they also dominate various spheres of public life of Baroda.

Table 5. Distribution of the Type of Course and Time for the Course in the Various Voluntary Organisations

N=18

Nature		*N*	%
Type of Course			
	Only theory is taught	00	-
	Only practicals are done	11	61.2
	Both (Theory and Practicals)	07	38.9
Time of Course			
	Fixed timing	14	77.9
	Learner chooses time according to convenience	17	94.4

Sixty per cent of the agencies offered only practical courses. This holds true as all the agencies are undertaking some or the other skill developing and practical oriented courses. Majority of the agencies (94%) reported that the learner choose timing according to their convenience. The women beneficiaries after finishing the household chores as and when they find free time they come to take part in the activities.

Table 6. Distribution of Beneficiaries according to the Number and Purpose of Attending Activities

N = 18

Characteristics	*N*	*%*
Average Number of Beneficiaries		
Less than 20	03	16.8
21–40	02	11.2
41–60	06	33.3
More than 60	07	38.9
Purpose of Attending		
Income generation	16	88.8
Recreational/cultural	06	33.3
Legal help	04	22.4

When average number of beneficiaries are analysed it is found that majority of the organisations have more than 60 women on an average.

Income generation is the main objective for which the women come to the organisation. The chance of getting extra income by working in leisure time have attracted many women to these voluntary organisations.

Besides income generation, women come to take part in recreational, cultural and socialization during their leisure time. These women enroll themselves so that these centres could provide them entertainment by offering cultural programmes. Competitions are held, with a view to encourage members to take up various activities. Various organisations organise dance, music, drama, and garba competition, reciting of Geeta, bhajanas. Besides these celebrations, the voluntary organisations have programmes like baby-shows, fun fairs, cooking contests and beauty classes, and so on. All these activities give them chance to take part and show their talents. Also, it gives them a feeling of satisfaction.

Counselling centre provides just and viable counselling to the distressed women. Out of eighteen women voluntary organisations contacted by the investigator, four of these organisations reported that women come to these agencies for getting legal help.

There are other than the routine activities not so commonly found in all the voluntary organisations in Baroda city as listed below :

- Giving hall on rent for marriage.
- Running working women hostel.
- Running own show rooms to sell their goods.
- Organising street plays, dharana, gherao.
- Running balwadis.

A detailed analysis of activities, services and projects of the voluntary organisation reveal striking similarities which indicate that they share a common cultural pattern. These similarities appear in recreational interests, income generating activities, religious, educational and social patterns of Baroda.

Although public authorities have chalked out a number of programmes for the welfare of women and they have been implemented also.

These ladies can be suggested new topics like file making and making of bakery items. Alongwith this they can be given information about various places where they could go and get more orders for sale.

The balwadi workers can be taught about clay moulding, and soft toys. Education about child care and health and nutrition education can be given to them so that they can perform their work more effectively.

In Baroda district, Social Welfare organisations fund several Mahila Mandals. In these Mahila Mandal's women only sing songs, Bhajans and Kirtans during meetings. This could be because of lack of training. Seminars and workshops can be conducted by Home Scientists to tell them about different productive activities which could be performed by these women.

Role of Home Scientists in these Organisations

The significance of voluntary organizations in the life of modern women is seen. The changing kinds of participation of women in education and social activities can be seen from the post-independence club activities. At the turn of the century women's clubs were limited to cultural and educational opportunities of upper class women.

Today the great variety of women's organisations reflect the greater range and differentiations of women's activities, interests and services in our society. Because they wanted to change to work with others, they wanted to develop latest talents in art, hobbies and organizational planning and the pride in being part of a special group.

Home Scientists can work extensively with neighbourhood groups and can show persistence in influencing the decisions of relevant government agencies. Home Scientists can help in some project areas where the problems may be of juvenile delinquency or atrocities on women and while outside agencies may deal with such cases, much can be done by the local community itself. A citizen juvenile delinquency committee can be formed to discuss the problems with the young people and the families involved. Home Scientist (who will be having knowledge of child development and psychology) can help to discover conditions in the family and community that may have given rise to delinquency.

Home Scientists can work in the different voluntary organisations and help people. For example, the income generating activities like tye and dye, different types of printing and making of handicraft and decorative articles.

One of the oldest agency "Lalita Devi Society" is doing very good work in the field of recreation, education and income generation. Home Scientists can help other agencies to establish rapport with such agency and learn its positive points, so that they can also run as efficiently.

In Baroda district, the social welfare authorities have the established "Mahila Mandals" where women sing songs and Bhajans during meetings. This is because they are not trained. Seminar and workshops can be conducted to teach them different activities which could be performed by these women. Home Scientists can give them training to perform their functions properly. The Balwadi workers can be taught about soft toys, wall hanging, soap making, pot holders and magazine holders, use of embroidery. They can be given education about child care and health and nutrition education and many such important topics.

Voluntary action in India has always been an integral part of the cultural and social tradition. Voluntary agencies have currently opted for several alternative roles depending on their objectives, location and resources available. The role of voluntary agencies in national development has been considered vital due to their direct and first hand experience and knowledge of local needs, problems and resources at the grassroots. The essential strength of voluntary agencies during from the fact that they are closer to the community and people.

Kaul 1990 in her Ph.D research, studied eight voluntary agencies marking in city of Baroda for training women from low SES for income generation.

This was the time when womens' decade for development (1975-85) had just ended and the government wanted NGO's to be involved in this crucial task. Thus, this study was of lot of importance.

A Profile of Voluntary Training Agencies for Training Low Socio-economic Status Women in Baroda City

Over centuries it was believed that women are experts only in dealing with the world inside the four walls of the house while men are experts in dealing with the outside world. Whereas, in reality if equal opportunity is given to women they can also prove to the world that they can compete with men in every field and can do certain jobs better than men.

With the changing times, women have realized their importance as mothers, wives and workers in the family and outside. They are becoming independent and are even going for self-employment and entrepreneurship. Women have succeeded in changing their image as weak dependent, passive and subservient persons to independent, active and strong human beings. They have changed their stereotype images to more positive ones.

Over half of the population, is represented by the women and thus for growth and development of a nation it is necessary that each and every citizen should participate and contribute towards this end. It is for this reason that each and every person should be educated and independent. As women represent half of the world's population, they should be educated and given access to necessary inputs required for enhancing their productivity, ability and for their equal share in the benefits of development.

A woman is an important element of the family who keeps the culture alive by transferring it from generation to generation through her children. Women are fully aware of the fact that they can bring grace and dignity to the place where they live. They can build a new nation, their role and effectiveness in a family, society and nation has been fully realized and accepted, now.

Many government and non-government agencies carry out many vocational training programmes for her socio-economic status in family, society and nation. The main aim of government training programmes is to provide necessary infrastructure for all-around development of the participants. Not only government but many voluntary women's organisations are also taking a lead in this field, these days.

Women can now choose from many new careers. They have a vast choice before them, now they can enter any field and even hold the highest positions which previously was considered the exclusive domain of men. Women can now become industrialists, entrepreneurs, exporters, beauticians, crafts-persons, technologists and so on for which of course, they would need proper training.

For the past three decades, employment of women is becoming an important issue even at national level in India. This trend has made it more essential that women have the potential to develop certain skills, get the right kind of training to join the work of employment with all the confidence and faith. So with the help of training agencies only, women's earning power can be developed. Women should turn from economic liabilities to economic assets and this is only possible when women have the earning power, which is further made possible by women's training agencies for income generation. Training programmes provide training in selected vocations to the women with skills which would enable them to earn through self-employment.

There are various kinds of training programmes undertaken by government, semi-government and voluntary organisations to train women in various income generating skills. The training programme should deal with the basic principles related to income generation. Training can be provided in the best way to overcome intermediate hurdles and restraints such as how to get access to a better price for their products, how to start production of goods, be it in the home or in the factory, and how to administer small shops or cooperatives. The most important activity is to train women to identify the local resources and raw materials which they can transfer into goods.

There are various agencies which provide vocational training to the women in the entire country. Gujarat ranks highest in vocational training facilities followed by Punjab, Maharashtra and Karnataka. There are in all 4565 training institutions and agencies in India, imparting training for women in income generation out of which 868 institutions are found in Gujarat.

A research was conducted in the city of Baroda in Gujarat to find out which are the training agencies, training women for income generation, the popular courses for which women are being trained and so on. This was done as a follow-up of a Ph.D/Doctoral study conducted in 1990 in Baroda to study eight voluntary organisations training women for income generation.

In Gujarat, training women for income generation in the following courses are very common–

– Cutting or tailoring	–Knitting	–Embroidery
-- Weaving	–Book Binding	–Typing
– Shorthand	–Beauty hair and skin care	
– Dyeing and printing	–*Masala, papad* and pickle making	

Objectives of the Study

The major objectives of the present study were to find out whether these training agencies were able to meet the following objectives:

- To enable women to generate supplementary income.
- To impart certain vocational skills to trainee to make them self-dependent.
- To raise their educational status by imparting certain basic general knowledge.
- To help trainees in setting up their own industries.
- To raise the social status of these trainees.
- To raise their standard of living by teaching them income generating skills.

The following agencies were studied:

1. Diamond Jubilee Trust

This is a state level unique Cottage Industries Training Institute of Government of Gujarat under the Directorate of Cottage Industries Institute. Which is headed by the Deputy Director of Cottage Industries (Training and Extension) Baroda, Gujarat.

The institute was first started in 1938. The training was given in only five vocational trades such as tailoring and cutting, wood-carving, leather work, sankheda lacquer work and metal work. Since then, it has been expanded as per the demands and requirements of the time. At present, it imparts training in eighteen, one year durational courses of engineering, vocational and handicrafts. There are twenty-three short durational courses in chemical, and fourteen short durational courses in cosmetic section. A special scheme is implemented for wearers of designable cloth weaving in textile section. The age limit for above one year courses is between 14–30 years and each trainee is paid a stipend of rupees one hundred and twenty-five per month.

Staffing Pattern of Diamond Jubilee Trust, is as follows :

Managerial	: Deputy Director–1, Assistant Director–1
Technical	: Office Superintendent–1, Assistant Wireman
Teaching	: Trained Teachers–10,
Non Teaching	: Head Clerk–1, Clerk–1.

2. Vikas Jyot Trust

Vikas Jyot Trust was started in 1973 for the multi-dimensional development of women to make them self-sufficient, self-reliant and thereby create confidence in them to develop better personalities. Vikas Jyot Trust conducts various vocational training programmes for women.

Source of the Finance of Vikas Jyot Trust

The source of finance of this agency is generated from all the three sources viz. by self, by the government and by donations. The family counselling centre is provided with 75 per cent of its finance through government and 25 per cent is incurred by the trust, rest of the projects are financed by the government, trust and donations.

Vikas Jyot Trust gives financial assistance to its trainees in the form of stipends. They also provide assistance to some of its trainees for job placement on completion of their training. They give help by calling the potential employers to the agency, for on the job training, job placement of their trainees. They also give the addresses to their trainees, of people who have the authority to employ them or enable them to seek an employment.

Staffing Pattern of Vikas Jyot Trust is as follows :

Project : chairman, president, managing trustee, trustee, executive secretary, production department, accountants, workers.

Central Body : president, secretary, board of directors (director of cottage industry, representatives of apex body and supply department), production department–accountants, workers.

Family Counselling Centre : social defence department, social worker.

3. Bhagini Samaj

Bhagini Samaj provides assistance to some trainees for job placement after completion of their training. They do give general guidance and knowledge to their trainees for job placement.

The Bhagini Samaj was established on 15th August 1971. The main activities of this agency are women's and children garment making, embroidery course. Apart from this, new courses offered are computers and English teaching course–for these two courses fees is charged from the students. They do get financial aid from government trust and donations.

Staffing Pattern of Bhagini Samaj is as follows

Managerial : Executive Secretary–1, Teaching : Teachers–6, Non-Teaching : Attendants–2, Helper Peon–1.

4. Kamubala Sahakari Audyogic Centre

Under this training agency the women are taught about different activities like book binding, file making, sewing etc. This agency was established on 8th August, 1950. The general training given to the girls is in : (1) Sewing and (2) Embroidery

For these courses examinations are conducted by the Government of Gujarat and for the examination, qualifications, attendance and other rules and regulations are taken into consideration. Government gives them certificate on passing. New courses introduced are beautician course, fabric painting, wooden craft-carving. Apart from giving training, its other activities are running a health centre for family, women and children's programmes, and immunization and family planning programme. Under family, women and children programme, they provide mother and children with vitamin tablets, health check-ups, pre-natal, post-natal guidance. These centres are totally regulated by government. Kamubala Agency covers around 50,000 population.

Staffing Pattern of Kamubala Sahakari Audygic Centre is as follows:

MANAGERIAL : Executive Secretary–1, TEACHING : Training Teachers–6, NON–TEACHING–Attendants–2, Watchman–1.

5. Chimnabai Trust

Chimnabai Trust was established in the year 1974. The source of finance is mainly generated by the agency itself. Besides, there is a bulk of financial help from the Maharani Chimnabai trust, and from Central Government, Municipality, and contributions from beneficiaries and donations.

The general courses conducted by this training agency are tailoring and typing. The fees charged from the students is rupees forty per month and rupees ten as admission fees.

In Shri Chimnabai Industrial Home for Women, no financial assistance is provided to the trainees, i.e. no stipends, scholarships or apprenticeship is given. They give the address of the people who according to them, have the authority to employ their trainees.

Staffing Pattern of Chimnabai Industrial Home is as follows:

Managerial : Superintendent–1, TECHNICAL : Supervisors–3, Teaching : Trained Teachers–5.

Minimum Level of Qualification Required for Admission in these Training Agencies

Name of the Training Agency	*Name of the Programme*	*Minimum Qualification Reqd.*
DIAMOND JUBILEE COTTAGE INDUSTRIES INSTITUTE	Tailoring	SSC Pass
	Dolls making	4th class
	Wood Carving	4th class
	Chemical Trade	Those who can read & write
	Cosmetic Trade	SSC Pass
VIKAS JYOT TRUST	Sewing	—
	Bakery	—
	Papad Making	—
	Book Binding	—
BHAGINI SAMAJ	Women's & Children	Govt. Course
	Garment Making	VII Std. Pass
	Computers	SSC Pass
	English Teaching	—
	Embroidery	W.C.G.M. General Course
	Fancy Work	No specific qualification required
KAMUBALA SAHAKARI AUDYOGIC VIKAS	W . C . G . M . –	
	Women's & Children Garment Making	8th Pass
	Embroidery Work	No specific qualification required
SHRI CHIMNABAI TRUST	W.C.G.M.-General Diploma in Women's & Children's Garment Making, Typing	7th Standard Pass SSC Pass

Conclusion

All the agencies are giving training to women in income generation skills, but no agency has any contact with the Industries for the placement of their trainees. Although, they have and do give information about the persons who can employ them, but no assurance is given.

In Vikas Jyot Trust and Bhagini Samaj, they accept orders from the Industries or people for making *buns*, *papads*, *masalas*, dry namkeen, etc. Some of these agencies employs their own trainees if he or she is perfect in doing work, active and well qualified and has the potential to carry out work.

Some of these agencies carry out Government Certificate Courses in tailoring, sewing, typing etc. They prepare the trainees for appearing in examinations.

These agencies are voluntary agencies except Diamond Jubilee Trust which is a Government Organisation. These agencies get financial help in the form of donations, funds and some minimal aid from the government. Some of these agencies even charge fee from the students for raising their own corpus fund.

A great change in the knowledge attitude and status in these current trainees is observed. Now well qualified and well to do students are also coming for training in these agencies.

One observation that was made, was that except in Diamond Jubilee Trust, no women came from rural areas. The women coming to these agencies are from the local areas only and mostly from low socio-economic status.

With the change in time and advancement in technology some of these agencies like Bhagini Samaj and Chimnabai Trust have started computer teaching course, typing etc. The criteria and eligibility for selection of the trainee too changed but to a very little extent.

To sum up, it may be added that there is still a lot of work which can be done provided that these organisations have good networking with academic institutions and industries. There is need for updating knowledge and skills, this is where Universities and colleges can play a vital role by way of imparting training to the administrators, Organisers and Supervisors or Teachers, of these organisations.

NGO's and Empowerment of Rural Women

It is the rural woman who need empowerment, the most. The two reasons for their empowerment, are that rural women being in majority, their enlightenment and liberation are utmost important; and, that rural women are less powerful and subservient, compared to urban and sub-urban women. The voluntary organizations are such institutions which can play a positive intervention role in the empowerment of women.

The empowerment means women assuming power to direct their lives in order to contribute to development of themselves and of the nation. Not only the Indian societies in general, but the educational system as well as the recruiting systems, have a systematic bias against women.

The most desirable level of empowerment of rural woman would be to bestow power on them in all decision making and participating activities, so that the women become the possessors and users of the fruits of their economic productivity.

What factors make empowerment of women difficult?

Several factors make women invisible–economically and socially. These factors are the general bias towards women in all sphere of life, and the general neglect of women in all activities, within and outside the home.

Gender bias

The gender bias against women is expressed in the denial of education and early marriage, which prevent the development of personality and rationality of women.

Legal structure

Although the current amendments to Indian Penal Code have removed certain biases from the laws, some still prevail.

The antiwoman norms and traditions of the family and society

Although the motherhood is over glorified in India, the womanhood is cruelly neglected. The woman of the house is expected to sacrifice her time, interest, food, clothing, and job in helping all other members of her family. These sacrifices are so great and so long-lasting that they strip the woman, of all her rights and abilities.

Role of voluntary organizations in empowerment of women

The basic requirement of the voluntary organizations to help rural women is to adopt a rural profile and view-point in their endeavours. If the organizations are suited and adapted to rural people, they will create necessary intervention in empowering women. The empowerment of rural women can be facilitated and achieved through the following measures :

Involvement of women in income-generating activities

Each rural woman must earn money to be an economic asset, even a partial one. The voluntary organizations can start appropriate income-generating activities for women only. The organizations can encourage women to invest part of their earning in their own name.

Establish women's co-operatives, banks and industrial societies

For empowerment of women at economic front, women's institutions for entrepreneurship will be needed. Cooperatives, banks and small scale industries operated by women, will empower women in the world of business and industry.

Sensitize women for leadership

Because women lack organizational and professional skills, a broad-based leadership training in leadership must be offered by the voluntary organizations. The women's overdependence on men in handling social and economic matters has to be removed by systematically training the women for leadership role. Sensitization of women to their abilities and aspirations are necessary to empower women in decision-making, especially at places outside the home.

Promote health

Due to over glorification of motherhood and subservient wifehood, the woman is not accepted and recognized in her own rights. The biggest toll taken by such roles assigned to women, is the health of women. The voluntary organizations must direct a strong thrust in raising the health status of women.

Promote child care agencies

The rural women are used to leave smaller children at home, under the care of older ones, while they go out to work. If crèches, day-care centres, nursery schools are opened, they will not only liberate the women from child care, but will also generate income for some women.

Provide middleman services to women facing family conflicts

The rural women are victims of atrocities, cruelty, and deprivations within the family. The voluntary organizations can open family courts, family peace centres and family reconciliation homes, to help women who are stranded. The intervention in family conflicts, created by voluntary agencies, will facilitate the empowerment of women.

Provide functional literacy to women

Probably literacy is the first requirement to empower women in all of their aspects of life. Without literacy, there can be no empowerment of women. So the voluntary organizations must start and continue literacy programmes for rural women.

Conclusion

The empowerment of women is a concept worth adopting and not confining it to the literature alone. The empowerment originates from possession of resources, the most important being the monetary resource.

The voluntary organizations are in a position to make empowerment a reality for women. The empowerment is realised in having control over one's body, possessions, and psychological assets, such as abilities, skills, aptitudes and inclinations.

Women in India are victims of a multiple socio-economic and cultural factors. Though women need to be empowered in all the areas it is economic independence, which is the most prominent means of empowerment. So, enhancing income-earning opportunities is increasingly viewed as an effective means for empowering women and improves their status. Thus, poverty reduction by way of income generating activities has become a significant strategic activity for any government or NGO working with women.

Women are assisted for income generation in a number of ways by NGOs. They are given financial assistance directly or facilitated by NGO functionaries. Many NGOs have special entrepreneurial development programmes under which they conduct training programmes to help women develop motivation and business skills.

At present, there are two types of voluntary groups working in the field of women. One is an organisation not necessarily of women, but working for women and secondly, an organisation of women, working for women. Although the number of women's own organisations need to be greatly increased, both types of organisations should be encouraged. The spread of these organisations is not uniform throughout the country; their numbers are small largely concentrated in townships, urban areas and district headquarters. The activities of these groups are also of a limited nature. Some of them take up welfare activities like child care, destitute women, short stay centres and crisis centres. Some of them have taken up developmental activities, but these are generally linked with the government schemes under which grants are available.

Since the voluntary organisations have the advantage of community involvement, and help to promote voluntary action, the national commission recommends that they should be actively assisted by providing finances training and managerial inputs.

The organisations, should be encouraged to enlarge their activities to:

(a) Create awareness.

(b) Mobilise and organise poor women.

(c) Carry out training programmes for creating awareness and leadership amongst women.

(d) Formulate and implement developmental and economic projects for women. Such projects should not be restricted to Government schemes only. They should carry out new projects which will meet the realistic needs of the women which have not been taken into account by developmental agencies.

(e) The creativity and innovativeness of the voluntary groups should be encouraged by providing flexibility in their programmes.

The Government should provide legislative support and removal of restrictive legislation, needs to be done, if voluntary agencies can play such a role. Greater coordination and cooperation among NGOs is called for to avoid duplication of services. Greater funding for net working among N.G.O's must be provided. This will ensure more efficient utilization of funds and greater coverage of programmes. Voluntary agencies must be increasingly involved in the provision of employment and supportive services for women.

The National Literacy Mission must involve women's organisations in a big way. The voluntary sector should increasingly be involved to act as a catalyst/intermediary in organising women for collective action. There is the need to document the success stories of major N.G.O.'s in India and learn from their success and failures. In order to ensure that the security and integrity of the nation are preserved, there is a need to adopt suitable policies to ensure that voluntary agencies abide by the rules governing the receipt and utilisation of foreign grants and submit audited accounts, returns and reports periodically.

Identity cards should be issued to workers of voluntary agencies who are dealing with cases of atrocities against women, as is already being done in some districts. In order to have sufficient infrastructure and facilities, there is need to mobilize more resources for voluntary agencies who are engaged in welfare and development of women. There is a need to decentralise the planning process to stimulate local people's participation in planning, implementation, monitoring and evaluation of development projects. A suitable mechanism should be evolved to involve voluntary agencies and other people's institutions at various stages of developmental programmes/projects. Voluntary agencies should further ensure the participation of poor women in the development process.

A number of programmes implemented by conventional voluntary agencies have emphasized imparting skills to improve the efficiency of women as housewives and mothers, and or to improve their earning capacities. Voluntary agencies have, tended to neglect the participative potential of women in the development process as well as conscientizing women on their rights and roles. There is the need for such efforts that could increase the awareness of women and improve their participation as equal citizens in national development. Further, voluntary agencies should play a surveillance role and observe, explore and analyse the extent to which social legislations implemented for women have actually benefitted them.

Empowerment of women cannot be ensured until they are enabled to organize themselves. Collective organizations spells strength. This is a prerequisite for initiating action, lobbying, pressurizing and bargaining. Grassroots organizations can greatly enhance the opportunities for poor women to participate in development programmes by providing an organizational base to operate from. By organising, working together, sharing experiences and resources, building pressure groups and so forth, women can find independent access to opportunities for their betterment.

References

Alfred Desouza. *The Indian City Poverty*, Manhar Publications, New Delhi, 1978.

Bhatia, S.S. Jobs, *Careers and Personality for Young Boys and Girls*, 1987, 88-94 and 97-104.

Bhatia. A. Women's Development and NGOs. Rawat Publication, Jaipur and New Delhi, 2000.

Brahmbhatt, U., Study of Marriage Counselling Service Provided by Karelibaug Bhagini Samaj Trust.

Chandra, S., *Social Participation in Urban Neighbourhood.* National Publishing House, New Delhi, 1977.

Chaudhary, D. Paul Voluntary Social Welfare in India, Sterling Publication (P) Ltd., New Delhi, 1971.

Dissertation (M.S.W).... M.S. University, Baroda, 1996.

Gaonkar, R. Role of SHGs in Empowerment of Women, Zuarinagar, Goa. Mimeographed paper read at ISTR Sixth International Conference, Contesting Citizenship and Civil Society in a divided world, Toronto, Canada, 11-14 July, 2004.

Goela Usha, *Training Schemes for Women in Government of India*, 1989, pp. 79 85 and 91-99.

India, Department of Women and Child Development. Ministry of Human Resource Development. National Perspective Plan for Women 1988-2000 A.D. Government of India, 1988.

J.K. Friend, J.M. Power, *Public Planning Dimension*. Tavistock Publications, London, 1982.

Kaul Anuradha, Educational economic and social impact of vocational training agencies offering income generating programmes on low socio-economic status women of Baroda city, Ph.D. Thesis 1990.

Marvin B. Sussman, Thomas, Y. *Community Structure and Analysis*. Thomas Y. Cromel Company. New York, 1989.

Mehta and Das, NGOs and Women Empowerment in Pandya R.M. and Mathu, A.A. (Eds.) Imbibing value education - various perspectives, Kalpaz Publications, 2003, pp. 163-167.

Parlikar Kalpana R. et.al. A Report of Workshop on Training & Development of Women for Participation in TRYSEM programme, Dec. 1990.

Paul, M. and E.H. Mizruchi, Urbanism, *Urbanization and Change–Comparative Perspectives*. Addison Weslly Publishing company, New York, 1980.

Rana, K., People's Participation and Voluntary Action. *Dimension, Roles and Strategies*, Kanishka Published, Distributed, New Delhi, 2001.

Robson, Lacke and Dawson, User Involvement in the control of Voluntary Organizations, 1997 (www.jrf.org.uk).

Sen, S. Voluntary Organisations and Women Development. Dissertation (MSW)..., M.S. University, 1994.

Shrivastava Ramesh, C., NGO's, Securing People's Partnership for Progress, *Social Welfare*, February, 2000.

Siwach, R.K. Perspective role of VOs in Tenth Plan. *Social Welfare*, Vol. 50, No. 11, February 2003, pp. 13-15.

Suresh K. A. Participation of beneficiaries in the developmental programmes of NGO in Kerala. *Journal of Rural Development*, Vol. 9, No. 5, September 1990, pp. 911-915.

Wadiwale, Role of SHGs in empowerment of women, *Social Welfare*, April 2004, Vol. 54, No. 11, pp. 20-25.

William, E. Cole. Urban Society. The Riverside Press, Cambridge, Massachusetts, 1980.

(www.jhu.edu/nistr/conferences/toronto/absracts/gaonkar.pdf)

Suggested Further Readings

Abhilasha Kumari (1990). Illusion of Power–The Women's Vote, *Women's Link*, Jan.–March.

Adult Education in India. Ministry of Education, Govt. of India, 1985.

Agarwal, N. (1993). *Women education and population in India*, Chugh Publications, Allahabad.

Aggarwal, N. (1993). *Women, education and population in India*. Chugh Publications, Allahabad.

Alva Margaret, (1997). *Women's Political Representation in Contemporary India*. Ed. by Mohanty Bidyut, Roy, Jaya and Gupta Smita Women and Political empowerment Institute of Social Science.

Anju Singh (1998). Demystification of Law for Women, WOMEN ON TRIAL Feb.

Annual Report, Ministry of Rural Development published by Government of India. 1993-94.

Ansari, N.A. (1984). *Adult Education in India*. Published by S. Chand and Co. New Delhi.

Ansari, N.A. *Adult Education in India*, New Delhi, S. Chand and Company Ltd., 1984.

Antony, M.J. (1989). Women's Rights. New Delhi Hind Pocket Books Pvt. Ltd.

Arputhamurthy Savitri, (1990). *Women work and discrimination*, Ashish Publishing Houses, New Delhi.

Arputhamurthy, S. (1990). *Ibid.*

Arya, A. Women and Press in India. *Communicator* 25(4): 9-11, 1988.

Athreya Ventesh B. *Literacy and Empowerment*, Sage Publication, New Delhi, 1996.

Bakshi, P.M. (1992). *The Constitution of India*, Universal Book Traders. Delhi.

Banerjee, A. and Sen, R. (1990). *Women and Economic Development*, Deep and Deep Publication, New Delhi.

Banerjee, N. "Women Workers and Development", *Social Scientist*, Vol. 6(8), March, 1978.

Barle, Shree Lakshmi, (1979). 'Role of women in rural Economic Development', *Yojana Journal*, Vol. XXVIII(21), Nov. 16.

Baroda, The M. S. University of Baroda. WOHTRAC and VVSRC "Workshop Report on Qualitative Research Approaches and Women Centred Health Care" Baroda: Centre for Operation Research and Training, 1997.

Batra, G.S. (1999). *Entrepreneurship and Small Scale Industries*. Deep and Deep Pub. New Delhi.

Behera, S.N. Rainfed Agriculture in Dryland Areas of Orissa, XXXVI (10) July 1998. pp. 47-50.

Bhadauria, Mridula, *Women in India: Some Issues*, APH Publishing Corporation, New Delhi, 1997.

Bhatia, S.S. (1987). *Jobs, Careers and personality for young boys and girls*, pp. 88-94 and 97-104.

Bhise, Lata and Bhansle, Leela, (1980). A sign of things to come Manushi May-June, 1980.

Bishnoi Indira. (1978). Reasons given by the women for not attending the adult education classes conducted by the labour welfare centre. Dissertation M.Sc. M.S.U. Baroda.

C. Gopalan, (1993). *Child Care in India Emerging Challenges*, Swasth Ltd.

CASE, Centre for Adult and Continuing Education (1993), Gender Development and Power : Some Issues and Methods for Gender Trainers". Cape.

Chatterji, S.A. (1988). *The Indian women's search for an identity*, Vikas Publishing House, New Delhi.

Chauhan Abha, Women in Politics. *Women's Link* Vol. 4, No. 2. April-June, 1998. pp. 13-18.

CHETNA, 'A Decade of Health Education', Ahmedabad, Chetna, 1993.

CHETNA, 'A Workshop on Women and Occupational health', June 13, Ahmedabad, Sardar Patel Institute of Public Administration, Chetna, 1995.

Contingency Action Plan for Natural Calamities. Ministry of Agriculture, Government of India. 1990.

Cormack, Margaret, (1978). *The Hindu Women*, Bombay. Asia Publishing House.

Country Report–Fourth World Conference on Women. Beijing 1995. Department of Women and Child Development, Ministry of Human Resource Development, Government of India, 1995.

Credit Needs of the Rural poor - Role of Self Help Groups and their linkages with the formal Credit Institutions NABARD, Annual Report 1990-91.

Datta, M.N. Rural drinking water supply in India, *Kurukshetra*, XXXVI (10). July 1988. pp. 16-21.

Datta, S.K. and Kapoor, S. Collective Action, Leadership and Success in Agricultural Co-operatives. A Study of Gujarat and West Bengal, 1997.

Desai Neera and Krishnaraj Maithreyi, (1987). *Women and Society*, Ajanta Press, New Delhi.

Desai, A.R. (1990). *Women's Liberation and Politics of Religious Personal Laws in India*, Published C.G. Shah, Memorial Trust, Bombay Printed by Impressions, Belgam.

Desai, N. and Patel, V., (1990). *Indian women–change and challenges*, Popular Prakashan, Bombay.

Devi Lalita. (1982). *Status and Employment of Women in India*. Delhi B.R. Publishing Corporation.

Devi, S. "Towards freedom for women", *Indian Express*, Delhi. Sept. 1, 1984.

Devi, S. Uma (1994). *Women, Work, Development and Ecology*, Har Anand Publication, New Delhi.

Dharmalingan, T. and Ramachandran, L. (1993). *Health Education, A New Approach*, Vikas Publishing House Pvt. Ltd.

Diman Paras and Diman Peeyashi (1994). *Women and Legal Protection*. Deep and Deep Publication, New Delhi.

Diman Paras, (1988). *Law of Marriage and Divorce*. Wadhwa & Company. Allahabad.

Dutta, S.C. (1987). *Adult education in third world*. Criterion Publishers. New Delhi.

Eekelaar, John, (1978). *Family Law and Social Policy* (Weidenfeld and Nicolson, London).

Elizabeth : *Women and the Welfare Status*. Taristock Publications Limited, London, 1999.

Evaluation of Traditional Birth Attendant Training Scheme in India: A Collaboration study. New Delhi: National Institute of Health and Family Welfare, 1983.

Gangopadhyay, A. Occupational Health: Psychological perspectives, *Indian Journal of Industrial Medicine*, Vol. 42(4), December, 1996.

Gates, W. (1995). *The Road Ahead*. The Penguin Group. USA.

Giri, V.M. (1998). *Emancipation and Empowerment of Women*, Gyan Publishing House, New Delhi.

Goa sets a lesson for "son preference" states. *The Times of India*, New Delhi, 2 July, 1995.

Goela Usha, (1989). *Training Schemes for women in Government of India*, pp. 79 to 85 and 91 to 99.

Goldetein, Rhoda, (1972). *Indian Women in transition - A Bangalore Case Study Metachen*, The Scarecrew, New Jersey.

Gopalan, S. Integrated approach to resolve the problem of water. *Kurukshetra*. XXXVI (10), July 1998. pp. 4-7.

Grieffen, V. (1987). Women Development and Empowerment, Kaula Lumpur, Asian and Pacific Development Centre.

Gupta, J. L. (1988). *Challenges to the Fair Sex - Indian Women : Problems, Plights, and Progresses*. 1988.

Gupta, S.K. (1982). Distance Education Problems of Co-ordination, Co-operation and Functional Autonomy, *Journal of Higher Education* 7(3).

Gupta, V.S. (1999). *Communication Technology Media Policy and National Development*, New Delhi : Concept Publishing Company.

H. Nakajima, (1996). "Health Promoting Schools" World Health Organisation Report.

Handa Rameshwari, Catalysts of Female Literacy - The empirical indicator. *Indian Journal of Adult Education*, Vol. 60, No. 4. Oct.-Dec. 1999. pp. 48-52.

Harish, (1991). *Economic Development and Role of Indian Women*, New Delhi, Commonwealth Publishing.

Hati Chittaranjan, (1992). "Girl Child: Mom long should she bear The Cross" *Yojana* : Vol. 36, No. 56, p. 15.

Hazarika Sultan, (1971). Reasons given by the adult women for not attending the adult education classes in Home Science with respect to their SES and age Dissertation (M.Sc.). M.S. University, Baroda.

Heldn, M. Mary, "Women and Politics in the Third Work", U.K. University of York, 1996.

Helen, A., Mary, M. (1996). Women and Politics in the Third World. U.K. University of York.

Hisrich R.D., Brush, C.G. (1986). *The Women Entrepreneurs* De Health & Co. Toronto.

Horan, N. (1997). Wastewater collection, Treatment, Disposal and Reuse in the book *The Global Environment, Science, Technology and Management* Vol. 2 Ed. By Brune. D : Chapman. D.V. A Wiley Company.

Jackson, Joseph et. al. (1982). Rayden's Law and Practice in Divorce and Family Matters. Butterworth Modern Text Books 14th ed.

Jha, K.N. (1985). *Women towards Modernization.* Janki Prakashan, Patna.

Joseph, C. (1985). *Toni Mass Media and Rural Development*, New Delhi, Rawat Publications.

Joseph, M.K. (1996). *Modern Media and Communication Sociology and Communication Revolution*, Vol. 1. Anmol Publication Pvt. Ltd. New Delhi.

Jot, Jivan, (1985). Is Women a Weaker Sex? Shackles and Women. Faridkot.

Kapur, P. (1970). *Marriage and the working women in India.* Vikas Publications, New Delhi.

Kapur, P. (1974). *The changing status of working women in India.* New Delhi.

Karl, M. (1995). *Women and Empowerment : Participation and Decision Making*, Zed Book Ltd., London and New Jersey.

Kaul Anuradha, (1990). Educational economic and social impact of vocational training agencies offering income generating programmes on low socio-economic status women of Baroda city, Ph.D. Thesis. The M.S. University of Baroda, Baroda.

Kaul Anuradha, Training Women of Baroda City for Income Generation–An Alternative to Employment, 1996.

Kaushik, V. and Sharma, B.R. (1990). *Women Power and Development*, Sarup and Sons, New Delhi.

Kotaiah, P. (1998). Policy on Institutional Credit to generate employment and marketing skills among the rural youth in Asia Pacific, NABARD, News letter Vol. 8. No. 12.

Kottern, D.C. and Felipe B.A. (1981). "Bureaucracy and the Poor : Closing the Gap" Asian Institute of Management, Manila.

Kumar Ashok, (1990). *Developing Women and Children in India*, Commonwealth Publishers, New Delhi.

Kumari, Ranjana and Dubey Anju, (1994), "Women Parliamentarians" New Delhi: Friedrick Elbert Staffing Centre for Sonal Research Development.

Lankester Ted, (1992). Setting up Community Health Programmes, a practical manual for use in developing countries.

Lawley, John (1990). Awareness is not enough. *People*, Vol. 13, No. 2.

Lichtenberg, J. (1990). *Democracy and the Mass Media*. Cambridge: Cambridge University Press.

M. Kunudini, (1989). "School health worker and supplementary nutrition in Indian Schools." Swasth Hind.

Magundar, M. (1990). Women and Media, *Communicator*, 25(4) 6-8.

Mahajan P. Mani and Siby K, Josep, "Human Resource Utilization" Musing on an Alternative Developing. Paradigm Kurukshetra, Dec. 1996, p. 11.

Malhan, P.N. (1992). Communication Media Yesterday, Today and Tomorrow. Ministry of Information and Broadcasting, New Delhi.

Manikyamba, P. (1990). *Women in Panchayati Raj*, Gyan Publishing House, New Delhi.

Mathur, M.B. (1989). *Adult education and social change*. The Indian Publication, Ambala Cantt.

Mazumdar, V. (1986). *Women in Political Process*. Popular Prakashan. Bombay, pp. 95-107.

Media Consultation on Women in Development 21-22 Feb. 1989. Delhi.

Mehta, T.U. Women's Quotes. *Times of India*, Ahmedabad, 17 July, 1998 : 10.

Melkote, R. (1991). *Srinivas Communication for development in the Third World: Theory and Practices*. New Delhi. Sage.

Menon, N.V.C. Role of NGOs in Disaster Management. *Indian Journal of Adult Education*. Vol. 59. No. 3. July-Sept. pp. 33-39.

Mirashi, H.N. Towards Better Occupational Health, *Indian Journal of Industrial Medicine*, Vol. 42(3), September, 1996.

Mitra, A. (1979). *Status of Women : Literacy and Empowerment*, Allied Publisher, New Delhi.

Mitra, A., Srimany, A.K. and Pathak, L.P. (1979). *Status of women : Household and non-household economic activity*, Allied Publisher, New Delhi.

Mitra, S.M. (1981). *The position of women in Indian life*, Neeraj Publication, New Delhi.

Mittal, D. N., Women and Education Development Process: *University News*, 31. (3), Sep. 1993, pp. 3-4.

Mody Bella. (1990). *Designing messages for Developmental Communication*, Sage Publications, New Delhi.

Mody, Bella (1991). *Designing Messages for Development Communication*, Sage Publications, New Delhi.

Nag, P.K. et.al., September Applied Ergonomics. 1986.

National Commission on Self-employed Women and Women in the Informal Sector 1988, New Delhi.

National Consultation on the Role of Women Development Corporation 11-12 Jan., 1989.

National Perspective Plan for Women–1988-2000 A.D. Department of Women and Child Development, Ministry of Human Resource Development, Government of India, 1988.

National workshop on Problem of Women Construction Workers (12-14 Nov., 1986), New Delhi.

Natural Disaster Reduction–South Asian Regional Report, Ministry of Agriculture, Government of India, 1994.

Nayan Usha, (1985) *Cultural Roots of Oppression Patterns of Women's Education in India*, Shakti Books, New Delhi.

Ninan, Sevanti, Tune in to Quality. *The Hindu*, July 29, 2001.

Ninth Five-Year Plan (1997-2002), Vol. II, Govt. of India, *Planning Commission*, New Delhi, pp. 8-9.

Omoruyi, F.E.O. The dilemma of Women in Adult Literacy Educational Programme in Benin Metropolis. *Indian Journal of Adult Education*. Vol. 62. No. 1. Jan. March 2001.

Osha, (Eds.) U.S. Dept. of Labour, Occupational Health and Safety Adminis. OSHA 2056, 2, 1982.

P.P. Ghosh "Implementation of Literacy and Continuing Education Activities for out of school girls and women in rural areas. State Resource Centre Asian Development Research Institute. Patna.

Panda, S. (1989). *Women's involvement in politics in India*. Tata McGraw Publishing Ltd., New Delhi.

Pandey, D. (1990). Empowerment of women participatory action research approach, SNDT Women's University, Bombay.

Pandey, R. (1989). *Women from subjection to liberation*, Mittal Publication, New Delhi.

Parlikar Kalpana R. et.al. A Report of Workshop on training and Development of Women for participation in TRYSEM programme, Dec. 1990.

Pasricha, J.S. (1991). Dermatological Problems faced by Female Workers in the Cashewnut Factories, Project Report, New Delhi.

Patel, Vibhuti, Women's participation in policy and decision making process: Need for a network a paper read at the Regional round table on the subject at SNDT Women's University, Bombay. August 1991.

Patri C.M. (1999). *Self Employment and Successful Entrepreneurship*, Kanishka Pub. Co. New Delhi.

Prasad, C. (1994). Training for Agricultural Development: A Basic Functional Area. *Journal of Rural Reconstruction* 27 (1). 1994.

Purushothaman, S. (1998). *Empowerment of Women in India : Grassroots Women's Networks and the State*, Sage Publication, New Delhi.

Ramdas, L. (1986). "Women, Education and Development questions and Reflections" paper presented at the National Conference on Women's Studies, 1-4 October, Punjab University, Chandigarh.

Ranade Sobhana: Women's role in politics stressed. Documentation on women's concerns. New Delhi. *All India Association Christian Higher Education*, July-Sept. 1996-99.

Rao, K.V. (2003). Health Planning and Development in Reproductive Health Gender and Development—an international perspective B.R. Publishing Company, Delhi.

Ravindran, R.K., (1999). *Handbook of Mass Media*, Anmol Publications Pvt. Ltd. New Delhi.

Reddy, KV. Mass Media in education, *University News*, Vol. XXX, No. 1. Jan. 6, 1992.

Roe, Anne, (1986). *The Psychology of Occupations*. John Wiley and Sons, New York.

Rogers Alan, (1986). 'Teaching Adults' Milton Keynes : Open University Press.

Rogers, (1999). Everest Quoted in V.S. Gupta, *Communication Technology Media Policy and National Development*, New Delhi: Concept Publishing.

Roy Kalpana, "Women's in Indian Politics", 1999, pp. 91-148. *Social Welfare*, Vol. 4.

S. Gopalan, (1995). "Educational for Nutrition Promotion" Swasth Hind Publications.

Saho, A.K. (1986). A study of the Correspondence Education in an Indian University. Unpublished Ph.D. Thesis. M.S. University of Baroda.

Saxena Radha Rani. Changing Roles of Indian Women in Society. *Social Welfare*, Vol. 48, No. 5. Aug. 2001, 25-27.

Seminar on Employment Opportunities for Women in Electronics, Computers and Communication 13th Dec., 1986.

Sen, S.R. Development of Drought Prone Area. *Kurukshetra* 12(8) 73-80. 1969.

Shah Anupama and Ojha Sulochana, (1990). *Women and Law–A compilation of speeches*, Mohe Printers, Baroda.

Shams Shamasuddin, (1991). *Women, Law and Social Change*, Ashish Publishing House, New Delhi.

Sharma Neerja, Kandai Hemlata, Moving Continuing Education towards learning society. *Indian Journal of Adult Education*. Vol. 62. No. 4, Oct.-Dec. 2001, 64-67.

Sharma, Atul, Sharan, G., D.R. Veena. Parikh, K. Bhanumati. Adult Education in India, Anmol Publication, New Delhi 1989.

Sharma, I.P. *Adult Education in India*, N.B.G. Publishers, New Delhi, 1985.

Sharma, O.P. and Retherford R.D. "Effect of female Literacy on Fertility in India" Occasional Paper No. 1 of 1990, Office of the Registrar General, India.

Sharma, R.D. "Crime against Women is on the Rise" 15th May, 1990. *The Times of India*.

Sharma, U. and Sharma, B.M. (1977). *Committees and Commission on Women Education*, Commonwealth Publishers, New Delhi.

Shramshakti (1988). The Report of National Commission on self-employed women and women in informal sector, Government of India, New Delhi.

Singh Madan, *Adult education in 21st century*, The Associated Publishers Ambala Cantt. 2001.

Singh Uma (2001). *New Women and Mass Media*. Surabhi Pub. Jaipur.

Singh, Mira, Revices : Grossing the Lakshman Rekha, *Manushi*, Sept.-Oct. 1994: 92.

Singh, Uma, (2001). *New Women and Man Media*. Surabhi Pub., Jaipur.

Sreenivas Chary P. 'DPAP Outlay and Expenditure' *Kurukshetra*, Vol. XXVII. No. 21, 1979.

Steeves, H.L. (1987). Femist Theories and Media Studies, *Critical Studies of Mass Communication* 4(2) 95-135.

Stevenson, N. (1995). *Understanding Media Culture - Social Theory and Mass Communication*. London: Sage Publication Ltd.

Subramanium, C. (1970). The new strategy in Indian Agriculture, Vikas, New Delhi.

Suguna, B. Women's Empowerment Concept and Framework, *Social Welfare*, Vol. 48. No. 9, 2001, 3-7.

Sunita, K. and Sunanda, G. Review of Researches in Women's Studies conducted in the M.S. University of Baroda (1962-1985).

Super, D.E. (1967). *Psychology of careers*, Harper and Sons, Inc., New York.

Surai, E.V. Women's Education Needs Analysis for alternative approach to Adult Education in Tanzania. A case study of Kiroka and Sembeti village in Morogoro and Kilimanaro, M.A. Thesis.

Tara, S. Narain (1993). "Education of the Girl Child" *Yojana*, Vol. 37, No. 10, p. 9.

The Constitution–Eighty First Amendment Bill 1996. Discussion organised by the National Commission for Women, compiled by Women's Studies Research Centre, M.S. University, Baroda.

The new economic policy and women Indian Association for women's studies. Tata Institute of Social Sciences, Bombay. 1993.

Town : CACE University Publications Institute of Development Studies, 1992, "Gender and World Development" East Sussex: Sussex University Publications.

Tripathi, R.S., Tiwari, R.P. (1999). *Perspectives an Indian Women*, A.P.H. Publishing Corporation, 5 Ansari Road, New Delhi.

UNDP (2001). *Human Development Report 2001*. Oxford University Press. Oxford.

UNESCO, Fourth International Conference on Adult Education. Final Report, UNESCO, Paris, 1985.

Upadhyay, J.N. Role of Education and Training in Disaster Mitigation, *Indian Journal of Adult Education*, Vol. 59, No. 3 July-Sept. 1998. pp. 27-32.

Varda Burnsting (1983). Masculine Dominance and the State. The Marlin Press, London.

Varma, S.C., Women's Vital Role in Rural Development, Integrating Women's Programmes in the Rural Development–Strategy and Women's Programmes as part of Rural Development efforts.

Venkateswaran, Sandhya (1995). *Environment, Development and the Gender Gap*. Sage Publications. New Delhi.

Verma, S. (1997). *Women's Struggle for Political Space*, Jaipur and New Delhi Rawat Publications.

Verma, S. (1997). *Women's struggle for political space*, Rawat Publications, Jaipur and New Delhi.

Vidya, K.C. (1997). "Political Empowerment of Women at the Grassroots", pp. 239-269.

Women Studies–In search of alternatives, *Social Welfare*, Vol. 43(7) October, 1996.

Women's studies, *A Current Awareness Bulletin*, Dec. 1990.

Workshop on Women's Studies, University News, Vol. 34(45), Nov. 5-11, 2001.

World Bank : Enhancing Women's Participation in Economic Development, 1994.

Yadav Singh Rajendra, *Adult education training and productivity*. The Indian Publication Ambala Cantt., 1991.

Sites : free.freespeech.org/manushi/97/politics.html.

www.indiatogether.org/women/authority/history.htmla

Index

V